ESTHER HIGGINS

SIERRA SOUTH

*100 Back-country trips
in California's Sierra*

by Karl Schwenke and Thomas Winnett

illustrated by Don Denison

cover by Karl Schwenke

Published by Wilderness Press
2440 Bancroft Way
Berkeley, California

Third printing March 1970

Library of Congress catalog card number 68-5595

SBN: 911824-01-4

Printed in the USA

foreword

In The Beginning

there is nothing quite so humbling as a long set of switch-backs or the start of a new book. One's conditioning and capacities make themselves known as the going becomes rocky, the way convoluted, and the grade steep. The End, consequently, takes on the aspect of a goal, and all too often we arrive only to find that we've forgotten what it was we saw and felt enroute. And so, at this inception, we pledge ourselves to enjoy the doing — not

The End.

K.S.

T.W.

acknowledgements

Don Denison, Lu Winnett, David Poast, Suzanne Schwenke, Thomas Dum, Jim Watters, Louise Moroney, Richard Wiebe, Dan Simon, John McElheney, David Pesonen, Rephah Berg, Luisa Sciutto, E. P. Pister, George Marks, Robert Swanson, Robert L. Simpson, Carl Schreck, Jack High, Chet Rice, Dave Buschman, Rudolph Hurwich, Cecelia Hurwich, J. W. Wright, A. I. Kelty.

Table of Contents

Introduction

Whether on foot or on horseback, the back-country traveler knows the exhilaration of the out-of-doors in a rich, personal way that is beyond the ken of the ordinary car camper. Far from the crowds that infest the roadside campgrounds, he comes to realize the value of solitude, and he learns the calmness of spirit that derives from a fundamental relationship with the mountains. He comes to know the simple satisfactions of deep breaths, hardened muscles, and a sound sleep under brilliant stars. But, above all, in renewing his bond with the wilderness he rekindles that cherished spark of child-like innocence that is so easily extinguished by the pressures of city life. It is these pressures that account for the dramatic increase in the demand for wilderness experiences. The Sierra, offering some of the finest and most spectacular wilderness in the United States, has drawn more than its share of the demand, and its back country sees thousands of new faces each year.

Together with the companion volume *Sierra North,* this small book is a discriminating effort to meet the demands of both the newcomer and the "old hand." Taking up where *Sierra North* left off, this book describes most of the back-country trails between Mono Creek and the southern end of Sequoia National Park. Here are trips ranging in length from overnighters to two-week expeditions; trips that will satisfy the beginner and challenge the expert; trips that will sate the appetite of the most avid angler, naturalist or camera bug.

These trips were chosen after considerable screening that entailed interviews with rangers, packers and mountaineers, and substantial research. Finally, they were walked — almost all by the authors, the rest under their direction in the field. After this screening, the final selections were made on the basis of: (1) scenic attraction; (2) wilderness character (remoteness, primitive condition); and (3) recreational potential (fishing, swimming, etc.).

After walking the trip the scout graded it for "Leisurely," "Moderate" and "Strenuous" paces. Many theories and methods about how this should be done were considered but rejected because they failed to take into consideration enough pertinent factors (elevation change, heat, exposure, ground cover, terrain, availability of water, etc.). The method settled upon is a combination of the above factors together with the subjective evaluation by the scout who walked the trail. The "Trail/layover days" designation is also the recommendation of this scout, and is directly involved in the grading. (A "layover" day is one on which one does not travel to a new camp.)

The scout's subjective consideration also carries over to the evaluation of campsites and abundance of firewood. Campsites are labeled poor, fair, good or excellent. The criteria for assigning these labels were amount of use, immediate surroundings, general scenery, presence of vandalization, availability of water, kind of ground cover, and recreational potential — angling, side trips, swimming, etc.

Two other terms used in the descriptive text warrant definition. "Packer" campsite is used to indicate a semipermanent camp (usually constructed by packers for the "comfort of their clients") characterized by a nailed-plank table and/or a large, "stand-up" rock fireplace. "Improved" campsite is a relatively new U. S. Forest Service designation for places where simple toilets have been installed.

Angling, for many, is a prime consideration when planning a trip. The recommendations in this book are the result of research into the California DF&G's fresh-water fish-stocking program, study of DF&G-sponsored surveys ("Anglers' Guides,"), "on the trail" sampling and feed evaluation, and interviews with commercial packers. When a conflict arose between "paper research" and trail sampling, the latter was given precedence, and, like the campsite designations, fishing was separated into poor, fair, good or excellent. It should be noted that these categories refer to the *quantity* of fish found in the stream or lake, and not the fishes' *inclination* to take the hook. Experienced anglers know that the size of their catch relates not only to quantity, type, and general size of the fishery, which are given, but also factors of water temperature, feed, angling skill, and that indefinable something known as "fisherman's luck." Generally speaking, the old "early and late" adage holds: fishing *is* better early and late in the day, and early and late in the season.

Defining high-country seasons is at best a difficult chore because of altitude and latitude variations. Low early-season temperatures and mountain shadows often keep some of the higher passes closed until well into August. Early snows have been known to whiten alpine country in July and August. Some of the trips described here are low-country ones, designed specifically for the itchy hiker who, stiff from a winter's inactivity, is searching for a "warm-up" excursion. These trips are labeled "early season," and this period extends roughly from late May to early July. "Mid-season" is here considered to be from early July to early September, and "late season" from then to early October.

Most of the trails described here are well maintained (the exceptions are noted), and they are usually properly signed. If the trail becomes indistinct, look for blazes (peeled bark at eye level on the trees) or "duck-on-the-rock" markings (cairns of two or more rocks piled one atop the other). Two other significant trail conditions have also been described in the text: (1) exposure (type and density of forest cover, meadow, brush, etc.); (2) underfooting (talus, granite, pumice, sand, "duff" — deep humus ground cover of rotting vegetation).

Blest silent groves!

O may you be
    Forever mirth's best nursery!

May pure contents
    Forever pitch their tents

Upon these downs, these meads, these rocks,
    these mountains,

And peace still slumber by these purling
    fountains:

Which we may every year

Meet when we come a-fishing here.*

*Venator's toast quote from Sir Henry Wotton in *The Compleat Angler*

Backpacking Basics

Backpackers are a delightfully individualistic and unusual lot. They pride themselves on their separateness — and this is not a false pride. For in the context of today's motor-powered outdoorsmen, the backpacker is indeed utterly unique. The backpacker's horizons are his own. He is unlimited by the fetters of machinery or four-footed stock, and inclination and stamina are the only bounds to his freedom to wander.

This individuality reflects itself in equipment. One will find, on any given trail, as many outfits as he finds backpackers. There are some basic similarities, however, that may (humbly) be construed to reflect agreement on three or four pieces of basic equipment.

For the trail, one needs adequate footgear. No piece of equipment is more intimate to the hiker than his boots, so selection becomes an important, and subjective, affair. Leather boots six to eight inches high with vibram lug soles are, by consensus, the choice for the rugged Sierra trails. Tennis shoes and low-tops are just not substantial enough. Care should be taken to acquire boots with a stiff heel counter, and the boot should fit snugly at the heel and loosely around the toes.

A good-quality down sleeping bag is desirable — if not essential. Since this is by far the most expensive equipment a backpacker will acquire, one hesitates to state that the success or failure of a wilderness backpack trip hinges on owning a down bag. But the amount and quality of one's sleep — particularly in the face of substantial expenditures of energy — influences one's feeling of well-being. In a sleeping bag, overlapping-tube and box construction baffle designs are superior, and the best "all-round" bag should weigh no more than five pounds. "Mummy" and rectangular-shaped bags each have their adherents. Some cannot tolerate the close-fitting "mummy" style despite its superior thermal and weight characteristics. This is an option that the individual must exercise.

The third piece of basic equipment is a pack frame and accompanying bag. Some rigs observed on the trail rival Rube Goldberg's contraptions, but generally speaking, the frame should be constructed of lightweight, tubular aluminum. The design should not impede free movement of the hips, arms or head, and the frame's weight should not exceed three pounds. The pack bag should be roomy (for longer trips), and exterior zippered pockets are convenient. Elaborate construction is not essential, but compartments make for easy organization and keep the load from shifting. The bag should have a long "weather" flap, and the material should be waterproof.

Summers in the Sierra are fairly dry; hence many "go-lighters" forego the comfort of a tent. Sceptics who have been caught without shelter in a "rare" high-country thunderstorm carry a plastic sheet or a plastic "tube tent." These temporary shelters are strung up with light nylon cord, and extra precautions are always taken to assure an adequate air supply.

Other equipment essentials include warm clothing, raingear, ground cloth (usually plastic), air mattress (or foam pad), Sierra cup, utensils, cooking gear (lightweight aluminum), flashlight, first-aid kit (bandaids, moleskin, compresses, antiseptic, soap, aspirin, eye wash, adhesive tape, individual prescriptions), bug dope, compass, nylon line, knife, snakebite kit, waterproof matches, toilet paper, bandanna, and pencil.

The following check list (courtesy of the Sierra Club) is included for the beginner who has doubts about putting in "last-minute extras":

last-minute check list

This is a check list only! Don't take everything here.

Taken by
1. **Almost** everyone
2. Most

3. About half
4. A few

5. Practically no one
? For consideration only

Knapsack	Pack Animals	TO WEAR OR CARRY	Approx. Wt. Ea. Article 16 oz. = 1 lb. (Ounces)
1	1	Hat or cap	
2	2	Dark glasses	3
1	1	Shirt	6-16
1	1	Trousers or shorts	6-16
1	1	Belt	3-5
1	1	Shoes — boots	32-96
1	1	Socks	2-6
2	2	Bandana — handkerchief	1
1	1	Underwear	6-24
2	2	Maps (Topo or Forest Service)	1
3	3	Compass	3-5
1	1	Matches in waterproof case	1-3
1	1	Toilet paper	
2	2	Watch — cheap	2
1	1	Pocket knife — not cheap	2
1	1	Sunburn preventive	2
2	2	Insect Repellent	1
1	1	Lip ice or lipstick	1
1	3	Knapsack or pack frame	16-64
1	1	Parka or jacket	16-34
2	2	Adhesive tape, moleskin, etc.	1
2	1	Raincoat, cape, poncho	3-24
1	1	Flashlight	3-9
1	1	Lunchbag, durable	1-2
1	1	Sierra Club Cup (2?)	4
1	1	Spoon	
2	1	Swim suit	3-24
2	2	Washing kit (self and clothes)	
4	3	Plastic lemonade shaker	3-6
4	..	Canteen or plastic bottle	6-12
4	3	Lemonade mix, soft drink mix	
5	5	Powdered coffee or tea or bouillon	
..	..	Water purifying tablets	
3	2	Fishing license	
3	2	Camera — FILM	

—5—

..	1	Dunnage bag	24-48
2	1	Tarp or tent	16-96
1	1	Sleeping bag	36-176
3	3	Inner bag	10-24
4	4	Outer bag	16-32
2	1	Ground cloth	3-32
3	2	Air mattress	32-82
5	4	Pillow or pad	3-12
5	4	Pajamas	14-16
1	1	Underwear (light) set	3-8
5	4	Undershirt (wool or quilted)	12
4	3	Under drawers (wool or quilted)	12
1	1	Extra socks	5-10
4	2	Camp shoes	6-32
3	2	Extra trousers	16-32
3	3	Hiking shorts	16
2	2	Shirts (light weight)	6-12
4	3	Shirts, wool	16
1	1	Sweater, light weight	8-16
4	2	Wool stocking cap or balaclava helmet	4
1	1	Bandanas	4
1	1	Powdered soap	4-8
4	2	Woolite or detergent	2
5	3	Sewing kit (small), safety pins	1
3	2	Extra optical glasses in case	3
5	3	Extra dark glasses in case	3
1	1	Flashlight (extra batteries, globes ?)	3-14
1	1	1/8" nylon or other cord	3-9
?	?	Kleenex (don't litter)	
?	?	Sanitary napkins	
5	2	Plastic wash basin	3-6
4	1	Collapsible plastic bucket	4
5	4	Cellulose sponge (small, thin)	2
?	?	Waterproof bags (strong) for camera, etc.	3
?	?	Small nail brush	1
?	?	Tickets, keys, money	
5	4	Mattress patching kit	
?	?	Clothespins, plastic	4
?	?	2 birthday candles or fire starters	1
?	?	Aluminum container (qt. filled)	39
..	4	Gloves or mittens	3
4	2	Towel (diaper)	2
1	1	Thin plastic bags (asst'd), rubber bands	

No list of backpacking basics would be complete without mention of some fundamental precautions that should become habit.

- Always leave your route itinerary, departure date and estimated date of return with a reliable friend and/or the nearest Ranger Station.

- Know in advance the nearest point(s) from which you can obtain emergency services.

- While enroute, sign all trail registers.

- Unless you are an accomplished mountaineer, always travel in company.

- Always acclimate before prolonged exertion at high altitudes.

wilderness courtesy

Traveling in the Sierra wilderness is a privilege, not a birthright! With the privilege comes the responsibility to keep it unspoiled for those who follow, and it is incumbent upon every wilderness traveler to be sensitive and responsible to that obligation. In recognition of that obligation, the Sierra Club, an organization dedicated to the preservation of wilderness, circulates the following policy on camping and trail conduct for their group outings. The authors concur.

As a member of a wilderness outing party you will become familiar with the rules enumerated below. You will discover an immense satisfaction in enjoying wilderness without depreciating it in any way, and in leaving no lasting sign.

Construction: Camp in the wilderness spirit. Minimize building, whether for kitchen emplacements or shelter. Don't disarrange scene with hard-to-eradicate ramparts of rock as fireplaces or windbreaks. Rig tents or tarps with line tied to rocks or trees. Never cut boughs or poles, or put nails in trees. Camp should be set up where foot traffic does the least damage to fragile vegetation.

Fires: Never leave a fire unattended! Build a minimum fireplace. Clear a wide circle around your fire down to mineral soil. Don't place a fire against a log or back rock. When breaking camp, drown fire completely, stir, and drown again until ashes are cold to touch. Bury ashes and charcoal. Use existing fire sites where found. If you start from scratch in places not camped before, return fireplace rocks to natural positions when you leave, blackened portions hidden. Never build fires on meadows, vegetation or duff.

Refrain from smoking while traveling; smoke only in camps and at rest stops.

Wood: Use down wood only; do not cut standing trees, living or dead nor break off their branches. Snags are picturesque and should not be molested. Axe work on down logs and stumps mars wilderness atmosphere. Conserve wood, especially where scarce. *Keep fires small.*

Bedsites: Don't excavate. Try to find naturally level and sheltered spot. Erase evidence of your bed when breaking camp. Double check area before you move on. Forgotten laundry is litter.

Sanitation: Latrines should be constructed when a large party plans a protracted camp. Use them when available. Latrines should be inconspicuous and placed well away from water. If no latrine, go far from camp and trail, dig deep and bury. Placing a rock over the site is not wholly satisfactory; it looks unnatural, and if small, is easily overturned by curious animals.

Swim or wash at distance or below from where camp water is drawn.

Washing: Use a small basin for laundry and sponge bathing. Prevent pollution by keeping soap or detergent out of lakes and streams. Even with care, soap is preferable to detergent for mountain use. Do your pot scrubbing and washing well back from the shoreline.

Garbage & Litter: Place candy wrappers, raisin boxes, orange peels, etc., in pocket or pack for later disposal in fire or garbage sack. Burn what will burn. *Foil does not burn!* Many packages have foil inner lining; look before you burn. Edibles may be concealed or scattered well away from camp and trail where animals can find them without digging. Carry cans, bottles, worn-out gear and foil out of the mountains. Remove ends of cans, flatten and burn cans preparatory to packing out. Garbage pits are no longer acceptable. Field-strip cigarettes.

Pack stock: Good grazing is limited, so take care to protect forage. Keep stock from concentrating on inadequate meadows; turn animals out at night whenever possible. Move picketed animals every few hours to avoid severe trampling and overgrazing of grassy areas. (Picketing per se is prohibited in Kings Canyon-Sequoia National Parks.) Saddle and groom stock away from camp to prevent accumulation of manure in camp area.

Trails: Don't cut corners. This breaks down trails and hurries erosion. Dislodged rocks may fall on others below you. Stock has right of way; stand quietly aside, preferably uphill, until animals have passed.

Off trail: Restrain impulse to blaze trees, or to build ducks (small rock cairns used as markers) where not essential. Let the next fellow find his way as you did.

Fish: Catch only as many as you need or can consume. After cleaning fish, conceal entrails ashore. Never throw entrails, head, etc., back into the water.

Noise: Be a considerate neighbor. Don't crowd others' camps or sleeping areas. Noise is out of harmony in a wilderness experience.

maps

Today's Sierra traveler is confronted by a bewildering array of maps, and it doesn't take much experience to learn that no single map fulfills all needs. There are base maps (U.S. Forest Service), shaded relief maps (National Park Service), artistically drawn representational maps (California Department of Fish and Game), aerial photograph maps, geologic maps, three-dimensional relief maps, soil-vegetation maps, etc. Each map has different information to impart (some more information than others), and the outdoorsman contemplating a back country trip is wise to utilize several of these maps in his planning.

For trip-planning purposes, the reader will find two plan maps in this book. Trails and trailheads used in the following trip descriptions are indicated on these maps in red, and all the access roads are numbered and delineated in black.

On the trail most backpackers prefer to use a topographic ("topo") map, because it affords a good deal of accurate information about conditions of terrain and forest cover. Topo maps come in a variety of sizes and scales, but the best, because they cover the whole Sierra in one useful scale, is the U.S. Geological Survey's 15' Topographic Quadrangle series. The 15' series scale is approximately 1"=1 mile; the contour interval (elevation difference between contour lines) is 80 feet in the Sierra; and the area covered by each map is about 13x17 miles. They show most of the maintained trails (exceptions noted in the text of this book), the elevations, the relief, the watercourses, the forest cover, and the works of man. "Reading" these maps takes a little practice, but the savings in shoe leather and frayed tempers make it a worthy undertaking. For the convenience of the reader, the appropriate topo maps for each trip are cited in the text.

A useful second map is the one published by the U.S. Forest Service. Being a base map, it lacks the contour lines, but it is revised with some frequency, and shows newer roads and trails. It also includes markings for water, man-made structures, and some elevations.

Anglers planning a fishing trip should acquire the "Anglers' Guides" published by the California Department of Fish and Game. These include both artistically drawn representational maps and descriptions of the fishing waters. Of this in-progress series, five guides apply to the regions of the southern Sierra covered by this book ("Mono Creek," "Bear Creek," "French Canyon/Humphreys Basin," "Upper Bishop Creek" and "Mineral King").

For those planning trips into the Kings/Sequoia Park back country, a plan map published by the National Park Service shows major trails, landmarks and watercourses.

how to acquire your maps

USFS base map: U.S. Forest Service,
                        630 Sansome St.,
                        San Francisco, Calif. 94111.
                        An index map and the set for one
                        National Forest per order are free.

DF&G "Anglers' Guides": DF&G, Resources Building,
                        9th and O Sts.,
                        Sacramento, Calif. 95814
                        Complete set is free.

Kings/Sequoia Park map: Superintendent,
                        Sequoia and Kings Canyon
                          National Parks,
                        Ash Mountain Headquarters,
                        Sequoia National Park.
                        Free.

USGS 15' Topo: U.S. Geological Survey,
                        Federal Center, Denver, Colo. 80225
                        50 cents each, less by bulk order.
                        Index map is free.

MONO CREEK TO GLACIER DIVIDE

Part of the 400,000 acre John Muir Wilderness Area, this region towers between Mono Creek and the northern boundary of Kings Canyon National Park. It is a roadless fastness of incredibly rugged alpine beauty composing a wilderness that beckons to the traveler. Barren summits rise above a dense mat of green conifers, and the landscape is stippled with a thousand blue-green lakes bound by connecting silver ribbons of mountain streams. Encompassing a small area of roughly 500 square miles, this section nevertheless contains enough trails and cross-country routes to satisfy the most dedicated back-country traveler for several summer seasons.

The profile of this region is classic. It boasts the typical, severe eastern escarpment, and, also typically, the western slopes tilt away in a long, gradual decline. The west side is cut by the Mono, Bear and Piute Creek drainages — all tributaries of the South Fork of the San Joaquin. And the east side is cleft by the precipitous, hurrying waters of Rock Creek, Pine Creek and the North Fork of Bishop Creek — all tributaries of the Owens River. These watersheds are separated by spectacular divides, which, together with the main Sierra Crest and a little imagination, form an interesting plan view. Seen from the air, the main crest and the ancillary divide spurs of this section take on the aspect of a very large frog — the head centering around Mt. Mills; Mono Divide and the Mt. Morgan/Wheeler Crest making the forelegs; and the Mt. Hooper/Mt. Senger complex and the Mt. Tom/Basin Mt. divide composing the two lower limbs. Naturalists would hasten to render this absurd analogy more "authentic" by pointing out that the frog's back is covered with warts (17 summits exceeding 13,000′), and that it should therefore be analogized to a toad. The reader is free to make his own Rorschach of the topography, but in any case it is vitally important — particularly in cross-country travel — for him to have a working map knowledge of the country and its terrain.

One soon learns, however, that his map knowledge never does justice to the country. This awareness comes with one's first glimpses of the majestic prominences and the awesome, blue-hazed canyons. With awareness comes wonderment — a pause to ponder the colossal forces required to move, pluck and sculpt the rock on such a scale. Clarence King, a member of the famous Brewer Survey party of 1864, was among the first white men to look at this portion of the Sierra and record his thoughts: "I believe no one can study from an elevated lookout the length and depth of one of these great Sierra canyons without asking himself some profound geological questions." Indeed, how did it happen?

The answer has mostly to do with ice — vast rivers of ice that ground, scoured and scraped their juggernaut way across the landscape. Were there an eye to witness it, in this area alone the fields of ice would be seen to extend over 1500 square miles.

Today there are but vestigial remnants to mark the icefield's extent, reminders that hang like gray ghosts on the shady northeast faces of the higher peaks. But today's visitor has only to look about him to understand the landforming powers of the glaciers. Huge U-shaped troughs mark the courses of the main glaciers that carved the Mono Creek, Bear Creek, Piute Creek, and South Fork of the San Joaquin River canyons. Shallow side valleys, usually suspended hundreds of feet above the floor of the U-canyon trough, mark the more ancient flow of tributary glaciers, and they have acquired the deserved appellation, "hanging valleys." Equally interesting to the traveler is the inevitable chain of lakes that stepladders down from the upper, amphitheatrelike cirque of a hanging valley. Called Paternoster Lakes, they string down the valley floor much like the beads of a rosary, and they are the joy of the lazy angler who likes to alternate between stream and lake fishing.

Those familiar with glacial phenomena will soon notice the absence of rounded domes. One imperfect example, Bear Dome, is the sole specimen touched by the trails of this section. Similarly isolated is the only evidence of post-glacial-age volcanic action — Volcanic Knob. This black-rocked, partial crater is seen by those following the John Muir Trail northward as it crosses Bear Ridge and turns up the Mono Creek drainage.

Other important, but less spectacular, glacial spoor include glacial polish and glacial smoothing caused by the abrasive action of sand and silt that moved at the bottom and sides of a glacier. In these scoured areas one often finds long gouges or scratches rent there by boulders caught in the flow of the ice river. The subsequent deposit of these boulders can now be witnessed in the form of various moraines.

But the process of landforming is still going on. River cutting, frequently taking advantage of fracture lines, has "Veed" sections of canyon that were previously of the U-configuration. Avalanche chutes and frost nivations flute vertical peak façades, and accumulations of scree and talus slope away at their feet. Subtler forms of weathering continue to attack the talus, reducing that rock to granuies, which then provide a suitable habitat for hardy plants. One can "watch" this ecological chain in "action" while walking the trails around timberline.

Basic to animals is the presence of an ample and healthy plant life, and one is sure to see more animals in this region's heavily wooded drainages. Birds are particularly plentiful, and the lakes and streams abound with fish. Among the most commonly seen mammals are mule deer. Early-season hikers working their way up Bear Creek are almost sure to come upon a grazing doe, and, with some luck, perhaps a pair of brand-new, spotted-back fawns. It should be noted that any wild-animal observation requires "freezing" — not necessarily stealth — but quiet and immobility. There isn't a naturalist observer worth his salt who hasn't experienced the dilemma of a hovering mosquito and a "once in a trip-time" wild-animal observation opportunity. In early and mid season both does and bucks have reddish coats, which are replaced in the fall with longer, gray hair. Because the buck is much warier, a sighting of him is rarer. One will also make trailside, passing acquaintance with the numerous squirrels that populate the heavily wooded areas, especially the fir belt. Easily recognizable because of the dual stripes running down his coppery-red back is the tiny golden-mantled ground squirrel. He is, perhaps, the most familiar of the family, and is found in both the lodgepole and subalpine belts. His less distinguished cousin, the California ground squirrel, will be seen near the trailheads — generally below 8000′, and the Belding ground squirrel, or "picketpin," seen in most of the meadows of this section. Not of the wooded country, but a constant companion to the high-country hiker are the cony, a tiny, rabbitlike creature, and the beaverlike marmot. Found in talus and rocky areas, these somnolent rodents pipe and chirp excitedly whenever approached.

Other less common, but consequently more exciting, sightings that one may make are of the black bear, mountain coyote, porcupine, flying squirrel, mountain lion and mountain sheep. The black bear, contrary to impressions one might well have gathered in heavily camped National Park areas, is not often observed in the back country. The notable exception to this rule occurs when one leaves food lying about untended. Although he is more often a clown, he can be a pest, and it is always advisable to remove temptations by hoisting food up out of reach. (As the signs say, bears are wild, and it is foolish to try to pet them.) The mountain lion, coyote and flying squirrel are more often heard than seen, and the happy occasion of hearing one of these animals usually transpires while one is busy setting up camp, bedding down or cooking a daybreak breakfast. A coyote's "singing" is a familiar sound to anyone who has watched a western movie, but the habitual birdlike whistling of a mountain lion is usually unrecognized because it seems totally out of character. This cat rarely screams, but he does meow, spit and growl in unmistakable feline fashion. Hearing a flying squirrel, contradictory as it may seem, is a fairly common occurrence. It takes place at night (the squirrel is nocturnal), usually with a *whhhist . . . splat* sound that characterizes their "flight" from one tree to another. Another creature that ostensibly disdains heights and is rarely seen is the mountain, or bighorn, sheep. These beautiful animals were once commonplace residents of this country, but are now exceedingly rare owing to severe depletion of their numbers by pioneer sheepherders and subsequent diseases. Found almost exclusively on the main crest and the ancillary spur ranges that point toward Owens Valley, they are usually sighted in small ram bands high atop inhospitable-looking rocky buttresses and peaks, and they are exceedingly difficult to approach.

The most commonly seen animal in this region is man. He is usually quite domesticated, and is exceedingly easy to approach. A query like, "Where've you been?" usually brings a flood of friendly information and advice that will keep the querying hiker shifting under his pack for fifteen minutes or more. In geologic terms this animal has been on the scene but an instant in time, and his written history consumes a minute sub-fraction of time's second hand. Despite his relative newness, his effect has been great, and the mark of his passage is on the land — temporarily.

In this section, man's trails, usually following those of other animals, are plentiful, clearly marked and well maintained. The trail following Mono Creek and crossing Mono Pass, and the one following the South Fork of the San Joaquin River and branching over Piute Pass are old trade routes of the Mono Indian tribes. Paralleling these ancient trails is the relatively newer Italy Pass trans-Sierra crossing, and bisecting all three of these routes is the renowned John Muir Trail which traverses the west slopes in a north-south direction.

There are six trailhead entry points to this country that are cited in this section — three on each side of the crest. Vermilion Campground, Bear Diversion Dam Jeep Road Junction and Florence Lake roadend, the three west side entries, are reached by taking paved State Route 168 to Huntington Lake, and then turning northeast on the narrow road that crosses Kaiser Pass. Mosquito Flat, the northernmost of the eastside entries to this country, is reached by turning west off Hiway 395 22 miles north of Bishop, and following the steeply ascending, paved road for seven miles. The trailhead on Pine Creek is similarly reached by turning off Hiway 395 about ten miles north of Bishop, and the partly paved road to the trailhead on the North Fork of Bishop Creek leaves Hiway 395 from the center of Bishop.

 1

TRIP   From BEAR DIVERSION DAM JEEP ROAD JUNCTION to UPPER BEAR CREEK (round trip). Topo map (15') Mt. Abbot; Profile 1. Best early or late season; 16 miles.

Grade	Trail/layover days	Total recommended days
Leisurely	2/0	2
Moderate	- - -	- - -
Strenuous	- - -	- - -

HILITES   Few creeks in the Sierra possess the simple, primitive appeal of Bear Creek. Never constant, it cascades, chutes and then tumbles down its rocky course, interrupted at graceful intervals by deep, slow-moving, sandy-bottomed pools. Fine brown and golden trout angling makes this trip a good fisherman's choice early or late season.

DESCRIPTION

1st Hiking Day (Bear Diversion Dam Jeep Road Junction to Upper Bear Creek, 8 miles): Lichen-covered, glacially-scoured granite

surrounds the trailhead for this trip. Actually, "trailhead" is somewhat misleading, for the first three miles (to the Bear Diversion
Dam) is an unmaintained Southern California Edison Co. jeep
road. From the point where the jeep road leaves the Mono Hot
Springs/Lake Thomas A. Edison road (7000') this route swings
first east and then south, undulating gently as it traverses the long
granite field that marks the southeast end of Bear Ridge. Rounding Bear Ridge, the jeep road ascends gently, and then drops down
to the Bear Diversion Dam spillway. This particular stretch of road
overlooks the gorge of the river to the west, and gives the traveler
a fine opportunity to watch the abundant population of birds that
frequent these broken slopes. Among the birds one is most likely
to see are the Steller jay, mountain chickadee, junco, dusky and
olive-sided flycatchers, cliff and barn swallows, red-tailed hawk,
and a variety of sparrows. Where the jeep road starts to descend
to the spillway, one can see upriver (southeast) to Ward Mtn. and
Mt. Shinn, and east to Bear Dome and the barren glacial cirques
above. Instructional in views, this route also offers the traveler on
foot or on horseback a chance to absorb a feeling for this glacially
scoured country. It is a feeling of openness that is emphasized
by the scattering of the forest cover. The mountain juniper and
Jeffrey pine occur in moderate stands amid broad expanses of
granite, where they have taken root in the granular sandswales
that have accumulated as a result of mechanical weathering. In
turn, the network of roots sprouting from pine, willow, ceanothus
and manzanita accelerates the continual process of granite-break-
ing. At the Bear Diversion Dam (7350') the traveler enters the
mouth of the canyon whose walls rise steeply on either side of
Bear Creek. The trail (unsigned) skirts the west and north sides
of the tiny Bear Diversion Dam reservoir and strikes out east-
northeast, along the north side of Bear Creek. It doesn't take one
long to realize he has left that feeling of openness behind. The
canyon walls close in, and the forest cover becomes moderate to
dense. Should one desire to try the fair-to-good fishing for brown
trout along the stream (they come in sizes up to 15"), he will also
more than likely encounter small stands of water-loving cottonwood and aspen en route, as well as some lodgepole, oak, and the
first fir. Near the creek, wildflower-fanciers will relish the luxuriant
growth of pentstemon, lupine, paintbrush, monkey flower, and
cinquefoil (pronounced "sink-foyl"). Bear Creek, in the stretch immediately above the reservoir, is a rock-bottomed, briskly flowing
stream with a surprising penchant for suddenly eddying out into
broad, emerald-green pools. Blessedly, the trail is never far from
the creek's banks, and one can make several worthwhile forays to
the water's edge without too much loss of trail time. For 1½ miles
above the reservoir, the trail ascends very gradually, and then as
the canyon narrows it begins to ascend more steeply. The duff
trail gives way to rocky underfooting, which prevails for the rest
of the trip, and about ½ mile farther this route encounters the
signed boundary of the John Muir Wilderness Area. At the boundary, one can catch his first V-notched glimpse of Recess Peak
directly up canyon. The trail drops down for a short distance and
then begins a steady, rocky ascent. Several good campsites dot
the nearby banks of Bear Creek, and the traveler can take his

choice of any of these primitive sites, or continue to ascend to the large "improved" packer site just below the confluence of Bear Creek and Cirque Creek. Though the emerald-green pools occur less often, they stand in dramatic contrast to the plunging white water, and, understandably, most of the campsites are located beside these stiller sections of water. In this country slight changes in altitude entail significant changes in the plant and animal life. For example, as the trail ascends steeply to the packer site mentioned above, fishermen find golden trout as well as brown in their catch, and exploring naturalists discover that the predominant forest cover is now Jeffrey pine and the shrubs are now mostly gooseberry and snow brush. Arrival at the packer site is presaged by several "corduroy" bridge crossings of marshy sections, and a stock drift fence. At the improved packer campsite (8000') there is a fine, large pool offering good fishing for brown and golden (8"-15"). Campers in this canyon are frequently serenaded by coyotes who range Bear Ridge. Swimming in mid or late season is excellent. Firewood is ample.

2nd Hiking Day (Upper Bear Creek to Bear Diversion Dam Jeep Road Junction, 8 miles): Retrace steps of 1st hiking day.

 2

TRIP From BEAR DIVERSION DAM JEEP ROAD JUNCTION to KIP CAMP, via Bear Creek (round trip). Topo map (15') Mt. Abbot; Profile 1. Best mid or late season; 19 miles.

Grade	Trail/layover days	Total recommended days
Leisurely	3/0	3
Moderate	2/0	2
Strenuous	- - -	- - -

HILITES This trip's route ascends Bear Creek to the densely forested flats of Kip Camp. The angler seeking varied sport will find good fishing from the time he first sees Bear Creek at Bear Diversion Dam. Brown trout, a particular favorite of the serious fisherman, populate the lower waters of this trip, and the justly famous golden trout inhabit the upper waters and nearby lakes.

DESCRIPTION (Moderate trip)
1st Hiking Day (Bear Diversion Dam Jeep Road Junction to Kip Camp, 9.5 miles): Proceed to the campsites on upper Bear Creek

as described in the 1st hiking day, trip 1. The improved packer campsite at the end of that hiking day marks the point where the trail veers away northerly from cascading Bear Creek. As it ascends steadily up the north wall of the canyon, one has good views of the jumbled cirque crest on the opposite side of the canyon to the southeast. Though rocky, this trail is well maintained as it rises above the floor of the valley. The moderate-to-dense forest cover of the creek bottom thins as the trail climbs to the slight granite-ribbed saddle that marks the start of the descent to Kip Camp and the reunion with Bear Creek. Flowers along this stretch of trail include pentstemon, larkspur, monkshood, elephant's head, lupine, goldenrod, fleabane, paintbrush, and western mountain aster. The descent reveals a marked change in the forest cover in that the predominant Jeffrey of the lower canyon has given way to lodgepole and juniper. Where the views during the ascent were of the down-canyon Bear Creek drainage, the descent brings views of the Mono Divide. Just above Kip Camp, a bend in the duff trail reveals Mt. Hilgard, and as one nears the flats of Kip Camp he finds that the timber now includes red fir. The aspen- and cottonwood-lined banks of Bear Creek reappear on the immediate right as our route strikes the John Muir Trail and turns right. Just a few yards to the southeast of the junction lies Kip Camp (8880′), where there are several good campsites (all improved) that offer the angler fair golden and brook fishing (to 10″) on nearby Bear Creek. Firewood is ample, and emergency services, should they be necessary, are available from the ranger patrolman stationed at Kip Camp. Those fishermen with enough enthusiasm remaining after the ascent will want to try the excellent golden fishing (to 14″) at Bear Twin Lakes. Access to these tiny lakes may be had either by following their outlet stream upward from its confluence with Bear Creek (opposite Kip Camp) or by continuing about 2 miles up the John Muir Trail to the improved packer campsites just north of the Hilgard Branch trail junction, and, after fording Bear Creek, ascending the west canyon wall.

2nd Hiking Day (Kip Camp to Bear Diversion Dam Jeep Road Junction, 9.5 miles): Retrace steps of 1st hiking day.

 3

TRIP   From BEAR DIVERSION DAM JEEP ROAD JUNCTION to VERMILION CAMPGROUND via Kip Camp, Quail Meadows (shuttle trip). Topo maps (15′) Kaiser Peak, Mt. Abbot; Profile 1. Best early or late season; 21 miles.

	Trail/layover	Total recom-
Grade	days	mended days
Leisurely	4/1	5
Moderate	3/1	4
Strenuous	2/1	3

HILITES   Varied scenery that ranges from the intimate confines of Bear Creek to the open expanses on Bear
Ridge gives this long-weekend trip a universal appeal. The trek circumnavigates Bear Ridge, visiting the
Bear and Mono Creek drainages, and the close proximity of the beginning and end of this horseshoe-
shaped route makes it a potential loop.

DESCRIPTION   (Moderate trip)

1st Hiking Day   (Bear Diversion Dam Jeep Road Junction to Kip
Camp, 9.5 miles): See 1st hiking day, trip 2.

2nd Hiking Day   (Kip Camp to Quail Meadows, 6 miles): From Kip
Camp (8880'), this hiking day's route follows the John Muir Trail
as it ascends steadily northwest, passing a stock drift fence, and
then climbing steeply through a thinning forest of lodgepole and
juniper. Views back into the Bear Creek drainage are excellent,
including Recess Peak, Mt. Hilgard and Seven Gables. Crossing
the rocky summit of Bear Ridge, one can view the geologically more
recent volcanic overlay typified by the breached crater of Volcanic
Knob to the east. As the trail begins the steep series of switchbacks that drop into the Mono Creek watershed, the traveler is
treated to excellent views of the Silver Divide, the immediate Mono
Creek watershed, and Lake Thomas A. Edison. This route stepladders near the foot of the descent, and then drops the final 400'
to the crossing at Mono Creek. At this writing, plans were under-
way for completion of a steel bridge to supersede a long and
sometimes hazardous ford of the creek. Several good campsites
line the north side of Mono Creek at Quail Meadows (7760'). Addi-
tional campsites can be found along the south side of the creek.
Firewood is ample, and fishing is good for brook and rainbow
(to 12") on Mono Creek.

3rd Hiking Day   (Quail Meadows to Vermilion Campground, 5.5
miles): Quail Meadows marks the junction of the John Muir Trail
and the Vermilion Campground trail. Our trail leaves the John
Muir Trail and proceeds downstream (west) toward Lake Thomas
A. Edison. This trail is relatively new, and is unmarked on the
latest topo map. The first mile of level going parallels the magnificent chutes and rapids that precede Mono Creek's absorption
by the Lake Edison reservoir. These white waters are periodically
interrupted by sand-bottomed granite potholes that offer excellent
swimming to the mid or late season traveler. One can easily
imagine the members of the famous Brewer Survey Party of 1864
stopping here for a few moments of relaxation and refreshment.
A few yards beyond these potholes an indistinct path branches
off to the left and leads to the boat landing at the northeast tip of
the lake. Here a boat-taxi service operates during the summer
months, and one may obtain the ferry schedule by writing the

High Sierra Resort/Lake Thomas A. Edison/Mono Hot Springs/ California. The ferry service is based at a resort adjoining Vermilion Campground. Those choosing to use the newly constructed trail along the north side of Lake Edison will find that the route undulates severely up and down the north wall of Vermilion Valley. However, the worst of these climbs and descents are over midway down the length of the lake, and the point where our trail passes the Goodale Pass trail marks the beginning of relatively level going. Along these leveler stretches the forest cover of Jeffrey, red fir, and lodgepole becomes somewhat denser. In one of these denser stands of lodgepole, a few yards from the Goodale Pass trail junction, our route meets a second boat-landing trail. Continuing westward, our trail crosses the Cold Creek Bridge, passes the trail lateral to Devils Bathtub, and winds down through a dense stand of Jeffrey to meet the Forest Service access road that leads to Vermilion Campground (7650′).

TRIP From BEAR DIVERSION DAM JEEP ROAD JUNCTION to LAKE ITALY via Kip Camp (round trip). Topo map (15′) Mt. Abbot; Profiles 1, 2. Best mid or late season; 37 miles.

Grade	Trail/layover days	Total recommended days
Leisurely	5/1	6
Moderate	4/1	5
Strenuous	3/1	4

HILITES This trip is tailor-made for the traveler who wants to experience the high, alpine country of the mid Sierra without having to contemplate cross-country walking. Lake Italy, the aim of this trip, is a frequently used base camp for climbers, and a fine trip selection for the photographer.

DESCRIPTION (Moderate trip)
1st Hiking Day (Bear Diversion Dam Jeep Road Junction to Kip Camp, 9.5 miles): See 1st hiking day, trip 2.

2nd Hiking Day (Kip Camp to Lake Italy, 9 miles): From Kip Camp (8880′), the moderately ascending trail stays very close to the east bank of Bear Creek. This moderate ascent soon leaves the flats of Kip Camp behind, and the forest cover changes to lodgepole. Within 2 miles after leaving the flats, one sees the last of the familiar quaking aspen, and the canyon takes on more of an open valley feeling. Three improved packer campsites (spaced at intervals of about 1 mile) line Bear Creek for the first 3 miles above Kip Camp, and their presence indicates the heavy use that the Muir trail is subjected to. On the left, below Mt. Hilgard, one can see the Hilgard Branch canyon come into view. At the confluence of Hilgard Branch and Bear Creek our route branches left (east) from the John Muir Trail. The Hilgard Branch trail ascends steadily through a thinning forest cover of lodgepole and then over large patches of glacially smoothed granite. Midway between the trail junction and Lake Italy, the trail levels out temporarily, only to begin climbing abruptly via short, rocky switchbacks. High on the left the rocky prominence of Mt. Hilgard dominates the skyline as the switchbacks temporarily end. The trail fords the stream, and then resumes its switchbacking. Just below Teddy Bear Lake, the trail passes timberline, and then crosses long granite ledges that alternate with grassy patches to the outlet of Lake Italy (11150'). This large, bootlike lake derives its name from its similarity to the European peninsula. Rounding the curve of the lake just above the outlet one can easily see the cirque basin where the feeder glacier had its beginnings. At the east end of the cirque, Bear Creek Spire marks the division between the western and eastern directional flows of the old glaciers. There are a number of fair exposed campsites along the turfy south shore of the lake near the outlet, but wood is scarce. However, the scenery surrounding this large granitoid lake compensates for the lack of firewood and forest cover. To the west towers Mt. Hilgard; to the north, Mt. Gabb; and to the east are Bear Creek Spire and Mt. Julius Caesar. To the immediate north of Bear Creek Spire, making up the distant skyline, are Mts. Dade, Abbot and Mills. A climber's heaven: every peak bordering on this lake towers well over 13000'. Poor spawning and feed conditions restrict the golden trout fishery (8"-12") to fair — a classification that applies to the surrounding Toe, Jumble, Brown Bear and Teddy Bear Lakes as well.

3rd Hiking Day (Lake Italy to Kip Camp, 9 miles): Retrace steps of 2nd hiking day.

4th Hiking Day (Kip Camp to Bear Diversion Dam Jeep Road Junction, 9.5 miles): Retrace steps of 1st hiking day.

5

TRIP	From BEAR DIVERSION DAM JEEP ROAD JUNCTION to LAKE ITALY via Kip Camp, return via Vee Lake, East Fork Bear Creek (semiloop trip). Topo map (15') Mt. Abbot; Profiles 1, 2. Best mid or late season; 43 miles.	

Grade	Trail/layover days	Total Recommended days
Leisurely	7/2	9
Moderate	5/2	7
Strenuous	4/2	6

HILITES   For intermediate and experienced knapsackers only, this varied and exciting cross-country trip seeks the kind of high country that is the exclusive province of the knapsacker.

DESCRIPTION (Moderate trip)

1st Hiking Day   (Bear Diversion Dam Jeep Road Junction to Kip Camp, 9.5 miles): See 1st hiking day, trip 2.

2nd Hiking Day   (Kip Camp to Lake Italy, 9 miles): See 2nd hiking day, trip 4.

3rd Hiking Day   (Lake Italy to Vee Lake, 5 miles cross country): Our route skirts the south side of Lake Italy, following the ducked and sometimes faint Italy Pass trail. As the trail ascends on the west side of the outlet stream from Jumble Lake, one has excellent views north along the Sierra Nevada crest. The trail then fords the stream, and at the east side of Jumble Lake our route branches away from the Italy Pass trail and begins the cross-country work by traversing the steep granite face on the south side of Jumble Lake to the rocky saddle that dents the ridge just above White Bear Lake. At this saddle, one can see the clear division that this ridge made between two small glaciers which once fed the main *mer de glace* that flowed down Bear Creek canyon. White Bear Lake and Black Bear Lake just to the east are the puddled remnants of the outermost extremities of the East Fork feeder glacier. By virtue of having come "through the back door," the hiker has the opportunity to trace the old glacier's path from its inception all the way to the main trunk. Anglers will probably want to try the fair-to-good golden trout fishing at White Bear and Black Bear lakes before proceeding, but as a rule of thumb the fishing gets better as one descends into the East Fork drainage. The descent to Big Bear, Bearpaw and Ursa lakes is made due south via a series of smooth granite ledges and talus. This cross-country travel requires careful route-picking and the inevitable scrambling. Hikers should take particular care in crossing these loosened talus slopes. At Big Bear and Bearpaw lakes fishermen will find some of the best fishing of the trip. Golden trout to 15″ are present in the lakes and the intervening streams, and because the fishing at Little Bear Lake is almost equally good, it isn't worth breaking down one's rod for the short walk between. From Little Bear Lake our route veers south-southwest across an easy granite ridge that is dotted with tiny tarns. This ridge brings the traveler to a point just above the outlet of Vee Lake, and it is an easy scramble down to the turfy but forest-barren fringes of the lake (11120′). As at Lake Italy, camping at Vee Lake is of the high, alpine, woodless variety. However, fishing on this large (50-acre) lake is good-to-excellent for golden trout (to 16″), and it is an ideal spur camp location for angling or exploratory side trips to the lakes in the upper part of the basin. From the fair campsites on the north and east sides of the lake the camper has excellent views to the east of Royce and Merriam peaks and to the west of Seven Gables.

4th Hiking Day   (Vee Lake to Kip Camp, 10 miles): Keeping to the east side of the outlet stream, our route descends steeply to the Seven Gables Lakes basin. The intimate falls and chutes found along this outlet stream are a pleasant contrast to the brooding heights of Seven Gables peak to the west. Just above the confluence of the outlet creek and the Seven Gables branch of the East Fork Bear Creek, our route fords the Seven Gables Branch and turns downstream. However, anglers electing to first test the good fishing for golden at the largest of the Seven Gables lake chain will alter their route upstream—½ mile of gentle ascent. Those continuing downstream reford the Seven Gables branch just below the lovely waterfalls that precede the stream's inlet into the L-shaped lake, the lowest of the Seven Gables chain, and there pick up the well-ducked trail. Fishing for golden (to 10″) in the L-shaped lake is good. Descending steadily, the trail veers north, fords the outlet stream from Coronet Lake, and then, turning west, crosses back and forth over the rushing creek. This steady descent encounters timberline just north of Seven Gables peak, and witnesses the typical hemlock/lodgepole/fir spectrum as it follows the length of a Veed canyon and emerges into the wide, more open expanses of Bear Creek Valley. Turning northward, the trail intercepts and turns right onto the John Muir Trail. The descent becomes moderate to gentle as the trail winds through alternating meadow and lodgepole stands to the fords of multibranched Hilgard Creek. A few yards beyond these fords the trail meets the Hilgard Branch trail lateral, and retraces the steps of the first part of the 2nd hiking day.

5th Hiking Day   (Kip Camp to Bear Diversion Dam Jeep Road Junction, 9.5 miles): Retrace steps of 1st hiking day.

TRIP   From BEAR DIVERSION DAM JEEP ROAD JUNCTION
              to SANDPIPER LAKE via Kip Camp (round trip). Topo
              map (15′) Mt. Abbot; Profiles 1, 2. Best mid or late
              season; 36 miles.

| | Trail/layover | Total recom- |
Grade	days	mended days
Leisurely	5/1	6
Moderate	4/1	5
Strenuous	3/1	4

HILITES   This trip provides the unusual opportunity for knap-
             sackers (or those with stock) to trace a river's course
             from its inception. Most of this route follows the
             famous John Muir Trail, but most of the campsites
             avoid that trail's heavily used stopover places.

DESCRIPTION   (Moderate trip)
1st Hiking Day   (Bear Diversion Dam Jeep Road Junction to Kip
Camp, 9.5 miles): See 1st hiking day, trip 2.

2nd Hiking Day   (Kip Camp to Sandpiper Lake, 8.5 miles): Kip
Camp (8880′), a sand flat situated in a moderately dense forest
cover of lodgepole, juniper, red fir, and quaking aspen, is a fine
place for the hiker who gets on the trail early to observe the many
animals that use the flats for grazing and watering. One is very
likely to see deer, or a black bear or coyote. Following the John
Muir Trail, our route swings south through thinning forest cover on
a moderate ascent that stays close to the river. The trail passes
several improved packer campsites situated near large, log-
jammed pools in the river, and the canyon takes on a valley aspect
as it nears Hilgard Branch. Our route passes the Italy Pass trail
and fords by footlog several branchlets of Hilgard Branch. Near
these wetter sections of trail, one will find abundant whorled blue-
purple pentstemon, yellow and purple shooting star, prickly red
gooseberry and yellow wallflower. The ascent is still gentle-to-
moderate as it passes several more improved campsites between
open granite slab sections with meadowy breaks, and arrives at the
trail junction where the Vee and Seven Gables lakes trail branches
left (east). This junction is just a few yards short of the Bear Creek
ford—a wade-across ford that is hazardous during high water.
Those on foot will find the going easier by using the footlog ford
⅛ mile downstream (due west of the last improved packer campsite). After fording the stream via this footlog, one rejoins our route
at the west side of the wade-across ford cited above via a short

section of the Orchid Lake trail. The trail then ascends steeply by switchbacks to the corduroy bridge crossing of the West Fork of Bear Creek at Rosemarie Meadow. At the signed junction, our route branches left, off the John Muir Trail, westward over an easy ridge to Lou Beverly Lake. (This well-established trail is not shown on the topo map.) The moderate forest cover of lodgepole through which the trail winds shows the effects of the higher altitude. The 2-needled trees take on a stunted appearance and one begins to see occasional hemlock and clumps of mountain heather. Lou Beverly Lake (10050') is a tiny (5-acre), shallow, moderately forested lake with one improved packer campsite (there are other primitive sites) at the southwest end. Fishing for golden (to 14") is good to excellent, which should be adequate reason for anglers to try their luck. For the camper who prefers a more protected and timbered lake, Lou Beverly is a fine alternative site to end this hiking day. For the camper who prefers a high alpine feel to his campsite, the choice should be Sandpiper Lake. The signed trail to that lake crosses the marshy inlet to Lou Beverly Lake, and ascends along the north and east side of the stream connecting the two lakes. This ascent, over rough, unmaintained trail, is steady until it reaches the abrupt granite face just below Sandpiper Lake, where the going becomes very steep. The waterfall outlet of Sandpiper Lake (10480') makes a musical accompaniment to end the climb by, as one arrives at the good campsites near the outlet and along the west side of the lake. This fair-sized granitoid lake (about 25 acres) has a very sparse forest cover of stunted lodgepole (firewood is somewhat scarce) but the view of the surrounding peaks is excellent—particularly from the granite shoulder just southwest of the lake. Despite fairly heavy fishing pressure in the last two years, angling for golden (to 13") is good, and this lake makes an excellent base camp for fishing and hiking excursions to the surrounding lakes on the headwaters of Bear Creek.

3rd Hiking Day (Sandpiper Lake to Kip Camp, 8.5 miles): Retrace steps of 2nd hiking day.

4th Hiking Day (Kip Camp to Bear Diversion Dam Jeep Road Junction, 9.5 miles): Retrace steps of 1st hiking day.

 7

TRIP   From BEAR DIVERSION DAM JEEP ROAD JUNCTION to LITTLE MOCCASIN LAKE via Kip Camp, Sandpiper Lake, cross-country return via West Pinnacles Creek drainage, Three Island Lake (semiloop trip). Topo map (15') Mt. Abbot; Profiles 1, 2. Best mid or late seasons; 50 miles.

| | Trail/layover | Total recom- |
Grade	days	mended days
Leisurely	7/3	10
Moderate	6/2	8
Strenuous	5/2	7

HILITES   Loop trips that include the variety of country this one does are rare. From the confines of Bear Creek, this route climbs above timberline, and circles 2 rarely visited watersheds. The cross-country work is often difficult, and this trip is recommended for intermediate and experienced hikers only.

DESCRIPTION   (Moderate trip)

1st Hiking Day   (Bear Diversion Dam Jeep Road Junction to Kip Camp, 9.5 miles): See 1st hiking day, trip 2.

2nd Hiking Day   (Kip Camp to Sandpiper Lake, 8.5 miles): See 2nd hiking day, trip 6.

3rd Hiking Day   (Sandpiper Lake to Little Moccasin Lake, 6.5 miles cross country): This rugged cross-country loop begins by rounding the south end of Sandpiper Lake (10480') and fording the inlet stream coming from Medley Lakes. From here the route ascends southeast by means of the granite ledge systems. Following the south fork of the east inlet stream to Medley Lakes, this route ascends steeply over smoothed, barren granite slabs and grassy pockets to a narrow unnamed lake at the head of the stream on the topo map. Views during the course of this climb include Mts. Senger and Hooper, Seven Gables, and Medley Lakes. From the unnamed lake, this route ascends up the drainage to the northeast to an obvious saddle. Just short of this saddle, one has superlative views to the west, and these views are matched to the east when the crest of the saddle is reached. From the saddle one can see Mts. Hilgard, Abbot, Gabb, Dade, Bear Creek Spire, Julius Caesar, Royce, Humphreys and Gemini. Route-finding on these rugged talus slopes is difficult at best, but the hiker will find the traverse around the steep north slope of Gemini a moderate one that descends to a broad saddle and down to the unnamed scree-ridden lake just north of Aweetasal Lake. This traverse offers excellent views down into the Seven Gables Lakes cirque until it crosses a saddle. The rock cairn at the saddle marks a point from which one can see the crest as it dwindles away to the southernmost skyline, including Glacier Divide, Emerald Peak, and Mts. McGee, Henry and Goddard. Immediately on the right are the twin peaks of Gemini and the spectacular jumbled crest of The Pinnacles. It is the latter that dominate the views to the west for the remainder of this hiking day's progress down the East Pinnacles Creek drainage. Descent into this drainage is first moderate (to the first unnamed, talus-cluttered lake), and then steeper as one drops down to shallow Aweetasal Lake. Typical of most of the lakes on this drainage, Aweetasal has virtually no timber, tundralike grassy spots between granite slabs, and poor fishing. Most of these lakes were air-planted with golden trout, but lack of adequate feed and spawning areas and winter kill soon depleted the populations. This rugged and somewhat sterile land is the alpine Sierra at its best. Here, despite the harsh, exposed environment, the tough yet delicate grasses grow. Near the streams one can rediscover the yellow columbine that is found only in these rarified heights. There are, of course, the usual whorled pentstemon, paintbrush, yellow cinquefoil and shooting star, but all are dwarfed, clinging close to the turf, as though they were foreign to this clime. Here the margin for life is slim, and the hardiest knapsacker finds himself imitating the plant life. When he rests or seeks sleep in the comfort of his bedroll, he instinctively curls up to conserve his precious body heat. This is perennial ice-touched land, always cold, and yet a place where one can come by a severe sunburn. Harsh and uninviting as the land seems, the hiker soon finds a beauty to wonder at as he progresses down the drainage. Only those who dare this harshness manage to view The Pinnacles from the east side, and that rugged, spiring rock mass towers on the right as one scrambles down the alternately moderate and steep granite slabs between Aweetasal and Jawbone lakes. Following the outlet stream from Jawbone Lake, one arrives at shallow, grassy Council Lake. Here route-finding becomes simpler as the going levels off, and by a series of grassy benches one passes Paoha and Negit lakes, and, rounding a granite shoulder, comes to Big Moccasin Lake. Stunted and solitary whitebark pines, a sure sign of high alpine country, dot the rocky fringes of this shallow lake. From Big Moccasin Lake it is an easy descent to Little Moccasin Lake, where one has fine views of the Piute Creek drainage. Above the U-shaped valley one can see Pilot Knob and the complex of avalanche chutes on the north face of Mt. Henry to the south. Majestic Mt. Humphreys dominates the Sierra crest, and the adjacent subrange is crowned by Emerald Peak. The top of Mt. Tom is visible. From this viewpoint, our route veers due west, descending a grassy chute to the campsites along the outlet streams from the upper lakes. These campsites (10800') are good, with excellent views, but the sparse forest cover of stunted whitebark and lodgepole makes firewood somewhat scarce.

4th Hiking Day (Little Moccasin Lake to Sandpiper Lake, 7.5 miles cross country): From the west fork of East Pinnacles Creek this cross-country route swings around the south end of The Pinnacles on a long talus and bouldered traverse to a point just north of Pemmican Lake. This scrambling traverse offers the views described in the 3rd hiking day until the drainage of West Pinnacles Creek is reached. A slight descent past several tarns unmarked on the topo map leads to Spearpoint Lake, which, unlike the lakes of the East Pinnacles Creek drainage, is deep, and populated by a few small golden (6-8"). The rugged terrain around the edges of Spearpoint Lake determines the best feasible route to be over the easy granite ridge separating Spearpoint and Pendant lakes, and thence north across the marshy section separating Pendant and Big Chief lakes. Skirting the east side of shallow Big Chief Lake (some golden, fry), this route ascends on a moderate grade from the meadowed north end of the lake to Old Squaw Lake. This lake is barren of trout, but it offers some of the best views of The Pinnacles obtained on this trip. Glacially smoothed granite slabs line the lake's edge on all sides, and progress is fairly easy along the east shore. Following the inlet stream, the route ascends steadily to Wampum Lake, where anglers may try their luck for the fair fishing (golden 6-8"). At Wampum Lake the twin peaks of Gemini once more come into view, and one has reached the cirque-basined headwaters of West Pinnacles Creek. This bowl-like cirque presents route-picking problems, and some care should be exercised in crossing the sometimes steep west wall, which divides the West Pinnacles Creek drainage from the South Fork of Bear Creek drainage. At the top of this wall one has a panoramic vista of Seven Gables, Gemini, The Pinnacles, Emerald Peak, Mt. Henry, Mt. Senger, Mt. Hooper and the Bear Creek drainage. Descent from this ridge presents no problems to the accomplished rock-climber, but the easiest route for the novice is found by picking one's way westward around the head of the Three Island Lake cirque to the saddle just east of Sharp Note Lake, and then traversing down the steep slopes on the west side of Three Island Lake. Anglers will find fair-to-good golden trout fishing in this large (80-acre) lake. These rockbound, deep waters provide a classic glacial setting for high-country enthusiasts, and they are a long-time favorite of camera-carrying visitors. Following the outlet stream at the north end of Three Island Lake past Medley Lake, an easy descent along a ledge system of granite leads to the inlet of Sandpiper Lake, the beginning point for this cross-country loop.

5th Hiking Day (Sandpiper Lake to Kip Camp, 8.5 miles): Retrace steps of 2nd hiking day.

6th Hiking Day (Kip Camp to Bear Diversion Dam Jeep Road Junction, 9.5 miles): Retrace steps of 1st hiking day.

TRIP   From BEAR DIVERSION DAM JEEP ROAD JUNCTION to FLORENCE LAKE ROADEND via Kip Camp, Sandpiper Lake, Selden Pass, Blaney Meadow (shuttle trip). Topo maps (15') Mt. Abbot, Blackcap Mtn.; Profiles 1, 2, 5. Best mid or late season; 36.5 miles.

Grade	Trail/layover days	Total recommended days
Leisurely	5/1	6
Moderate	4/1	5
Strenuous	3/1	4

HILITES   This popular shuttle trip circles the Mt. Hooper complex and visits some of the best creek and lake fishing in the Sierra. Part of this trip's popularity stems from the near proximity of the trailhead to the conclusion of this trip—making the shuttle fairly simple.

DESCRIPTION (Moderate trip)

1st Hiking Day   (Bear Diversion Dam Jeep Road Junction to Kip Camp, 9.5 miles): See 1st hiking day, trip 2.

2nd Hiking Day   (Kip Camp to Sandpiper Lake, 8.5 miles): See 2nd hiking day, trip 6.

3rd Hiking Day (Sandpiper Lake to Lower Blaney Meadows Campground, 11 miles — 2 miles cross country): The first 2 miles of this hiking day are cross country. Starting from the campsites along the west side of Sandpiper Lake (10480'), this route ascends the easy, tarn-dotted swale at the southwest end of the lake. This line of route takes one around the granite-slabbed nose of the ridge extending north from Mt. Senger. From the nose of the ridge, one has excellent views down the Bear Creek drainage to Bear Ridge, and beyond to the barren tops of the Silver Divide. Immediately below is Lou Beverly Lake. In its mirrorlike green surface one sees the reflection of Recess Peak. Looking north, views from left to right include Mt. Hooper, the Bear Creek drainage, and Lou Beverly Lake; and beyond, Graveyard Peak, Mt. Izaak Walton and Red and White Mountain. Given a clear atmosphere, one can see all the way north to the Minarets and the Mammoth Crest. To the immediate right is the bouldery crest of Mt. Hilgard, and to the right of that towers the multipeaked Seven Gables, with Mt. Gabb peeking over its left shoulder. Turning toward the south, one looks into the immense cirque basin headed by Mt. Senger. From the top of this ridge, it is a moderate descent to large, granitoid Marie Lake, where our route skirts the meadowy northern edge. Walking the turfy fringes of the lake (poor-to-fair brook and golden fishing), one will find lousewort and western mountain aster mixed among the heather. This lake fringe marks timberline, and as our route turns south on the west side of Marie Lake, the mixed sparse forest of hemlock and lodgepole pine is left behind. At the outlet of Marie Lake our route rejoins the John Muir Trail as it winds along the west banks of the lake. From the south end of the lake, the trail ascends on a moderate-to-steep grade to Selden Pass (10873'). Breather stops on this climb offer fine views back to Mt. Hilgard and the granitoid Marie Lake cirque. From Selden Pass the trail descends over short, steep switchbacks to Heart Lake. This rockbound, heart-shaped lake has a meadow-turfed fringe delicately colored with heather, primrose and yellow columbine. Fair angling for golden (6-8") makes this lake an interesting rest stop. Non-fishermen will find the views a fine way to pass the time while anglers practice their art. From the outlet, one can see Mts. Goddard and Henry to the southeast; to the southwest Ward Mtn. and Mt. Shinn dominate the visible peaks. Continuing the moderate descent from Heart Lake along its outlet stream, the trail arrives at Sally Keyes Lakes. This short walk is lined with an abundance of wildflowers including corn lily, Indian paintbrush, Douglas phlox, shooting star, yellow cinquefoil, milfoil, pentstemon, lupine, red heather, wallflower, nude buckwheat and western mountain aster. Fishermen who have not dismantled their rods will find the fishing here about the same as at Heart Lake. The trail crosses the short stream joining the two Sally Keyes Lakes and descends on a duff and sand trail through a thickening forest cover of lodgepole. There are several good, but heavily used, campsites at the outlet and along the west shore of the lower of the two lakes. Wood is plentiful. Our route crosses the outlet stream and in a long meadow ¼ mile south branches right, away from the John Muir Trail. Appropriately, a sign at the edge of the meadowed trail junction warns that this route is "not for stock." Although the trail is dusty and steep, one can enjoy the unusual cross-section of Sierra flora encountered in the course of its 4000′ descent. At first, altitude-loving whitebark pines are mixed with the dense forest cover of lodgepole, but within a few miles the whitebark disappears and fir makes a brief appearance, only to be replaced by Jeffrey at lower altitudes. Juniper is found in both the high and low altitudes; quaking aspen are not seen until the trail nears Senger Creek, near the foot of a descent. The dry canyon walls are generally brush-covered, with heavy manzanita around the middle of the descent, but with some surprise the trail traveler will also find many wildflowers along these same stretches. In the drier regions are Douglas phlox, streptanthus and Mariposa lily; in the wetter sections are shooting star, red columbine, corn lily, cinquefoil and pentstemon; almost everywhere are lupine, white Mariposa, Bigelow sneezeweed, golden brodiaea and groundsel. The switchbacking descent ends above Blaney Meadows (visible from the trail) and then this route turns right onto the Florence Lake/Evolution Valley trail. From this junction the duff trail descends through a moderately dense mixed forest cover of lodgepole, juniper, Jeffrey and quaking aspen, and arrives at Lower Blaney Meadows and the signed public campground (7650′). Several fair campsites, including 2 improved packer sites, are available, and firewood is ample. Fishing on the South Fork San Joaquin River for brook and some rainbow (to 12″) is fair to good — mostly downstream.

4th Hiking Day   (Lower Blaney Meadows Campground to Florence Lake Roadend, 7.5 miles): Following the well-used route east from Lower Blaney Meadows the trail ascends steadily over sand and rock to the footlog ford of the unnamed creek just east of Double Meadow. Here, the trail has been rerouted around the fringes of the grassland. Damage to fragile meadows like these, particularly during the wet spring months, has finally made a sufficient impression on the Forest Service and the National Park Service that they are now deemed worthy of appropriate conservation measures to guarantee their survival. As the trail rounds the north side of the meadow it affords excellent views of Ward Mtn. and high, pointed Mt. Shinn, and then it makes a moderate descent through a moderate forest cover of Jeffrey, juniper and white fir to the ford of the South Fork of the San Joaquin, just above the southeastern end of Florence Lake. Crossing the smooth granite just west of the bridge, this trail passes the short lateral branching right to the edge of Florence Lake, and a heavily used campground (primarily boaters' use). At Boulder Creek the trail fords by means of a footlog. The ford bears a caution sign reading, "Dangerous crossing during heavy runoff." This route then passes the Thomson Lake/Hot Springs Pass trail junction, and commences a series of moderate-to-steep ups and downs through a mixed forest cover of Jeffrey and juniper, with occasional aspen, white fir and lodgepole. This route skirts the west side of man-made Florence Lake, sometimes ascending to granite ledges 300′ above the lake's surface. Views to the south always include Mt. Shinn and Ward Mtn. and glimpses up the South Fork San Joaquin River drainage. To the north is the Silver Divide, foregrounded by the blue waters of Florence Lake. Just before this route meets the Southern California Edison Dam Road (no public auto travel) the trail has climbed high on the ridge; it then descends steeply to the roadend.

TRIP   From BEAR DIVERSION DAM JEEP ROAD JUNCTION to VEE LAKE via Kip Camp, Sandpiper Lake, cross country to Vee Lake, return via cross-country route to Lake Italy, Hilgard Branch Creek, Kip Camp (semi-loop trip). Topo map (15′) Mt. Abbot; Profiles 1, 2. Best mid or late season; 47 miles.

Grade	Trail/layover days	Total recom-mended days
Leisurely	8/3	11
Moderate	6/2	8
Strenuous	5/2	7

HILITES   A fine fishing trip combined with a short, rugged cross-country segment, this route should appeal to the intermediate knapsacker.

DESCRIPTION (Moderate trip)

1st Hiking Day (Bear Diversion Dam Jeep Road Junction to Kip Camp, 9.5 miles): See 1st hiking day, trip 2.

2nd Hiking Day (Kip Camp to Sandpiper Lake, 8.5 miles): See 2nd hiking day, trip 6.

3rd Hiking Day (Sandpiper Lake to Vee Lake, 5.5 miles cross country): This route circles the west side of Sandpiper Lake, fords the westernmost inlet stream, and ascends the granite ledge systems south of the lake. On this southeastward ascent, our route meets and follows the south fork of the east inlet stream to Medley Lakes. This cross-country route crosses steep, glacially smoothed granite that is interspersed with grassy, wildflower-colored pockets, and arrives at the narrow, barren unnamed lake that lies at the head of this stream fork. The rarified air of the climb (crossing the 12000′ level) brings fine views of Mts. Senger, Hooper and Seven Gables. A rest break is probably in order before beginning the final ascent to the obvious saddle on the northeast horizon. The climb begins easily, soon becomes steep, and concludes by a scramble to the crest. At this saddle, one has unmatched views to the east. Besides the immediate summits of Seven Gables and the twin spires of Gemini, one can see Mts. Hilgard, Abbot, Gabb, Dade, Bear Creek Spire, Julius Caesar, Royce and Humphreys. Every one of these peaks towers over 13000'. Also from this saddle, one can pick out the natural route to the southernmost of the Seven Gables lakes. Though steep, this descent is made mostly over glacially smoothed rock. Route-picking, however, is sometimes made difficult by interruptions of talus and scree slides. The upper lakes of the Seven Gables chain are talus-bound, shallow bodies of water having no fish, but anglers will want to try the good fishing on the lower lakes (golden trout to 12") before making the final ascent to Vee Lake. These lower lakes and the intersecting stream are a fly fisherman's paradise. The ascent to Vee Lake is made over granite and talus along the outlet stream from that lake. The ascent terminates at the turfy east end (11120'), where there are fair campsites. Hikers who do not care for the high, alpine kind of camping (usually woodless) should plan on ending their day at the lowest of the Seven Gables lakes, where there are several good campsites and firewood is ample. Fishing on large Vee Lake (50 acres) is good to excellent for golden (to 16"). Views from the campsites on the east and north sides of the lake are excellent of the striking, white-granited faces of Royce and Merriam peaks.

4th Hiking Day (Vee Lake to Lake Italy, 5 miles cross country): Beginning at the north side of the north arm of Vee Lake, this hiking day's route ascends the granite shoulder to the string of rockbound tarns just south of Little Bear Lake. This moderate ascent is accomplished over a granite ledge system broken by talus. Fishing on tiny Little Bear Lake for golden is fair to good, and this evaluation holds for Big Bear and White Bear lakes upstream. Following the inlet stream of Little Bear Lake, the route ascends to the outlet of Big Bear, Ursa, Bearpaw Lake basin, crosses the stream joining Big Bear and White Bear lakes, and ascends steeply along the eastern side of this stream. Above the abrupt northeastern side of White Bear Lake one can make out the obvious saddle that separates the drainage of the East Fork of Bear Creek from that of Hilgard Branch. Our route crosses this saddle, traverses the southeast end of the Jumble Lake cirque, and strikes the Italy Pass trail, where it turns left. The saddle and the traverse offer unusual end-on views of Mts. Julius Caesar, Dade, Abbot, Mills and Bear Creek Spire. Descending the moderate-to-steep slopes above Jumble Lake, one cannot help feeling awed by the forces that carved this basin. The smoothed rock is mute testimony to the grinding action of the glaciers that found their start here, and, as the trail continues to descend along the north shore of Jumble Lake, one pursues the course of the glacier as it forged its way into the much larger Lake Italy cirque. This descent fords the stream that joins Jumble Lake and Lake Italy, and drops down to the shores of the lake about a mile above the outlet (11150'). This very large lake (124 acres) is granite-enclosed, with narrow, meadowed fringes. Fair campsites that are quite exposed can be found along the south shore near the outlet. Firewood is very scarce, but this defect is more than compensated for by the superlative views of the surrounding peaks. Fishing for golden (8-12″) is fair.

5th Hiking Day (Lake Italy to Kip Camp, 9 miles): The trail descends along the east bank of Hilgard Branch past the short lateral to Teddy Bear and Brown Bear Lakes (fair fishing for golden to 12″) and then switchbacks down steeply to the ford of the creek. Then the trail levels out as it winds through a sparse forest cover of lodgepole. About a mile farther, it descends steeply once more, via rocky switchbacks, and after losing 500′ then levels out. The loss of altitude brings an increase in density of the forest cover — mostly lodgepole — and the individual trees no longer appear gnarled and stunted. The route then fords the outlet stream draining Hilgard Lake, and a few yards beyond that fords Hilgard Branch, only to recross ¼ mile below. This last ford precedes the final switchbacking drop into the main canyon of Bear Creek. Our route meets and turns right onto the John Muir Trail, descending moderately past several improved packer campsites to the sand flats of Kip Camp (8880′). Several good improved campsites are situated near the creek. Firewood is ample. Fishing along Bear Creek for golden and brook is fair (to 10″). Serious anglers will, however, want to test the excellent fishing for golden (to 14″) at nearby Bear Twin Lakes. Although they are only about 3 miles away (the last mile being cross country) these beautifully set lakes draw very few visitors from travelers of the John Muir Trail. Bear Twin Lakes are best reached by retracing the above-described route to the footlog crossing of Bear Creek just north of the Hilgard Branch junction. From the west side of Bear Creek the best route follows a very faint, mostly cross-country fisherman's trail that ascends northwest, and arrives at the southeast end of the larger of the two lakes.

6th Hiking Day (Kip Camp to Bear Diversion Dam Jeep Road Junction, 9.5 miles): Retrace steps of 1st hiking day.

TRIP   From BEAR DIVERSION DAM JEEP ROAD JUNCTION to SECOND RECESS via Kip Camp, Hilgard Branch, Lake Italy, cross-country route to Lower Mills Creek Lake, Second Recess, return via Fish Camp, Quail Meadows, Kip Camp (semiloop trip). Topo map (15′) Mt. Abbot; Profile 1, 2, 3. Best late season; 48.5 miles.

	Trail/layover	Total recom-
Grade	days	mended days
Leisurely	8/3	11
Moderate	6/2	8
Strenuous	5/2	7

HILITES   Another fine cross-country route, this trip is frequently used by climbers making ascents of the cluster of peaks that line the route. Anglers, photographers, naturalists and garden-variety trail-pounders will all find something to excite them en route. Because of the cross country, this route is recommended for intermediate and experienced knapsackers only.

DESCRIPTION   (Moderate trip)

1st Hiking Day   (Bear Diversion Dam Jeep Road Junction to Kip Camp, 9.5 miles): See 1st hiking day, trip 2.

2nd Hiking Day   (Kip Camp to Lake Italy, 9 miles): See 2nd hiking day, trip 4.

3rd Hiking Day   (Lake Italy to Lower Mills Creek Lake, 5 miles cross country): This scenic cross-country route rounds the granite-bound north side of Lake Italy to Toe Lake, and then ascends the increasingly steep north cirque wall to Gabbot Pass (the saddle between Mt. Gabb and Mt. Abbot). The ascent involves a strenuous workout, but does not require rock-climbing skills. As a reward, the hiker acquires some of the finest views obtainable in this part of the Sierra. This route is generally considered a climber's access route for ascents of Mts. Gabb and Abbot, and is seldom used by casual hikers, and almost never by side-excursion-minded packer parties (not passable to stock). Peaks in line of sight during the ascent and at the pass include, to the west, Mts. Hilgard and Gabb; to the south, Mt. Julius Caesar and Royce Peak; to the east, Mts. Dade, Abbot and Mills, and Bear Creek Spire; and to the north, the crest of the Silver Divide. From the pass, this route descends just east of the Mt. Gabb glacier to the steep headwall of the Upper Mills Creek Lake cirque. Traversing the east side of this cirque, it continues down the east side of the cascading creek between the lakes to the good campsites at the timberlined outlet of Lower Mills Creek Lake. Both Upper and Lower Mills Creek lakes are meadow-fringed, though mostly rockbound, and offer good-to-excellent golden fishing (to 13"). Firewood takes a bit of looking for, but is ample. Views from the campsites are excellent of the Mono and Silver divides.

4th Hiking Day   (Lower Mills Creek Lake to Quail Meadows, 9.5 miles): Staying on the east side of Mills Creek, a faint fisherman's trail descends the sparsely timbered slopes below Lower Mills Creek Lake past two small lakelets (good fishing for golden to 10"). At the final drop into Second Recess Creek canyon, this faint, often washed-out trail switchbacks down steeply to the confluence of the two creeks. The forest cover alters during the course of this descent from stunted lodgepole and some whitebark to flat-needled fir, lodgepole pine, and occasional quaking aspen and yellow pine. This route, now following a distinct trail, descends on a moderate slope along the east side of Second Recess Creek. As one nears the brink of Mono Creek Canyon he achieves a clear picture of the glacial story that left these spectacular landforms. It is clear that the valley of the Second Recess was a secondary (or feeder) arm of the greater ice mass that once filled the deeper Mono Creek canyon. After accomplishing the moderate-to-steep descent to the bridge crossing of Mono Creek, the traveler can look back whence he came and fully understand the nature of the geologic term "hanging valley." Here, the receding rivers of ice, and later water, continued their grinding course of attrition long after the feeder glaciers had ceased to flow. The greater ice mass of the main trunk ground deeper, leaving these valleys literally hanging. At Fish Camp this route passes several improved packer campsites and turns left (west) onto the Mono Creek trail. This creekside trail descends moderately, offering between-the-trees views into First Recess, and of the abrupt, dark, northern face of Volcanic Knob. Frequent groves of quaking aspen line this route, and late season sees the banks of Mono Creek clad in golden hues. At the point where the canyon walls appear to be closing in (about 2½ miles below Fish Camp), the trail veers away from the creek on a steep, switchbacking ascent that crosses the long-nosed ridge that separates the North Fork from the main drainage of Mono Creek. On the west side of this ridge, our route descends a short distance to the John Muir Trail junction, and turns left along the east side of the North Fork of Mono Creek. The trail then switchbacks down steeply to ford the North Fork a few yards above its confluence with the main stream. From the ford it is less than a mile of relatively level going through a dense lodgepole forest cover to the good campsites at Quail Meadows (7760'). Here fishing for brook and some golden (to 14") is good, and a camp firewood supply is abundant.

5th Hiking Day (Quail Meadows to Kip Camp, 6 miles): From Quail Meadows our trail crosses Mono Creek via the steel bridge, and promptly begins the steep, switchbacking ascent of Bear Ridge. This 2200' climb, particularly if taken in the early morning hours, offers dramatically lit views of the Silver Divide to the north. Foregrounding the Silver Divide are the aptly named Vermilion Cliffs, and the green clefts of the Cold Creek and North Fork of Mono Creek drainages. The ascent begins to level out near the rocky crest of the ridge, and then begins a switchbacking descent on the south side. Views along this descent include Recess Peak, Mt. Hilgard, Seven Gables, and the U-shaped Bear Creek drainage. Midway down the ridge, the trail passes into denser forest cover, and as it reaches the stock fence just above Kip Camp, it encounters dense stands of juniper, lodgepole, and a few fir. At Kip Camp (8880') one also finds cottonwood and quaking aspen lining the banks of Bear Creek. Good campsites can be found just a few yards southeast of the Bear Creek trail junction, and, should they be necessary, emergency services are available from the ranger patrolman stationed at Kip Camp. Fishing for golden and brook (to 10") along Bear Creek is fair, but those anglers with enough ambition for some cross-country walking (about 3 miles) will find fishing at Bear Twin Lakes. These tiny lakes lie hidden behind the timbered knoll that rises just to the south, across the creek.

6th Hiking Day (Kip Camp to Bear Diversion Dam Jeep Road Junction, 9.5 miles): Retrace steps of 1st hiking day.

TRIP From BEAR DIVERSION DAM JEEP ROAD JUNCTION to VERMILION CAMPGROUND via Kip Camp, Hilgard Branch Creek, Lake Italy, cross-country route to Lower Mills Creek Lake, Second Recess, return via Fish Camp, Quail Meadows (shuttle trip). Topo maps (15′) Mt. Abbot, Kaiser Peak; Profiles 1, 2, 3. Best late season; 38.5 miles.

Grade	Trail/layover days	Total recommended days
Leisurely	7/2	9
Moderate	5/2	7
Strenuous	4/2	6

HILITES Using the same access route (cross country) to Second Recess as the previous trip, this trek finishes by emerging at Vermilion Campground. A complete loop (instead of a shuttle) can be made by hiking the short road section separating Vermilion Campground and Bear Diversion Dam Jeep Road Junction. For intermediate and experienced hikers only.

DESCRIPTION (Moderate trip)

1st Hiking Day (Bear Diversion Dam Jeep Road Junction to Kip Camp, 9.5 miles): See 1st hiking day, trip 2.

2nd Hiking Day (Kip Camp to Lake Italy, 9 miles): See 2nd hiking day, trip 4.

3rd Hiking Day (Lake Italy to Lower Mills Creek Lake, 5 miles cross country): See 3rd hiking day, trip 10.

4th Hiking Day (Lower Mills Creek Lake to Quail Meadows, 9.5 miles): See 4th hiking day, trip 10.

5th Hiking Day (Quail Meadows to Vermilion Campground, 5.5 miles): See 3rd hiking day, trip 3.

12

TRIP From BEAR DIVERSION DAM JEEP ROAD JUNCTION to VERMILION CAMPGROUND via Kip Camp, Sandpiper Lake, cross country to Vee Lake, Lake Italy, Lower Mills Creek Lake, return via Fish Camp, Quail Meadows (shuttle trip). Topo maps (15') Mt. Abbot, Kaiser Peak; Profiles 1, 2, 3. Best late season; 48.5 miles.

Grade	Trail/layover days	Total recommended days
Leisurely	9/2	11
Moderate	7/2	9
Strenuous	5/2	7

HILITES A lengthier version of the previous trip, this route traverses a considerable length of the Sierra Crest, offering exciting vistas, excellent fishing, and adventurous cross-country walking. For intermediate and experienced knapsackers only.

DESCRIPTION (Moderate trip)

1st Hiking Day (Bear Diversion Dam Jeep Road Junction to Kip Camp, 9.5 miles): See 1st hiking day, trip 2.

2nd Hiking Day (Kip Camp to Sandpiper Lake, 8.5 miles): See 2nd hiking day, trip 6.

3rd Hiking Day (Sandpiper Lake to Vee Lake, 5.5 miles cross country): See 3rd hiking day, trip 9.

4th Hiking Day (Vee Lake to Lake Italy, 5 miles cross country): See 4th hiking day, trip 9.

5th Hiking Day (Lake Italy to Lower Mills Creek Lake, 5 miles cross country): See 3rd hiking day, trip 10.

6th Hiking Day (Lower Mills Creek Lake to Quail Meadows, 9.5 miles): See 4th hiking day, trip 10.

7th Hiking Day (Quail Meadows to Vermilion Campground, 5.5 miles): See 3rd hiking day, trip 3.

13

TRIP   From BEAR DIVERSION DAM JEEP ROAD JUNCTION to LAKE ITALY via Kip Camp, Sandpiper Lake, cross country to Vee Lake, Lake Italy, return via cross-country route to Lower Mills Creek Lake, Fish Camp, Quail Meadows, Kip Camp (semiloop trip). Topo map (15′) Mt. Abbot; Profiles 1, 2. Best late season; 58.5 miles.

Grade	Trail/layover days	Total recommended days
Leisurely	10/2	12
Moderate	8/2	10
Strenuous	6/2	8

HILITES   To many, cross-country walking is what sets hikers apart from those using stock, and this trip is tailor-made for intermediate and experienced hikers. Few hiking pilgrimages offer a more condensed exposure to the magnificent Sierra crest than this one.

DESCRIPTION   (Moderate trip)

1st Hiking Day   (Bear Diversion Dam Jeep Road Junction to Kip Camp, 9.5 miles): See 1st hiking day, trip 2.

2nd Hiking Day   (Kip Camp to Sandpiper Lake, 8.5 miles): See 2nd hiking day, trip 6.

3rd Hiking Day   (Sandpiper Lake to Vee Lake, 5.5 miles cross country): See 3rd hiking day, trip 9.

4th Hiking Day   (Vee Lake to Lake Italy, 5 miles cross country): See 4th hiking day, trip 9.

5th Hiking Day   (Lake Italy to Lower Mills Creek Lake, 5 miles cross country): See 3rd hiking day, trip 10.

6th Hiking Day   (Lower Mills Creek Lake to Quail Meadows, 9.5 miles): See 4th hiking day, trip 10.

7th Hiking Day   (Quail Meadows to Kip Camp, 6 miles): See 5th hiking day, trip 10.

8th Hiking Day   (Kip Camp to Bear Diversion Dam Jeep Road Junction, 9.5 miles): Retrace steps of 1st hiking day.

14

TRIP   From BEAR DIVERSION DAM JEEP ROAD JUNCTION
            to PINE CREEK ROADEND via Kip Camp, Sandpiper
            Lake, Selden Pass, Sally Keyes Lakes, Hutchinson
            Meadow, Pine Creek Pass, Upper Pine Lake (shuttle
            trip). Topo maps (15') Mt. Abbot, Blackcap Mtn., Mt.
            Tom; Profiles 1, 2, 5, 4. Best mid or late season; 49.5
            miles.

	Grade	Trail/layover days	Total recommended days
	Leisurely	8/2	10
	Moderate	6/2	8
	Strenuous	- - -	- - -

HILITES   This fine trail route zigzags to cross the Sierra crest
            at Pine Creek Pass. Starting at Bear Creek, the route
            joins the John Muir Trail, crosses Selden Pass, and
            then turns up Piute canyon. En route, this trip tours
            canyon bottoms, lofty passes and open meadows —
            a full range of wilderness experience included in a
            gratifying trans-Sierra route.

DESCRIPTION (Moderate trip)

1st Hiking Day (Bear Diversion Dam Jeep Road Junction to
Kip Camp, 9.5 miles): See 1st hiking day, trip 2.

2nd Hiking Day (Kip Camp to Sandpiper Lake, 8.5 miles): See
2nd hiking day, trip 6.

3rd Hiking Day (Sandpiper Lake to lower Sally Keyes Lake, 5
miles cross country): See first part of 3rd hiking day, trip 8.

4th Hiking Day (Lower Sally Keyes Lake to Hutchinson Meadow,
12.5 miles): See 5th hiking day, trip 22.

5th Hiking Day (Hutchinson Meadow to Upper Pine Lake, 9
miles): See 6th hiking day, trip 22.

6th Hiking Day: (Upper Pine Lake to Pine Creek Roadend, 5
miles): See 1st hiking day, trip 17.

15

TRIP From MOSQUITO FLAT (Rock Creek) to SECOND RECESS via Mono Pass (round trip). Topo maps (15') Mt. Tom, Mt. Abbot; Profile 3. Best mid or late season; 32 miles.

Grade	Trail/layover days	Total recommended days
Leisurely	6/2	8
Moderate	5/2	7
Strenuous	4/2	6

HILITES The exciting eastern escarpment makes the first part of this trip a memorable experience. Mono Pass offers sweeping vistas that vie for the traveler's consideration with the intimacy of the beautiful, cirque-bound lakes of Second Recess.

DESCRIPTION (Leisurely trip)

1st Hiking Day (Mosquito Flat to Ruby Lake, 2.5 miles): The magnificent Sierra Crest confronts the traveler at the very outset of this trip. From the trailhead at Mosquito Flat ((10400') the trail starts southwest toward the imposing, skylined Mts. Mills, Abbot, Dade and Bear Creek Spire. A short distance from the trailhead, our route passes the short lateral to Eastern Brook Lakes, and tops a low rocky ridge just west of Mack Lake. From this ridge one has good views of the Little Lakes Valley, and cannot help but feel a sense of satisfaction that this beautiful valley enjoys the protection of Wilderness Area designation (John Muir Wilderness Area). Aside from some early, abortive mining ventures, this region remains relatively unspoiled. The trail crosses the ridge, and descends a short distance to the junction of the Little Lakes Valley/Mono Pass trails. Our route branches right (west) and ascends steeply over rocky switchbacks. In the course of this switchbacking ascent, the traveler will see the moderate-to-dense forest cover of whitebark and lodgepole diminish in density, and the trail finally rises above timberline. Views during the climb include the glacier-fronted peaks named above, and Mt. Morgan midway up the ascent. Immediately below and to the east, the deep blue of Heart, Box and some of the Hidden Lakes reflect the sky above, and the viewer looking at the panorama of the valley can readily trace the glacial history that left these "puddles" behind. As the trail nears the meadowed edge of the outlet stream from Ruby Lake, it becomes apparent that a cirque basin is opening up. One cannot see Ruby Lake, which completely fills the cirque bottom, until actually at water's edge (11100'). This first breathtaking view of the lake and its towering cirque walls makes the climb worth the effort. Sheer granite makes up the upper walls of the cirque, and the crown is topped by a series of spectacular pinnacles, particularly to the west. To the north, also on the crest, a notch marks Mono Pass, and close scrutiny will reveal the switchbacking trail that ascends the south ridge of Mt. Starr. The lower walls of the cirque are mostly made up of talus and scree that curve outward to the lake's edge, and it is over this jumbled rock that ambitious anglers must scramble to sample the fair fishing for brook, rainbow and brown (to 12"). Good campsites with ample firewood can be found below the outlet of the lake. Lakeside campsites are exposed, usually windy, and offer little available wood.

2nd Hiking Day (Ruby Lake to Fish Camp, 9 miles): Following a general east-to-west course, the trail climbs by long, steady switchbacks up the north wall of the cirque, and after a long steady traverse veers northward by steeper switchbacks to the summit of Mono Pass (12000'). The best views from the pass area are obtained by climbing the easy granite shoulder of Mt. Starr, to the east. Views from this shoulder include: Mts. Stanford, Huntington, Crocker and Hopkins and Red and White Mountain to the north; and Mts. Abbot and Dade, Bear Creek Spire, and Mt. Humphreys to the south. The trail continues north from the pass, descending steadily over granite. It traverses the west side of rockbound Summit Lake (poor fishing), and then descends more steeply to the slopes above Trail Lakes (poor-to-fair brook fishing). The westerly descent around Trail Lakes turns northward, and the trail drops to the Golden Creek ford. Here, this route re-enters forest cover (moderate stands of lodgepole), and it continues to descend as it passes by the lateral to Pioneer Basin and the lateral to Fourth Recess Lake. Serious anglers may wish to alter their hiking plan with a rewarding excursion to the excellent brook (some rainbow and golden) fishing obtainable at the lower Pioneer lakes. Fishing at nearby Fourth Recess Lake is good for brook (to 14"). Beyond these laterals, the trail fords the outlet streams from Pioneer Basin. Mono Rock towers on the left as our route passes the Third Recess trail lateral, and, about a mile farther, the lateral to Hopkins Lakes and Hopkins Pass. Anglers who wish to sample the good fishing for brook, rainbow and occasional golden will find many fine, deep holes along this stretch of trail. For the most part, Mono Creek rushes along briskly, but occasional potholes and level stretches in the streambed contribute to the good spawning areas that any good Sierra trout stream requires. Anglers and hikers alike will appreciate the colorful abundance of quaking aspens that line Mono Creek. For those with color film in their cameras, the best time to capture the aspen color is usually late September or early October. This route then passes the Grinnell Lakes lateral, and descends to the good improved campsites on both sides of the bridge spanning Mono Creek at Fish Camp (8500'). Firewood is ample.

3rd Hiking Day (Fish Camp to Lower Mills Creek Lake, 4.5 miles): See 1st part of 4th hiking day, trip 10.

4th Hiking Day (Lower Mills Creek Lake to Fish Camp, 4.5 miles): Retrace steps of 3rd hiking day.

5th Hiking Day (Fish Camp to Ruby Lake, 9 miles): Retrace steps of 2nd hiking day.

6th Hiking Day (Ruby Lake to Mosquito Flat, 2.5 miles): Retrace steps of 1st hiking day.

 16

TRIP　From MOSQUITO FLAT to BEAR DIVERSION DAM JEEP ROAD JUNCTION via Ruby Lake, Mono Pass, Fish Camp, Lower Mills Creek Lake, Lake Italy, Kip Camp (shuttle trip). Topo maps (15') Mt. Tom, Mt. Abbot; Profiles 3, 2, 1. Best mid or late season; 39.5 miles.

Grade	Trail/layover days	Total recommended days
Leisurely	6/2	8
Moderate	5/2	7
Strenuous	4/2	6

HILITES　Everyone needs to traverse the Sierra — at least once — and this route provides a fine way to do it. Following an old Indian trade route, this trip visits two remarkably different watersheds, joined by the John Muir Trail, and boasts fishing for golden, brook, brown and rainbow trout that ranges from good to excellent.

DESCRIPTION (Leisurely trip)
1st Hiking Day (Mosquito Flat to Ruby Lake, 2.5 miles): See 1st hiking day, trip 15.

2nd Hiking Day (Ruby Lake to Fish Camp, 9 miles): See 2nd hiking day, trip 15.

3rd Hiking Day (Fish Camp to Lower Mills Creek Lake, 4.5 miles): See 1st part of 4th hiking day, trip 10.

4th Hiking Day (Lower Mills Creek Lake to Lake Italy, 5 miles cross country): See 3rd hiking day, trip 10.

5th Hiking Day (Lake Italy to Kip Camp, 9 miles): See 2nd hiking day, trip 4.

6th Hiking Day (Kip Camp to Bear Diversion Dam Jeep Road Junction, 9.5 miles): See 1st hiking day, trip 2.

17

TRIP   From PINE CREEK ROADEND to HONEYMOON LAKE (round trip). Topo map (15') Mt. Tom; Profile 4. Best mid season; 11 miles.

Grade	Trail/layover days	Total recommended days
Leisurely	2/2	4
Moderate	2/0	2
Strenuous	- - -	- - -

HILITES   The steep, winding ascent to Honeymoon Lake offers breathtaking over-the-shoulder views of the Pine Creek watershed, and the Honeymoon Lake campsite views of the Sierra Crest make this one of the best choices for a base camp location on the east side of the Sierra.

DESCRIPTION *(Leisurely trip)*

1st Hiking Day (Pine Creek Roadend to Honeymoon Lake, 5.5 miles): The trailhead (7580') is located at the pack station just south of Pine Creek. The dusty duff trail ascends gently from the pack station through a dense, mixed forest cover of Jeffrey, red fir and quaking aspen, and fords several branchlets of an unnamed creek that feeds Pine Creek. A few yards beyond these fords, the trail emerges from the forest cover, directly opposite the Union Carbide tungsten mill, and then merges with an old mining road. This tortuously twisted, rocky road was once used for access to the now-dormant Brownstone Mine, but now sees only the mark of a few wild animals, many pack strings and the shuffling track of a solitary backpacker. Although the slope into the Pine Creek canyon is steep, the road's grade is, for the most part, gentle, and this segment is simply a matter of slog-and-pant. Two welcome streams break the monotony of the climb, and the view (despite the ugly tramway that scars Morgan Creek) is spectacular. Through the Pine Creek valley that slopes away to the northeast, one can look across the Owens River drainage to the volcanic tableland and White Mountain (14242') on the skyline. There is one advantage to the presence of the mining activities across the canyon—and that is the dramatic contrast between industrial and recreational use of wilderness country. Coincident to this is the contrasting tempi of the two sides of the valley. One has only to watch the juggernaut flow of the tramway buckets and the antlike scurrying of trucks and people across the way to fully appreciate the slow, peaceful pace of the wilderness traveler. The road ends just above the clapboard and corrugated shacks (the terminus of an overhead tramway wire) marking the Brownstone

Mine, and the trail ascends from there over talus and scree by short, steep switchbacks. Trees along this ascent are juniper, incense cedar, and lodgepole. The latter have left beautiful, weathered snags of a dramatic golden hue that are a constant delight to color photographers. With the steepest part of the ascent behind, the trail fords another unnamed tributary and veers northerly to join Pine Creek just below Pine Lake. Here, the creek alternates cascades, falls and chutes in a riot of white water. The trail fords the stream, and amidst a moderate forest cover of lodgepole arrives at the northeast end of Pine Lake. This medium-sized lake (16 acres) is a popular overnight camping place (campsites along the northeast shore), and fishermen may wish to tarry here to sample the fair brook (to 10"); fishing, however, is generally better at Upper Pine Lake. The trail to Upper Pine Lake proceeds by skirting the rocky northwest side of Pine Lake and ascending the sometimes marshy section that crosses the seepage flow from Birchim Lake (¼ mile cross country to the west—fair fishing for Paiute cutthroat). Leveling out, the trail parallels the outlet stream from Upper Pine Lake (excellent campsites) and arrives at the west side of the lake (10200'). Anglers will find that brook, rainbow and some golden (to 12") frequent these waters, and angling is good. At the southwest inlet, the trail ascends moderately, fording that inlet stream, and arrives at the Pine Creek Pass/Italy Pass trail junction. Our route turns right, away from the Pine Creek Pass trail and onto the Italy Pass trail (incorrectly signed as the "Hilgard Pass" trail), and ascends steeply to the rockbound shores of Honeymoon Lake (10480'). This moderate-sized lake (10 acres) has good campsites near the outlet stream, and excellent meadowed sites at the head of the waterfall on the inlet stream on the west side. Fishing for brook and rainbow (to 10") is good. This lovely lake makes an excellent base camp for side excursions to 40 surrounding lakes in 4 drainages, or for climbing of 6 nearby peaks that exceed 13000' in elevation.

2nd Hiking Day (Honeymoon Lake to Pine Creek Roadend, 5.5 miles): Retrace steps of 1st hiking day.

18

TRIP   From PINE CREEK ROADEND to MOON LAKE via Pine Creek Pass (round trip). Topo map (15') Mt. Tom; Profile 4. Best mid season; 20 miles.

Grade	Trail/layover days	Total recommended days
Leisurely	4/1	5
Moderate	3/1	4
Strenuous	2/1	3

HILITES   The juggernaut tramways and snarling trucks that sur-
round the trailhead belie the primitive country that
lies beyond the first climb. Pine Creek, from its lower
aspen-clad banks to its tundra-meadow birth place,
is a kind of stream that hiker, angler, photographer
and naturalist can take a fancy to. At Moon Lake the
visitor will experience memorable open, alpine surroundings at their finest.

DESCRIPTION   (Leisurely trip)

1st Hiking Day   (Pine Creek Roadend to Upper Pine Lake, 5
miles): See 1st hiking day, trip 17.

2nd Hiking Day   (Upper Pine Lake to Moon Lake, 5 miles): From
the outlet stream at the north end of Upper Pine Lake (10200'), the
trail rounds the west side of the lake, ascends moderately, and
then fords the stream joining Honeymoon Lake and Upper Pine
Lake. A few yards beyond the ford, the trail meets the junction of
the Italy Pass and Pine Creek Pass trails. Our route bears left on
a steady ascent toward Pine Creek Pass. Originally a Mono Indian
trading route, this trail and pass have been used by man for almost
five hundred years. The moderate forest cover of lodgepole thins
as the trail climbs, and soon emerges above timberline. Tiny, emerald-green, subalpine meadows break the long granite slabs, and
wildflower fanciers will find clumps of color that include wallflower,
shooting star, pentstemon, lupine, primrose, and yellow columbine.
The trail parallels a seepage making up the headwaters of Pine
Creek as it ascends a long swale between two white granite walls,
and then makes the final steep rocky climb to Pine Creek Pass
(11100'). From the vicinity of the pass, one has excellent views to
the north of Mt. Julius Caesar (with Bear Creek Spire protruding
over the right shoulder); to the northwest of Merriam and Royce
peaks; to the south of Pilot Knob, Glacier Divide, and parts of the
great Humphreys Basin; and to the southeast of Four Gables and
Mt. Humphreys. This pass marks the division between the east and
west drainage flows at the Sierra crest. The trail to French Canyon
then descends steeply to a long, fairly level, rocky bench, and then
drops again over talus and slab ledges for about ¼ mile, to meet
the faint fisherman's trail branching left to Elba and Moon lakes.
Our route leaves the main trail, following this fisherman's trail
as it ascends the fairly steep south wall of French Canyon. This
400' climb brings one to fair-sized Elba Lake (unnamed on the topo
map). Typical of these high, montane lakes, Elba seems virtually
devoid of vegetation and life. It is understandable that the first-
time visitor to this country often refers to it as "moon country," but
those who come to know and love the high country soon discover
the beauty that hides close beneath the sterile veneer. Spots of
green between the tumbled talus blocks indicate grassy tundra
patches or clumps of willows, and occasionally the weathered landscape is broken by a dwarfed lodgepole or whitebark pine. Steady,
silent scrutiny will usually discover movement that indicates life.
A bird is usually the first to be detected, and most likely it will be
either a rosy finch or a hummingbird. Four-footed movement among
the rocks is most likely a cony or a marmot, or it just might be a

wolverine or a bushy-tailed wood rat. Fishermen will soon find life in the lake, for Elba Lake has a good population of golden and golden hybrids (to 12"). Following the inlet stream, our route then ascends steadily to larger Moon Lake (10998'). Fair campsites (exposed, no wood) can be found along the north side of the lake. Fishing for golden (to 12") is excellent, and, using Moon Lake as a base, anglers can explore 8 more fishing lakes sharing this same bench system.

3rd Hiking Day   (Moon Lake to Upper Pine Lake, 5 miles): Retrace steps of 2nd hiking day.

4th Hiking Day   (Upper Pine Lake to Pine Creek Roadend, 5 miles): Retrace steps of 1st hiking day.

 19

TRIP	From PINE CREEK ROADEND to BEAR DIVERSION DAM JEEP ROAD JUNCTION via Honeymoon Lake, Italy Pass, Kip Camp (shuttle trip). Topo maps (15') Mt. Tom, Mt. Abbot; Profiles 4, 2, 1. Best mid or late season; 30 miles.

Grade	Trail/layover days	Total recommended days
Leisurely	4/2	6
Moderate	4/1	5
Strenuous	3/1	4

HILITES	This is one of the best and shortest routes for an ambitious beginner desiring to get the "feel" of a trans-Sierra crossing. Bound up in this route is the steep eastern escarpment; the barren, glaciated granite of the Sierra crest; and the long, densely wooded slopes of the west side.

DESCRIPTION   (Leisurely trip)

1st Hiking Day   (Pine Creek Roadend to Honeymoon Lake, 5.5 miles): See 1st hiking day, trip 17.

2nd Hiking Day   (Honeymoon Lake to Lake Italy, 6 miles): The trail from Honeymoon Lake ascends steadily along the north side of the North Fork of Pine Creek through thinning lodgepole forest cover, and emerges on a rocky ridge dividing 2 lake basins composing the headwaters of Pine Creek. On the right, to the north, Chalfant Lakes (fair fishing for rainbow to 10") sparkle at the foot of Mt. Julius Caesar. On the left the Granite Park lakes compose the drainage on the south side of the ridge. Scooped, scoured and scraped by a river of ice, the granite of the upper cirque was left massive and smooth. Subsequent prying by expanding ice widened tiny crevices until chunks of granite broke loose and tumbled to the foot of the slope. Talus slopes born of this ice erosion are added to each year, and the occasional passerby who witnesses the thunderous crash of a large slab of freed granite can count himself lucky. Among large boulders, across talus, and along smoothed granite this trail ascends steadily to the east side of the uppermost lake in the Granite Park chain. From this lake, the trail ascends steeply on short switchbacks to Italy Pass (12300'). Views from this notch are dominated by massive Mt. Julius Caesar immediately to the northeast, but the view back to the east of the unusual, unnamed chocolate layer-cake peak (so typified because of the light dikes striating the mountain face) just east of Chalfant Lakes is excellent. From the pass, the trail descends steeply into the Jumble Lake basin, traverses the north slope above the lake, and then drops over the lip of the hanging valley into the Lake Italy basin. This large lake (124 acres) nestles at the foot of 7 of the highest peaks in the Sierra. It was named Lake Italy by the USGS in about 1907 because of its resemblance to that country in shape. Our descending route fords the outlet stream from Jumble Lake, strikes that profile "just above the heel," and then parallels the south shore to the fair exposed campsites there and at the outlet. Firewood is very scarce, and although the population of golden trout is somewhat depleted, their size (sometimes up to 12") makes this a fair lake for angling.

3rd Hiking Day (Lake Italy to Kip Camp, 9 miles): See 2nd hiking day, trip 4.

4th Hiking Day (Kip Camp to Bear Diversion Dam Jeep Road Junction, 9.5 miles): See 1st hiking day, trip 2.

TRIP	From PINE CREEK ROADEND to FLORENCE LAKE via Honeymoon Lake, Italy Pass, Sandpiper Lake, Selden Pass (shuttle trip). Topo maps (15') Mt. Tom, Mt. Abbot, Blackcap Mtn.; Profiles 4, 2, 5. Best mid or late season; 41.5 miles.

Grade	Trail/layover days	Total recommended days
Leisurely	6/2	8
Moderate	5/2	7
Strenuous	4/2	6

HILITES   Like the previous trip, this is a stirring trans-Sierra route. But, unlike it, this route visits three impressive drainages, and three lake basins, and crosses two major passes. Despite the trek's contact with the renowned John Muir Trail, campsites are remotely located, and the fishing en route ranges from good to excellent.

DESCRIPTION (Leisurely trip)

1st Hiking Day   (Pine Creek Roadend to Honeymoon Lake, 5.5 miles): See 1st hiking day, trip 17.

2nd Hiking Day   (Honeymoon Lake to Lake Italy, 6 miles): See 2nd hiking day, trip 19.

3rd Hiking Day   (Lake Italy to Improved Campsites on Bear Creek 1 mile south of Hilgard Branch/Bear Creek trail junction, 7 miles): Proceed to the John Muir Trail junction as described in 5th hiking day, trip 9, where our route turns left and ascends gently through stands of lodgepole that alternate with tiny meadows. Several fine fishing holes interrupt the fast flow of Bear Creek, and anglers may elect to tarry along this stretch in order to wet their lines in a try for the golden and some brook (to 10″) that populate the stream. The good, improved packer campsites lie just off the trail to the right about a mile beyond the junction. These sites make a fine layover spot to investigate the fishing and scenery of Orchid and Apollo Lakes. (The signed access trail to these lakes can be reached by fording Bear Creek via the footlog just upstream from the campsites.) Firewood is plentiful.

4th Hiking Day   (Improved Campsites on Bear Creek to Sandpiper Lake, 4.5 miles): See 2nd hiking day, trip 6.

5th Hiking Day   (Sandpiper Lake to Lower Blaney Meadows Campground, 11 miles—2 miles cross country): See 3rd hiking day, trip 8.

6th Hiking Day   (Lower Blaney Meadows Campground to Florence Lake Roadend, 7.5 miles): See 4th hiking day, trip 8.

 21

TRIP   From PINE CREEK ROADEND to SANDPIPER LAKE via Honeymoon Lake, Italy Pass, Sandpiper Lake, return via cross country to Vee Lake, Lake Italy, Honeymoon Lake (semiloop trip). Topo maps (15′) Mt. Tom, Mt. Abbot; Profiles 4, 2. Best late season; 45 miles.

| | Trail/layover | Total recom- |
Grade	days	mended days
Leisurely	8/3	11
Moderate	7/2	9
Strenuous	5/2	7

HILITES   This trip offers the intermediate or experienced hiker
a chance to cross the Sierra crest, via Italy Pass, and
return by that pass after cross-countrying the exciting Bear Lakes basin and touring a brief section of
the John Muir Trail. Unparalleled scenery, challenging route-finding, fine lake and stream fishing, and numerous opportunities for layover-day side trips make
this a trip designed to whet the appetite of the adven-
ture-seeking backpacker.

DESCRIPTION   (Moderate trip)

1st Hiking Day   (Pine Creek Roadend to Honeymoon Lake, 5.5
miles): See 1st hiking day, trip 17.

2nd Hiking Day   (Honeymoon Lake to Lake Italy, 6 miles): See 2nd
hiking day, trip 19.

3rd Hiking Day   (Lake Italy to Sandpiper Lake, 11.5 miles): See
5th hiking day, trip 9; and 2nd hiking day, trip 6.

4th Hiking Day   (Sandpiper Lake to Vee Lake, 5.5 miles cross
country): See 3rd hiking day, trip 9.

5th Hiking Day   (Vee Lake to Lake Italy, 5 miles cross country):
See 4th hiking day, trip 9.

6th Hiking Day   (Lake Italy to Honeymoon Lake, 6 miles): Retrace
steps of 2nd hiking day.

7th Hiking Day   (Honeymoon Lake to Pine Creek Roadend, 5.5
miles): Retrace steps of 1st hiking day.

TRIP   From PINE CREEK ROADEND to SANDPIPER LAKE
via Honeymoon Lake, Italy Pass, Sandpiper Lake, Selden Pass, Hutchinson Meadow, French Canyon, Pine
Creek Pass (loop trip). Topo maps (15′) Mt. Tom, Mt.
Abbot, Blackcap Mtn.; Profiles 4, 2, 5. Best mid or
late season; 54.5 miles.

	Trail/layover	Total recom-
Grade	days	mended days
Leisurely	9/2	11
Moderate	7/2	9
Strenuous	5/2	7

HILITES   The intermediate trail traveler (or the ambitious beginner) will find this long trip a rewarding choice. After leaving beautiful Pine Creek, this trail route tours Granite Basin and Italy Pass, and then joins the John Muir Trail. Traveling south, this singular trail crosses Selden Pass, and ascends the South Fork of the San Joaquin River watershed. Leaving the Muir Trail at Piute Creek, this route then loops back to rejoin the Pine Creek trail via Pine Creek Pass.

DESCRIPTION   (Moderate trip)

1st Hiking Day   (Pine Creek Roadend to Honeymoon Lake, 5.5 miles): See 1st hiking day, trip 17.

2nd Hiking Day   (Honeymoon Lake to Lake Italy, 6 miles): See 2nd hiking day, trip 19.

3rd Hiking Day   (Lake Italy to Sandpiper Lake, 11.5 miles): See 5th hiking day, trip 9; and 2nd hiking day, trip 6.

4th Hiking Day   (Sandpiper Lake to lower Sally Keyes Lakes, 5 miles): See 1st part of 3rd hiking day, trip 8.

5th Hiking Day   (Lower Sally Keyes Lake to Hutchinson Meadow, 12.5 miles): An early start for this hiking day is advisable in order to complete the long, sometimes steep, always dusty descent into the South Fork of the San Joaquin River drainage. From Sally Keyes Lakes (10200′), the duff trail descends through heavy stands of lodgepole interspersed with tiny meadows. Colorful wildflowers, often in patches, dot this stretch of trail: Indian paintbrush, Douglas phlox, shooting star, yellow and white cinquefoil, pentstemon, lupine, red heather, western wallflower, buckwheat, and rocky mountain aster. This route passes the first of two trail laterals to Blaney Meadows, swings eastward, and crosses two terminal moraine ridges. The sometimes rocky trail then descends to ford Senger Creek in a lovely forested flat, and then leaves the heavy concentrations of lodgepole behind. Alternately steep and moderate descents characterize the southeastward course of trail, and the traveler soon finds that he is entering a drier area of manzanita and fractured granite. Views are excellent to the south and west of the unfractured granite slopes of Mt. Shinn and Ward Mtn. To the southeast, the skylined peaks of the Le Conte Divide and Emerald Peak dominate the view until the trail passes by the second lateral to Blaney Meadows and makes the final descent to the junction with the main Florence Lake trail. A prelunch swim in the nice holes on the South Fork of the San Joaquin River to the west of the junction is in order, and fishermen will find fair fishing for brook in the same vicinity. Several fair-to-good primitive campsites and one packer campsite are near the junction, where firewood is ample. From this junction, our route continues east on a duff and granite sand trail through a mixed forest cover of Jeffrey and juniper interspersed with occasional red and white fir. The trail crosses an easy series of ridges and descends past several good campsites to the Hutchinson Meadow trail junction, where our route branches left, away from the John Muir Trail. Sporadic appearances of quaking aspen (in the wetter spots) line this rocky ascent up Piute canyon. The trail keeps to the west side of briskly flowing Piute Creek, and fords the multi-branched Turret Creek. This climbing, rocky trail affords excellent views of highly fractured Pavilion Dome and the surrounding, unnamed domes composing the west end of Glacier Divide. The trail then swings easterly through a narrowing canyon, fords tiny West Pinnacles Creek, and pursues a rocky course until it enters a moderate lodgepole forest cover before reaching the East Pinnacles Creek ford. Views of the cascading tributary streams are frequent along this trail section. From the ford, the trail ascends gently to beautiful Hutchinson Meadow (9439'), where travelers will find excellent campsites near the Pine Creek Pass trail junction. Fishing for golden and brook is good-to-excellent (to 9"). Firewood is ample, and the lovely meadow setting provides excellent campsite views of several granite domes (Pilot Knob and Peak 12432') to the east and west, and of the lower south slope of Merriam Peak to the north.

6th Hiking Day (Hutchinson Meadow to Upper Pine Lake, 9 miles): This hiking day's route leaves the Piute Pass trail and ascends moderately up French Canyon. Rocky stretches alternate with the soft underfooting of grassy sections. Fishing along these upper reaches of French Canyon Creek is good to excellent, despite the diminishing size of the stream. The trail crosses several unnamed tributaries draining the east and west slopes of Royce and Merriam peaks, and soon climbs above timberline. The character of the canyon walls reflects the increase in altitude. Barren granite, mostly white and heavily fractured, scoops away to the east, making a broad-headed, typical cirque basin. The footing becomes very rocky as the trail passes the faint fisherman's trail to Moon Lake, and then veers northerly, climbs steeply, and crosses a long granite bench. From the bench, it is but a short, easy climb to the summit of Pine Creek Pass, where there are excellent views to the north of Mt. Julius Caesar and the tip of Bear Creek Spire. Slightly to the west are Merriam and Royce peaks, and to the south one can see Pilot Knob, Glacier Divide and the Piute Creek drainage. Directly ahead, the trail descends a long, talus-ridden swale. This descent soon enters a sparse forest cover of lodgepole, winding between large slabs of granite. Tiny subalpine meadows fill the gaps in the rock, and the traveler is sure to encounter western wallflower, shooting star, pentstemon, lupine, primrose, and yellow columbine. The trail veers away from the trickling Pine Creek seepage, crosses a slight rise, and then drops to the junction with the Italy Pass trail (incorrectly marked as the "Hilgard Pass" trail). Our route keeps to the right, fords the North Fork of Pine Creek just above the cascading inlet to Upper Pine Lake, and arrives at the excellent campsites along the west side of the lake and below the outlet (10200'). Good fishing for brook, rainbow, and some golden (to 12") can be had on Upper Pine Lake, and there is an ample supply of firewood.

7th Hiking Day (Upper Pine Lake to Pine Creek Roadend, 5 miles): See 1st hiking day, trip 17.

TRIP From NORTH LAKE CAMPGROUND to PIUTE LAKE (round trip). Topo map (15') Mt. Goddard; Profile 6. Best mid or late season; 7 miles.

Grade	Trail/layover days	Total recommended days
Leisurely	2/0	2
Moderate	- - -	- - -
Strenuous	- - -	- - -

HILITES This trip offers an easy walk into the high country and a lake with large trout. It is an excellent choice for beginning knapsackers who want to sample the high country with a modest effort.

DESCRIPTION

1st Hiking Day (North Lake Campground to Piute Lake, 3.5 miles): Shortly after leaving the trailhead (9380'), this route enters the John Muir Wilderness Area and then ascends gently along slopes dotted with meadows, aspen groves and stands of lodgepole pine. In season the traveler will find a wealth of wildflowers in these little meadows and in the sandy patches among the granite slabs, including: paintbrush, columbine, monkshood, tiger lily, spiraea and pentstemon. After the trail fords the North Fork of Bishop Creek several times, the ascent becomes moderate. Aspen is left behind, the lodgepole becomes sparse, and some limber is seen. The glaciated canyon is flanked by slab-topped Peak 12707 on the south and rust-colored, 13225-foot Mt. Emerson on the north. The newcomer to the High Sierra will marvel at how the great granite slabs maintain their precarious perches atop Peak 12707, seeming to be almost vertically above him. But they all topple eventually, due to the action of frost wedging, and add to the piles of talus at the foot of the peak. Approaching Loch Leven Lake, the trail levels off, and the angler may wish to try the lake waters for rainbow and brown trout (to 10"). The trail then ascends moderately again, through a cover of sparse lodgepole and whitebark, winds among large, rounded boulders, and skirts a small lake before arriving at the next bench up the canyon, which contains this day's destination, Piute Lake (10950'). The traveler may wish to consider the wind in selecting a campsite, as it often blows stiffly in this Piute Pass country. There are good campsites on the north side close to the water. Fishing for brook and rainbow is good (to 24") and wood is adequate.

2nd Hiking Day (Piute Lake to North Lake Campground, 3.5 miles): Retrace steps of 1st hiking day.

TRIP   From NORTH LAKE CAMPGROUND to HUTCHINSON MEADOW via Piute Lake, Piute Pass (round trip). Topo maps (15') Mt. Goddard, Mt. Tom, Mt. Abbot; Profile 6. Best mid or late season; 11 miles.

Grade	Trail/layover days	Total recom- mended days
Leisurely	4/1	5
Moderate	3/1	4
Strenuous	2/0	2

HILITES   Hutchinson Meadow is one of the finest in the High Sierra, and the trail to it beside Piute Creek takes the traveler through several miles of wild mountain "lawns" and gardens, where Sierra wildflowers are at their best. Add the views of Mt. Humphreys and the spectacular Glacier Divide, and this trip becomes one of the most scenic in all the Sierra. Yet the Humphreys Basin is equally famous for its golden trout.

DESCRIPTION (Moderate trip)

1st Hiking Day (North Lake Campground to Piute Lake, 3.5 miles): See 1st hiking day, trip 23.

2nd Hiking Day (Piute Lake to Hutchinson Meadow, 7.5 miles): The trail ascends an open, rocky slope to timberline, and switchbacks up to the last traverse before Piute Pass. Here the traveler in midsummer will probably pass through a "road cut" in a snowbank, created by packers using sand and shovels. At the pass (11423') there are grand views west to the canyon of the South Fork San Joaquin River, south to Glacier Divide (the north boundary of Kings Canyon National Park) and north to Mt. Humphreys, highest peak this far north in the Sierra. (If it could acquire 14' from somewhere, Bishop residents would have their own 14000' Sierra peak.) The rocky trail descends moderately to Summit Lake, and levels off as it fords a stream and enters the great, high lake basin called Humphreys Basin, which contains 31 lakes that have golden trout. The sandy trail contours through alpine grasses and then descends to ford the outlet stream of Big and Little Desolation lakes. There is good fishing in Big Desolation for golden to 20", reached by going 2 miles north on the trail that turns right from our route shortly after this ford. Or the angler may wish to sample the waters of Golden Trout Lake, just south of the trail, for the fair fishing for golden (to 10"). Entering timber, the route begins a moderate descent on a rocky trail through sparse lodgepole which soon becomes moderate. Breaks in the timber cover afford views of the residual glaciers that give the Glacier Divide its name. Shortly after the trail passes the sign reading "Piute Pass 4 miles" the display of flower-studded green "lawns" begins, and from here to Hutchinson Meadow the traveler is seldom out of sight of these subalpine gardens. The amateur botanist will discern paintbrush, shooting star, fleabane, swamp onion, red mountain heather, buttercup, cinquefoil, pentstemon, buckwheat, yarrow milfoil, groundsel and Douglas phlox, along with Labrador tea, lemon willow and alpine willow. Rollicking Piute Creek is always close at hand, lending its music to complete this scene of mountain beauty. The trail levels out and fords the distributaries of French Canyon Creek, arriving at the good campsites at Hutchinson Meadow (9439'). Here beneath Pilot Knob and Peak 12432 the angler will find the riffles of Piute Creek good to excellent fishing for brook and some golden (to 9"), or he may cautiously approach the little pools on the distributaries of French Canyon Creek, which spread out through the east side of the meadow and offer equally good fishing.

3rd Hiking Day (Hutchinson Meadow to North Lake Campground, 11 miles): Retrace steps of 1st and 2nd hiking days.

TRIP   From NORTH LAKE CAMPGROUND to PINE CREEK ROADEND via Piute Lake, Piute Pass, Hutchinson Meadow, Pine Creek Pass (shuttle trip). Topo maps (15') Mt. Goddard, Mt. Abbot; Profiles 6, 4. Best mid or late season; 26.5 miles.

Grade	Trail/layover days	Total recommended days
Leisurely	5/2	7
Moderate	4/1	5
Strenuous	2/1	3

HILITES   Crossing Piute Pass this route tours the rocky expanses of fish-filled Humphreys Basin before returning to the east side of the Sierra via Pine Creek Pass. Travelers of this alpine circuit will often hear the raucous, crowlike cry of the Clark nutcracker and the repetitive *chenk, chenk, chenk* of the cony.

DESCRIPTION *(Leisurely trip)*

1st Hiking Day (North Lake Campground to Piute Lake, 3.5 miles): See 1st hiking day, trip 23.

2nd Hiking Day (Piute Lake to Hutchinson Meadow, 7.5 miles): See 2nd hiking day, trip 24.

3rd Hiking Day (Hutchinson Meadow to Moon Lake, 5.5 miles): See parts of 6th hiking day, trip 22; and 2nd hiking day, trip 18.

4th Hiking Day (Moon Lake to Upper Pine Lake, 5 miles): See 2nd hiking day, trip 18.

5th Hiking Day (Upper Pine Lake to Pine Creek Roadend, 5 miles): See 1st hiking day, trip 17.

TRIP   From NORTH LAKE CAMPGROUND to FLORENCE LAKE ROADEND via Piute Lake, Piute Pass, Hutchinson Meadows, Lower Blaney Meadows (shuttle trip). Topo maps (15′) Mt. Abbot, Blackcap Mtn., Mt. Tom, Mt. Goddard; Profiles 6, 5. Best mid or late season; 28.5 miles.

Grade	Trail/layover days	Total recommended days
Leisurely	4/1	5
Moderate	3/1	4
Strenuous	3/0	3

HILITES   Following an old Indian trade route, this trip tours nearly every life zone and type of forest belt found in the Sierra. Well suited to foot or stock travel, the trail crosses Piute Pass and descends the west slopes via the San Joaquin drainage. Good angling in the Humphreys Basin waters, fine views of the Sierra crest and Glacier Divide, and well-maintained trails make this a good, solid beginner's trip.

DESCRIPTION *(Leisurely trip)*

1st Hiking Day (North Lake Campground to Piute Lake, 3.5 miles): See 1st hiking day, trip 23.

2nd Hiking Day (Piute Lake to Hutchinson Meadow, 7.5 miles): See 2nd hiking day, trip 24.

3rd Hiking Day (Hutchinson Meadow to Lower Blaney Meadows Campground, 10.5 miles): Staying on the north side of Piute Creek, the alternately duff and rocky trail descends gently through a moderate forest cover of lodgepole. After the easy ford of East Pinnacles Creek, the timber thins, and the precipitous valley walls narrow. There are excellent views of the cascading tributaries. Meadowy patches of grass lace the rockier sections of trail, and it drops over a moderate slope to a tiny lakelet that interrupts the brisk, bouncing flow of Piute Creek. Although the fish are somewhat smaller than in the lakes passed on the 2nd hiking day, they are plentiful, and anglers may wish to sample some of these pansized golden. Our route then swings westerly to ford West Pinnacles Creek, and southerly as it approaches the ford of multibranched Turret Creek. Crossing the easy granite nose protruding from the west wall of the canyon, the trail descends over steep and then moderate slopes to the junction with the John Muir Trail. Our route turns right (west), and undulates via rocky trail down the South Fork San Joaquin River drainage. The mostly sparse forest cover has changed from a predominance of lodgepole to Jeffrey, juniper, some red and white fir, and the seepage-loving quaking aspen. The underfooting of this trail exhibits the effects of both chemical and physical weathering of the granite walls, with its deep pockets of heavy, coarse quartz sand. Where this sand has mixed with alluvial deposits, trees and shrubs have taken root, and along these stretches the ground is frequently carpeted with a shallow layer of duff. The trail junction where our route leaves the John Muir Trail, keeping to the left, makes an excellent lunch or swimming stop. However, those desiring their water on the warmer side can wait until they reach the public hot springs 2 miles down the trail. In a forest cover that has become heavy, the trail from the junction continues by a series of moderate ups and downs past a second short lateral (ascending northward to join the John Muir Trail) to the Hot Springs campground. Here, a signed trail leads off to the left to the public hot springs less than .4 miles away (via a wide, fast water ford). A few yards beyond the campground, the trail meets the fenced boundary of the Diamond D Guest Ranch. Several of the outbuildings of this commercial establishment are in view as the trail skirts the boundaries and fords the noisy branchlets of Senger Creek. The heavy traffic (both stock and mechanical conveyance) that is the spoor of the guest ranch upstream interrupts the primitive appeal of the subsequent trail. Our route winds through the heavy forest cover surrounding Blaney Meadows, and strikes the Sally Keyes "shortcut trail." Our route continues past this trail and around the fringes of the meadow to the fair campsites at Lower Blaney Meadows (7650'). Firewood at this public campground is ample, and fishing for brook and some rainbow is fair to good (mostly downstream).

4th Hiking Day (Lower Blaney Meadows Campground to Florence Lake Roadend, 7.5 miles): See 4th hiking day, trip 8.

GLACIER DIVIDE TO BUBBS CREEK

This area is bounded by Glacier Divide on the north, the Owens Valley on the east, Courtright and Wishon reservoirs on the west, and Bubbs Creek on the south, and it contains the greatest single bloc of unbroken wilderness in the southern Sierra. Still untainted by roads, the core of it enjoys the protection of National Park status, and the adjacent peripheral zones to the west, north and east are declared Wilderness Areas. Spread out over an area of roughly 1200 square miles, it boasts some of the most remote and scenic sections of the Sierra, and it is replete with scores of peaks that soar above 13,000', hundreds of lakes and thousands of miles of sparkling streams. Were the hiker able to take every trip suggested in this section, he would have a solid sampling of four life zones ranging in altitude from 5,000' to well over 12,000'. Further, he would have crossed ten major divides, visited three major watersheds, and enjoyed a wilderness experience unequaled anywhere in the world.

Topographically, the country divides neatly into three disparate types: the west slopes, Kings Canyon National Park, and the eastern escarpment. The Park, the heart of the high country, was established in 1940 when the Congress recognized the obvious need to protect this fragile wilderness from the increasing encroachment of stockmen and local, shortsighted business interests. Although the Park makes up the largest part of this section, the potential visitor should not ignore trips into the Wilderness Areas on the east and west sides of the Park.

The Park "heartland" is the rugged, comparatively barren, mostly alpine zone that lies between the Sierra crest and the Le Conte/White Divide. Here are the headwaters of the South Fork of the San Joaquin and the Middle and South Forks of the Kings River. The latitudinal watershed divides, within the Park, are Goddard Divide (separating the South Fork of the San Joaquin River from the Middle Fork of the Kings River), and the Monarch/Cirque Crest divide (splitting the watersheds of the Middle Fork and the South Fork of the Kings River). Within the Park are several longitudinal divides that serrate the topography into a complex ridge-chasm conformation. Most outstanding among these secondary divides are White Divide, Ragged Spur, Black Divide and the King Spur.

In contrast to the Park, the east escarpment enjoys a diverse and sometimes dense forest cover — a cover that diminishes as it rises to the Sierra crest. All of the many east-side streams flow into the Owens River, and they are separated by towering spur ranges that protrude from the backbone of the crest. The escarpment is nowhere more severe and forbidding than the stretch from South Lake to Onion Valley — accounting in part for the absence of heavily used trailheads in this interval. Peculiar also to the east side is the lower juniper woodland belt replete with the scattered grasses, pinon pine, Utah juniper (sometimes mistakenly referred to as Utah Cedar) and brush plants associated with the Great Basin. Fortunately, for those of us who enjoy and would preserve the east escarpment's native primitive appeal, this region is protected by a long, narrow belt of Wilderness Area designation.

Similarly, the west slopes (west of the Park boundary) enjoy this immunity, but it is a sad political commentary that policy-makers and boundary-setters did not initially establish the Wilderness Area limit along the obvious demarcation indicated by the present roadends at Courtright and Wishon reservoirs. The terrain of these western slopes is remarkable for its absence of outstanding peaks. In general it is a gradual, steady ascent to the Le Conte/White Divide and the timbered rise of Kettle Ridge. The pleasant, rolling landscape of Woodchuck Country and the three alpine basins nestled at the foot of the Le Conte Divide make up the headwaters of the North Fork of the Kings River, the sole drainage of this particular area.

Looking at topo maps of this section (Blackcap Mountain, Mt. Goddard) one can readily ascertain the comparative heavy forestation of the region west of the Le Conte Divide. Travelers working their way up any one of the various dendritic tributaries of the North Fork of the Kings River will discover for themselves the magnificent spectrum of Sierra flora that attends these westside entries to the high country. Beginning in the lower elevations around 6500' are the stately mixed conifers such as the sugar pine, Ponderosa pine, and incense cedar. The Ponderosa pine, with its distinctive bark plates and its long needles, is frequently mistaken for its close cousin the Jeffrey pine which is of a higher elevation but sometimes found in the same locale. There are many distinguishing characteristics, but the surest is the difference in their cones. The naturalist's rule of thumb is, "If you can comfortably catch a tossed cone, it is a cone of the Jeffrey pine." This differentiation arises from the fact that the prickle found on the end of each scale of the Jeffrey cone is turned inward, whereas the prickle on the Ponderosa cone turns outward. But the most distinctive cone of all belongs to the sugar pine. Sometimes as long as a man's arm, it is an impressive fruit whether it be found on the ground or seen hanging in clusters at the ends of massive branches.

Climbing a little higher, one enters the fir belt. First comes the white fir, along with occasional groves of Jeffrey pine, and finally the noble stands of red fir. Being rather brittle, red firs are frequently associated with a heavily littered forest floor, but the atmosphere engendered by their open, parklike groves is entirely unique. Perhaps it is the soft, filtered green light that sifts through their dense, short-needled crowns, or it may be the gentle line of their graceful, down-sweeping branches. Whatever the reason, there are a hush and a feeling of needing to tip-toe through these stands that do not exist in other kinds of forests. Standing in one of these cathedral-like groves, it is the easiest thing in the world to empathize with John's Muir's bitterness when he wrote:

> Any fool can destroy trees. They cannot run away; and if they could, they would still be destroyed — chased and hunted down as long as fun or a dollar could be got out of their bark hides, branching horns, or magnificent bole backbones. Few that fell trees plant them; nor

would planting avail much toward getting back anything like the noble primeval forests. During a man's life only saplings can be grown, in the place of the old trees —tens of centuries old—that have been destroyed. It took more than three thousand years to make some of the trees in these Western woods — trees that are still standing in perfect strength and beauty, waving and singing in the mighty forests of the Sierra. Through all the wonderful, eventful centuries since Christ's time — and long before that — God has cared for these trees, saved them from drought, disease, avalanches, and a thousand straining, leveling tempests and floods; but he cannot save them from fools — only Uncle Sam can do that.*

*Our National Parks, by John Muir, 1901.

The "gentle country" of the trees continues as the trails wind upward through dense groves of the two-needled lodgepole pine. Near timberline, solitary gnarled sentinels in the form of Sierra juniper guard the ridges, and cling tenuously to rocky slopes. The slim lodgepole pine no longer appears in tall, dense stands — now its trunk is bent to the unchecked winds of alpine country. Occasional clumps of whitebark pine and mountain hemlock dot those spaces among the granite that are not already filled with the tender-yet-tough grasses of an alpine meadow.

This is the land and the forests of the west slopes — an environment that has nurtured and awed man since his first acquaintance with it. It is an often-ignored fact that the first visitor to these slopes was the Indian, and there is adequate evidence to show that he was leaching his ground acorn meal at the sites of Simpson and Zumwalt Meadows long before the white man had settled the eastern shores of America. While Englishmen and Spaniards fought sea battles for supremacy of ocean trade routes, the Indians of the Mono and Monache groups were peacefully plying their primitive trade routes over Piute, Bishop and Kearsarge passes. Using laurel-wood bows and cane arrows that were dipped in a poison concoction of crushed, rattlesnake-venomed deer liver, Indian hunting parties ranged the upper watersheds of the Kings and San Joaquin rivers — this, while the white man was establishing the first Presidio-Mission complexes in Alta California. In Philadelphia, civilized men of 1776 used a bird feather and decomposed animal fat to paint their names on a piece of wood pulp — historians now refer to it as an historic document. At almost the same time, in Tehipite Valley, an unknown Indian artisan using a similar stain produced a series of amebalike figures — and today's archeologist/historian refers to them as primitive graffiti.

The first meetings of these original inhabitants and exploring white men had a predilection to disaster. Gabriel Moraga, among the first white men to penetrate this country, was called "the greatest pathfinder and Indian fighter of his day." Subsequent incursions by trappers, pioneer settlers and gold seekers brought the inevitable confrontation, and, to the white man's discredit, the inevitable eradication of the red man. Like the grizzly bear, he was judged a nuisance, and was considered "fair game." Today, both species are extinct in this region.

Early exploratory ventures from west to east into the heartland of this region were so arduous as to render their continuation impractical. This is quite understandable, as any examination of the topography will show. Numerous divides, nearly all exceeding 12,000', cross-hatch the landscape, making passage even to this day lengthy and arduous. Fremont, in December 1845, endeavoring to carry out a rendezvous with Talbot and Walker on the westside river they called "Lake Fork," led an unsuccessful sally into the reaches of the North Fork of the Kings River. He was turned back by snow and "impossible" going. Jedediah Smith's party, in an earlier attempt during spring, had suffered the same travails, and the subsequent annals of the Brewer Survey parties of 1864 and 1870 tell a similar story.

The actual trail-blazers of currently used trails were, however, not the Spaniards or the trappers. The earliest trails were usually those of the sheepherders who grazed their flocks in the backcountry during the last half of the 19th century. Among the better known of these sheepherders were Bill Helm and Frank Dusy, whose early exploratory efforts on the west slopes culminated in the discovery of the Tehipite Valley and in the building of the Tunemah trail. W. Baird, operating in the same vicinity, established what is now known as the Hell-for-Sure Pass trail, and although the 1864 Brewer Survey party was the first to visit the area, it is assumed that Portuguese sheepmen were the first to establish the current western access route to the Evolution region. No route in the Sierra has received more attention than the comparatively recently established John Muir Trail. This scenic route traverses the Park just west of the Sierra crest. It is, in final acknowledgement, the combined results of trails explored and established by many people, including trappers, sheepherders and mountaineers.

Access to the Muir trail, and to other trails described in this section can be had via a half-dozen trailheads on the east side, but only two of these (South Lake and Onion Valley) are cited. South Lake can be reached via the partly paved road that branches west in Bishop from Hiway 395. Onion Valley is also reached from Hiway 395 — turn west at Independence.

Western access is provided at three trailheads: Courtright Reservoir, Wishon Reservoir Roadend and Cedar Grove Roadend. Courtright and Wishon are reached by taking State Route 168 to the Shaver Lake Y, and then turning right on the alternately paved and graveled road past Dinkey Creek and the McKinley Grove of Big Trees. To reach the Cedar Grove Roadend, simply follow State Route 180 into Kings Canyon National Park, and thence to Cedar Grove Roadend.

27

TRIP	From COURTRIGHT RESERVOIR to POST CORRAL MEADOWS (round trip). Topo map (15') Blackcap Mtn.: Profile 9. Best early to mid season; 16 miles.

Grade	Trail/layover days	Total recommended days
Leisurely	2/0	2
Moderate	- - -	- - -
Strenuous	- - -	- - -

HILITES	A fine weekend selection, this two-day trip visits enchanting Long and Post Corral Meadows. Dense forests of fir and lodgepole that line the trail route are a pleasant habitat for a variety of wildlife. This trip is an excellent selection for the beginning knapsacker.

DESCRIPTION (Leisurely trip)

1st Hiking Day (Courtright Reservoir to Post Corral Meadows, 8 miles): (The trail segment from the reservoir dam to Chamberlain's Camp has been changed from that shown on the topo map, and the changes are incorporated in the text below.) From man-made Courtright Reservoir (8170') the route crosses the dam and, following a brief section of maintenance road, skirts the granite shoulder of the ridge that lines the east shore of Courtright Reservoir. Excellent views to the north of spectacular Maxson Dome greet the traveler while crossing the dam, and the view down the Helms Creek gorge just below the spillway is a dizzying one that leaves the traveler feeling as though he were treading the brink of hell's abyss. A few yards down the rocky maintenance road, the trail branches left (north), descending at first through an area of granite slabbing, and then leveling out. This leveler section offers fine views of Long Top mountain and the East Fork of Helms Creek watershed. From this viewpoint, the trail descends past the meadowed foot of a long sheet of glacially smoothed granite on the left that sports numerous spectacular glacial erratics. The trail then fords the East Fork of Helms Creek, and, by a newly worked trail, winds through a dense forest cover of young lodgepole around the east side of Maxson Meadows. Ascending gently, the trail passes Chamberlain's Camp (a Forest Service trail-maintenance camp that is manned intermittently) and the Dusy Meadows trail. Just beyond the Chamberlain's Camp cabin, the trail ascends steeply by short, dusty switchbacks, and then tops this climb in a beautiful mixed stand of red fir and lodgepole. This rocky slope reveals the typical rounded boulders set in a dusty silt matrix of a glacial moraine. The trail then fords an unnamed, intermittently flowing stream, and descends gently to the head of beautiful Long Meadow. Aptly named, this grassland stretches away to the northeast for about a mile, and the route winds through the middle — seldom more than a few yards away from the sluggishly flowing South Fork of Post Corral Creek. Indicative of the heavy use this trail is subjected to (primarily stock), the meadow section of the trail is frequently armpit-deep to a walking man, and this blight is the reason for the enlightened Forest Service policy of rerouting trails around fragile meadows. Our route passes the Burnt Corral Meadow trail midway through the meadow, fords the South Fork of Post Corral Creek, and then leaves the sandy-surfaced trail of the meadow behind as it swings easterly. Through the moderate-to-dense forest cover one can occasionally hear Post Corral Creek, and although it is out of sight, one can clearly hear the sound difference due to the increased volume of water resulting from the contribution of Burnt Corral Creek. Our route passes a faint trail branching left to a privately owned line cabin (Forest Service Multiple-Use land policy allows cattlemen to graze these lands), and then descends gently to the excellent campgrounds at the head of Post Corral Meadows (8201'). There are several primitive campgrounds at the head of the meadow, and one packer site. Other sites can be found at the foot of the meadow (ford Post Corral Creek) adjacent to the trail junction of the Hell-for-Sure Pass trail. Fair-to-good fishing for pan-sized brook trout and some rainbow (to 7") can be had along Post Corral Creek. Firewood is plentiful.

2nd Hiking Day (Post Corral Meadows to Courtright Reservoir, 8 miles): Retrace steps of 1st hiking day.

TRIP   From COURTRIGHT RESERVOIR to NORTH FORK KINGS RIVER via Post Corral Meadows (round trip). Topo map (15') Blackcap Mtn.; Profile 9. Best early to mid season; 24 miles.

Grade	Trail/layover days	Total recommended days
Leisurely	4/1	5
Moderate	3/1	4
Strenuous	2/1	3

HILITES   The winding, horseshoe-shaped route-plan of this trip tours magnificent back-country meadows and lush forests, and terminates alongside the racing, potholedotted North Fork of the Kings River. Excellent fishing and swimming on the Kings River make this a good trip selection for the beginner desiring maximum wilderness exposure for a minimum of hiking days.

DESCRIPTION (Leisurely trip)

1st Hiking Day (Courtright Reservoir to Post Corral Meadows, 8 miles): See 1st hiking day, trip 27.

2nd Hiking Day (Post Corral Meadows to North Fork Kings River Campsites, 4 miles): From the campsites at the lower end of Post Corral Meadows (8201'), the trail passes the Hell-for-Sure Pass trail (branching left), and winds through a densely forested stretch of mixed stands of red fir, lodgepole, silver pine, and Douglas fir. The duff-and-sand trail surface makes for very pleasant walking, and the relatively level going allows the trail traveler to keep a sharp eye out for the commonly seen mule deer and the sometimes seen black bear. Tiny meadowy sections interrupt the dense forest sections, and the experienced silent hiker will pause at the fringe of these fens to watch for betraying movement. The general southward progress of the trail changes to a staggering course eastward as the trail ascends a rocky, moderate slope, and finally emerges on an open, manzanita-covered ridge above the North Fork Kings River drainage. This open slope is a fine point from which to view the unfractured granite river chasm to the west and the dramatic U-shaped valley to the southeast. From this point, it is interesting to speculate on the probable route followed by Captain John Fremont, the "Pathfinder." Historians are still speculating on this subject, but on one thing they do agree — Fremont's party got lost in the upper reaches of the North Fork of the Kings River. They suffered terribly during an early winter storm, were forced to eat their saddle stock, and finally retreated. From this ridge, the trail descends on a traverse over infrequently jointed granite to the banks of the river (8029'). Excellent campsites can be found a short distance up or downstream. Firewood is ample, and angling for brook, rainbow and some brown (to 12") is excellent. Swimming in some of the finest sand-bottomed potholes in the Sierra is available just downstream, and photographers seeking a worthy subject will find Sue Falls, about ¼ mile downstream, interesting.

3rd Hiking Day (North Fork Kings River to Post Corral Meadows, 4 miles): Retrace steps of 2nd hiking day.

4th Hiking Day (Post Corral Meadows to Courtright Reservoir, 8 miles): Retrace steps of 1st hiking day.

	Trail / layover	*Total-recom-*
Grade	*days*	*mended days*

TRIP   From COURTRIGHT RESERVOIR to RAE LAKE via Post Corral Meadows (round trip). Topo map (15') Blackcap Mtn.; Profile 9. Best mid to late season; 28 miles.

	Trail / layover	*Total-recom-*
Grade	*days*	*mended days*
Leisurely	4/2	6
Moderate	3/2	5
Strenuous	2/2	4

HILITES   Rae Lake, an alpine gem surrounded by meadow on two sides and tumbled granite slopes on the other two, has long been a favorite of anglers and other high-country visitors. Situated beneath Fleming Mountain, this lake's innate beauty and its proximity to 25 other lakes and the intervening streams make it a choice base camp for discovery explorations of Red Mountain Basin,

DESCRIPTION   (Leisurely trip)

1st Hiking Day   (Courtright Reservoir to Post Corral Meadows, 8 miles): See 1st hiking day, trip 27.

2nd Hiking Day   (Post Corral Meadows to Rae Lake, 6 miles): Our route leaves the Blackcap Basin trail at the campground at the foot of Post Corral Meadows (8201') and ascends the divide separating the Fleming Creek and Post Corral Creek drainages. The ascent climbs eastward, passes a Forest Service spur trail maintenance camp (sometimes manned), and then crosses several unnecessarily dynamited sections of granite. To dynamite these granite slabs is a policy decision — an unfortunate and unrepresentative policy that sees the Forest Service maintaining backcountry trails for horses and pack animals when the overwhelming use of the trails is by those on foot. The trail crosses the John Muir Wilderness Area boundary, switchbacks over the crest of the divide, and begins a long, steady, rocky ascent through a moderately dense forest cover of lodgepole, incense cedar and red fir. As the trail nears Fleming Creek it climbs steeply, and there are spots along this ascent from which the passerby has beautiful views of the long, silver chutes of the West Fork of Fleming Creek as it plunges over the glacially smoothed, unfractured granite of this upper basin. The lodgepoles begin to take on the stunted look characteristic of high country as the trail emerges at the subalpine meadows surrounding Fleming Lake. Itchy anglers may wish to sample the fair-to-good brook-trout fishing (to 10") at Fleming Lake, but fishing is generally better as one ascends the drainage. The trail passes a packer campsite at the outlet of Fleming Lake and crosses a lovely subalpine meadow to the Hellfor-Sure Pass trail junction. Here, our route branches left and ascends steeply past the fisherman's trail to Lower Indian Lake. This rocky, morainal trail brings one to the excellent campsites along the south and east sides of Rae Lake (9894'). Almost ringed by meadow, this charming lake exhibits a timbered east wall, a mostly meadowed south side, and precipitous rocky faces on the west and north sides. Originally named "Wolverine Lake" (they are still occasionally seen here), 13-acre Rae Lake makes a fine base camp for day-hiking excursions to Lower Indian Lake, Upper Indian Lake, and the lakes of the Red Mountain Basin. Fishing for brook (to 12") is good. Firewood is ample.

3rd Hiking Day (Rae Lake to Post Corral Meadows, 6 miles): Retrace steps of 2nd hiking day.

4th Hiking Day (Post Corral Meadows to Courtright Reservoir, 8 miles): Retrace steps of 1st hiking day.

TRIP   From COURTRIGHT RESERVOIR to DEVILS PUNCH-BOWL return via Meadow Brook and North Fork Kings River (semiloop). Topo map (15') Blackcap Mtn.; Profile 9. Best mid to late season; 37.5 miles.

Grade	Trail/layover days	Total recom-mended days
Leisurely	6/2	8
Moderate	5/2	7
Strenuous	4/2	6

HILITES   Traveling what was originally known as the "Baird Trail" (an old sheepherder's trail that remained for years the primary access to the Evolution Valley country) this route culminates at regal Devils Punchbowl Lake. Here, excellent fishing and magnificent views greet the visitor, and a prolonged stay — using the lake as a base camp — will compensate the hiker with excellent fishing and views from the surrounding lakes.

DESCRIPTION (Leisurely trip)

1st Hiking Day (Courtright Reservoir to Post Corral Meadows, 8 miles): See 1st hiking day, trip 27.

2nd Hiking Day (Post Corral Meadows to Rae Lake, 6 miles): See 2nd hiking day, trip 29.

3rd Hiking Day (Rae Lake to Devils Punchbowl, 5.5 miles): Descending from Rae Lake (9894'), the trail meets and joins the fisherman's trail from Lower Indian Lake, and a few yards farther (in the meadow) joins the Hell-for-Sure Pass trail. Our route turns left, fords the West Fork of Fleming Creek, and ascends the steep moraine divide to the east. The forest cover diminishes as the trail ascends, and through the thinning timber one has good views of the northern reaches of the Le Conte Divide and of Fleming Mountain. Recent trail changes near the top of this divide alter the direction of the trail indicated on the topo map. The new trail veers somewhat more southerly, and rounds a granite-nosed ridge before ascending the grassy swale to the Devils Punchbowl trail junction. From this junction, one can look up the benched drainage containing Hell-for-Sure Lake to the notch that marks Hell-for-Sure Pass. Our route turns right onto the Devils Punchbowl trail, skirts a ridge, and descends past several streamside campsites at the headwaters of the East Fork of Fleming Creek. Climbing out of this drainage, the rocky trail reaches the good campsites at the north end of Devils Punchbowl (10100'). Timber cover on three sides of this charming, fairly large (33-acre) lake is moderate-to-sparse lodgepole mixed with willow in the wetter areas. Firewood is ample, and fishing for brook (to 13") is excellent. Anglers with extra layover days may wish to use this lake as a base camp for further angling adventures in the Red Mountain Basin. This angling varies from excellent at Horseshoe and Hell-for-Sure lakes to fair at Blackrock Lake. Equally varied is the range of trout. At Blackrock Lake there is a fair population of rainbow, while Horseshoe has a mixed fishery of brook, rainbow and (says the DF&G) golden hybrids. Whether the reason for excursions into the Red Mountain Basin be angling or just enjoying the rugged, alpine country, the basin merits investigation. Those visitors with the inclination for a somewhat more strenuous, but very satisfying, cross-country trip may elect to trek to the Bench Valley Basin (see trip 32).

4th Hiking Day (Devils Punchbowl to North Fork Kings River Campsites, 6 miles): Walking around the west fringe of Devils Punchbowl Lake, the hiker should take time out to step a few yards to the right of the trail for the breathtaking view west to the 2 tiny lakes and the wooded upper drainages of the East Fork of Fleming Creek. The trail then becomes somewhat faint as it crosses the rocky saddle at the southwest end of Devils Punchbowl, and descends the heavily timbered slopes to the rolling meadows of Meadow Brook. These meadows exhibit an unusual amount of seepage, and it is well that the winding, duff trail keeps to the lodgepole forest fringe on the west side. Along the trail and on the fringes of the stream, one will find a luxurious growth of shooting star, swamp onion, and knee-high lupine. There is a serene quality to a rolling alpine meadow that touches all who visit it. The meadows that stepladder down with Meadow Brook are a particular delight, and the brief two miles of trail that wind in and out of these grasslands are a rare pleasure. There is, however, a disturbing factor, which grates on the sensitivities of all experienced high-country travelers. That factor is the presence of the privately owned cattle that summer-graze here. Because of the heavy seepage, these grasslands are vulnerable, and they are undergoing irremediable harm. A close-up examination will reveal the torn turf and polluted waters caused by this stock. Further, the presence of these domestic bovines dramatically detracts from the meadow's magical wilderness quality. The trail passes the second large meadow section, and then swings away from Meadow Brook.

It then makes the final, steep descent into the North Fork of the Kings River valley. Views during this descent include large segments of Woodchuck Country, Nichols Canyon, and the U-shaped contour of the North Fork Kings River valley. This dusty, down-winding trail reflects the lower altitude, with the reintroduction of the golden, shaggy-barked incense cedar and the vanilla-scented, plate-barked Jeffrey pine. Our route then meets and turns right onto the Blackcap Basin trail. A short distance downstream, the trail crosses granite slabs, and then passes a snow-survey cabin with its nearby waterfall and fine, deep pool (good swimming). Immediately leaving the vicinity of the river, the trail swings right, crosses a rocky granite ridge, and then descends through a heavy stand of lodgepole, Jeffrey, and occasional red fir and incense cedar. This route fords Fleming Creek and arrives at the excellent riverside campsites situated at the point where the trail begins to climb out of the North Fork Kings River watershed. Fishing for brook (to 12″) is excellent, and swimming in the nearby potholes (just downstream) is also excellent. There is ample firewood just upstream.

5th Hiking Day (North Fork Kings River to Post Corral Meadows, 4 miles): See 2nd hiking day, trip 28.

6th Hiking Day (Post Corral Meadows to Courtright Reservoir, 8 miles): See 1st hiking day, trip 27.

TRIP   From COURTRIGHT RESERVOIR to GUEST LAKE (Bench Valley) via Post Corral Meadows, North Fork Kings River (round trip). Topo map (15′) Blackcap Mtn.; Profile 9. Best mid to late season; 38 miles.

Grade	Trail/layover days	Total recommended days
Leisurely	6/3	9
Moderate	5/2	7
Strenuous	4/2	6

HILITES   Of the three lake basins lying close under towering Le Conte Divide, Bench Valley is the least known and least-visited. This is surprising in view of the excellent angling available at McGuire Lakes and Guest Lake. The other lakes of this basin are among the most picturesque in the Sierra, and the angler with an inclination to visit stirring subalpine scenery enroute should give this trip serious consideration.

DESCRIPTION   (Leisurely trip)
1st Hiking Day   (Courtright Reservoir to Post Corral Meadows, 8 miles): See 1st hiking day, trip 27.
2nd Hiking Day   (Post Corral Meadows to North Fork Kings River Campsites, 4 miles): See 2nd hiking day, trip 28.

3rd Hiking Day   (North Fork Kings River Campsites to Guest Lake, 7 miles): From the river's edge, the trail swings left through a dense stand of lodgepole, Jeffrey, and occasional red fir and incense cedar, and fords Fleming Creek just above its confluence with North Fork Kings River. In these shady timber stands, heavy coats of green moss cover rock and tree alike; bright orange shelf bracts flash like eyes against the forest green; and sounds seem muted on the carpet of pine needles. But the soft duff trail is soon left behind as the trail climbs above the river valley over the granite nose of a ridge, and then descends to the snow-survey cabin nestled in granite slabs at river's edge. A nearby waterfall on the river and the subsequent pool makes a nice spot for a fast pre-lunch swim, and anglers will find good fishing for brook (to 11") immediately up or downstream. The trail then passes the Meadow Brook trail branching left to Hell-for-Sure Pass and the Nichols Canyon trail branching right, before fording an unnamed tributary and Meadow Brook. Ascending gently, this trail route winds through moderate-to-dense stands of lodgepole and red fir. After fording Fall Creek, the route leaves the Blackcap Basin trail by branching left onto the unmaintained, shortcut trail (signed) that ascends along the south side of Fall Creek. The route is level at first, and easy to follow, but this condition changes as soon as the area of the broad granite walls is reached. Here, the trail peters out, and the hiker keeps his bearings by staying close to the creek on the south side. This is a pleasant chore, for the creek forms a lovely silver ribbon as it chutes hundreds of feet across glacially smoothed granite. Where ledges interrupt the flow, pockets of wild flowers (including tasty swamp onion) have taken root, and a well-deserved lunch break is in order here. It becomes apparent that this ducked route is ascending the lip of a "hanging valley," but an understanding of the true nature of this geologic term awaits the conclusion of this hiking day. Our ascending route meets another trail lateral at the foot of the valley, and together they wind alongside the luxuriant foliaged banks of Fall Creek. Wildflowers fill the valley floor: shooting star, pentstemon, larkspur, monks-hood, monkey flower, columbine, wallflower, and Indian paint-brush. Frequently the trail is overhung by the rank, fast-growing false solomon's seal, which, because of soaked pant legs, is considered an annoyance by walkers. The trick to keeping one's pants legs dry is: (1) travel in a party of two or more; (2) finagle to be the last person in the walking file. After traveling a short distance along the river, the trail begins the steep ascent of the valley's east wall. Short switchbacks, which soon become rocky and steep, mark this strenuous climb, and the first, water-level view of lower McGuire Lake comes as a welcome and pleasant surprise. The lake's waters appear suddenly only a few feet from the precipitous drop-off, and from this point one can indeed ascertain the true meaning of the term "hanging valley." Our route passes several primitive and packer campsites as it rounds the north side of lower and upper McGuire Lakes. Both of these lakes afford excellent fishing for brook (to 18"). Through moderate-to-sparse timber, the trail crosses an easy ridge to the fisherman's lateral that turns off the main trail and leads to Guest Lake (10160'). Excellent packer and primitive campsites with unobstructed views of Blackcap Mountain line the north shore of this lovely granitoid lake, and it is a fine choice as a base camp for excursions to 20 nearby lakes of this basin. At Guest Lake fishing for brook (to 12") is good; firewood is ample. Fishing in the lakes of the upper Bench Valley Basin varies from good to excellent, and offers the angling sportsman a creel of both brook and rainbow.

4th Hiking Day (Guest Lake to North Fork Kings River Campsites, 7 miles): Retrace steps of 3rd hiking day.

5th Hiking Day (North Fork Kings River Campsites to Post Corral Meadows, 4 miles): Retrace steps of 2nd hiking day.

6th Hiking Day (Post Corral Meadows to Courtright Reservoir, 8 miles): Retrace steps of 1st hiking day.

TRIP

From COURTRIGHT RESERVOIR to GUEST LAKE via Post Corral Meadows, North Fork Kings River, and return via cross country route to Devils Punchbowl, then by trail to North Fork Kings, Post Corral Meadows (semiloop trip). Topo map (15') Blackcap Mtn.; Profile 9. Best mid or late season; 43.5 miles.

Grade	Trail/layover days	Total recom- mended days
Leisurely	7/3	10
Moderate	5/3	8
Strenuous	4/2	6

HILITES

This looping trip circuits two of the finest angling basins found on the west side of the Sierra. The rugged cross-country route between the basins makes it a choice limited to intermediate and experienced knapsackers, and the grand vistas encountered along this route more than compensate for the skill and energy required. The return leg of this trip through Meadow Brook valley is an exposure to subalpine meadows that will kindle an appreciation of and dedication to preservation of these sedentary grasslands.

DESCRIPTION   (Leisurely trip)

1st Hiking Day   (Courtright Reservoir to Post Corral Meadows, 8 miles): See 1st hiking day, trip 27.

2nd Hiking Day   (Post Corral Meadows to North Fork Kings River Campsites, 4 miles): See 2nd hiking day, trip 28.

3rd Hiking Day   (North Fork Kings River Campsites to Guest Lake, 7 miles): See 3rd hiking day, trip 31.

4th Hiking Day   (Guest Lake to Devils Punchbowl via cross-country route, 6.5 miles): The trail from Guest Lake is a fisherman's trail that joins the main Bench Valley Basin trail ascending to Horsehead Lake. This ascent winds through sparse, stunted lodgepole and alpine meadows. Mostly rocky, the trail is sometimes faint, but in the grassy sections it is easy to follow. When the trail arrives at the grassy fringes of open Horsehead Lake, the traveler has excellent views to the east and northeast of the barren crest of the Le Conte Divide. From this lake's open shores one can readily see that he has surmounted a series of hanging valleys, and that this hanging-valley chain continues in the tiny cirques carved out of the granite divide to the east and northeast. Crossing the marshy inlet to Horsehead Lake, this route rounds the east side of the lake, fords the east inlet (from Filly Lake), and parallels the north inlet stream as it ascends above timberline. Faint fisherman's routes crisscross this drainage, and the conflicting ducking placed by misguided but well-meaning visitors should be taken with a grain of salt. The general route direction is north, past Twin Buck Lakes, and around the granite-nosed ridge to Schoolmarm Lake. Anglers passing through this country will be able to sample the brook and rainbow (to 10″) at Horsehead Lake; brook (to 8″) at Roman Four Lake; rainbow (to 11″) at West Twin Buck Lake (East Twin Buck Lake is barren); and rainbow (to 7″) at Schoolmarm Lake. Our route crosses the outlet of Schoolmarm Lake and continues north and somewhat westerly, ascending steeply over heavily fractured granite and talus. Maintaining elevation, this route traverses the rugged, fractured, and talus-ridden headwaters basin of Fall Creek in an east-to-west fashion. This traverse brings one to a point above the jumbled granite and metamorphic rock divide between the Fall Creek and Meadow Brook watersheds. From this point, the route descends the long cirque basin directly to the west down the steep east side of the cirque basin. This descent should be undertaken only by experienced hikers with rudimentary climbing skills. The foot of this descent is a long, sloping cirque bench that is easily negotiated. Then it is another steep climb down to the tiny lakelets just above Devils Punchbowl. This final steep descent brings one to the sparse-to-moderate lodgepole forest cover at the north end of Devils Punchbowl Lake (10100′). There are several excellent campsites here, and firewood is ample. Fishing for brook (to 13″) is excellent, and this lake is a perennial choice among anglers as a base camp for further side-trips into Red Mountain Basin.

5th Hiking Day   (Devils Punchbowl to North Fork Kings River Campsites, 6 miles): See 4th hiking day, trip 30.

6th Hiking Day   (North Fork Kings River Campsites to Post Corral Meadows, 4 miles): Retrace steps of 2nd hiking day.

7th Hiking Day   (Post Corral Meadows to Courtright Reservoir, 8 miles): Retrace steps of 1st hiking day.

TRIP   From COURTRIGHT RESERVOIR to DEVILS PUNCH-BOWL via Post Corral Meadows, North Fork Kings River, Guest Lake, cross country to Devils Punchbowl, and return via Rae Lake (semiloop trip). Topo map (15') Blackcap Mtn.; Profile 9. Best mid or late season; 45 miles.

Grade	Trail/layover days	Total recommended days
Leisurely	7/3	10
Moderate	6/3	9
Strenuous	5/3	8

HILITES   This loop trip follows the same cross-country route suggested in the previous trip, but returns via Rae Lake and the Hell-for-Sure Pass trail. Having both Rae and Devils Punchbowl lakes on the trip itinerary allows the traveler a choice of two excellent sites for subsequent exploratory or angling trips in Red Mountain Basin. Because of the somewhat difficult cross-country work required by this route, it is recommended for intermediate and experienced knapsackers only.

DESCRIPTION   (Leisurely trip)

1st Hiking Day   (Courtright Reservoir to Post Corral Meadows, 8 miles): See 1st hiking day, trip 27.

2nd Hiking Day   (Post Corral Meadows to North Fork Kings River, 4 miles): See 2nd hiking day, trip 28.

3rd Hiking Day   (North Fork Kings River Campsites to Guest Lake, 7 miles): See 3rd hiking day, trip 31.

4th Hiking Day   (Guest Lake to Devils Punchbowl, via cross-country route, 6.5 miles): See 4th hiking day, trip 32.

5th Hiking Day   (Devils Punchbowl to Rae Lake, 5.5 miles): See 3rd hiking day, trip 30.

6th Hiking Day   (Rae Lake to Post Corral Meadows, 6 miles): See 2nd hiking day, trip 29.

7th Hiking Day (Post Corral Meadows to Courtright Reservoir, 8 miles): Retrace steps of 1st hiking day.

TRIP   From COURTRIGHT RESERVOIR to PORTAL LAKE (Blackcap Basin) via Post Corral Meadows, North Fork Kings River (round trip). Topo map (15') Blackcap Mtn.; Profile 9. Best mid or late season; 47 miles.

Grade	Trail/layover days	Total recommended days
Leisurely	6/4	10
Moderate	5/4	9
Strenuous	4/4	8

HILITES   Portal Lake lives up to its name. It is indeed the door to Blackcap Basin, a beautiful, barren, granite basin forming the headwaters of the Middle Fork of the Kings River. This trip boasts an encompassing look at the west-slope ecology over a 2500' elevation span.

DESCRIPTION (Leisurely trip)

1st Hiking Day (Courtright Reservoir to Post Corral Meadows, 8 miles): See 1st hiking day, trip 27.

2nd Hiking Day (Post Corral Meadows to Big Maxson Meadow, 8 miles): See 2nd hiking day, trip 28 for description to North Fork Kings River. Then proceed to the Bench Valley trail junction as described for 3rd hiking day, trip 31. From this junction, the Blackcap Basin trail continues south along the North Fork of the Kings River. Fishing along the river continues to be good for brook and rainbow (to 12″), and occasional pools, usually located at the foot of a chute or fall, make for fine late-season swimming. The narrowing canyon walls open briefly as the trail reaches wide Big Maxson Meadow (9000'). Formerly a sheepherders camp, and more recently grazed by cattle, this meadow offers fair-to-good campsites at its northwest and southeast ends. Firewood is plentiful. If used as a base camp location, these meadow campsites are central for side trips to Halfmoon Lake and the Scepter Creek drainage to the south, and the alpine lakes of upper Bench Valley.

3rd Hiking Day (Big Maxson Meadow to Portal Lake, 7.5 miles): As the trail leaves the open flats of the meadow, the traveler has excellent views east-southeast to the glacially smoothed, narrowing walls of the canyon. Bearing in the direction of these canyon narrows, our duff trail passes the second of the Bench Valley trail laterals and the first of the Scepter Pass trail laterals. The louder river sounds on the right reflect the steepening slopes as our trail begins a steady-to-steep climb, which levels out as its direction turns south through a thinning lodgepole forest cover. This direction soon brings the trail back to the river, which it fords, and subsequently passes the second Scepter Pass trail lateral. Staying close to the south side of the river, our trail swings easterly beneath the steep granite south wall of the canyon. This steady, often rocky ascent offers excellent views eastward into great Blackcap Basin. Obviously glacial in origin, the basin shows the usual smoothed granite, striae, hanging valleys and morainal debris. Rimmed by Blackcap Mountain on the northwest, Le Conte Divide on the east and Kettle Ridge on the south, this basin encloses over 50 alpine lakes. These deep, crystal-blue lakes nestle up against basaltic-lava-topped cirque walls and peaks, and constitute the last material evidence of the ice river that began here. Our trail ascends to the head of a sparsely timbered (lodgepole and some hemlock) basin, and then fords the Portal Lake outlet stream to the good campsites at tiny Portal Lake (10300'). Although granitoid in general nature, Portal Lake has some sparse timber cover, and the deep, cold waters contain a fair population of brook trout (to 12"). Firewood is somewhat scarce.

4th Hiking Day   (Portal Lake to Big Maxson Meadow, 7.5 miles): Retrace steps of 3rd hiking day.

5th Hiking Day   (Big Maxson Meadow to Post Corral Meadows, 8 miles): Retrace steps of 2nd hiking day.

6th Hiking Day   (Post Corral Meadows to Courtright Reservoir, 8 miles): Retrace steps of 1st hiking day.

TRIP   From COURTRIGHT RESERVOIR to FLORENCE LAKE ROADEND via Post Corral Meadows, Hell-for-Sure Pass, John Muir Trail, Blaney Meadows (shuttle trip). Topo maps (15') Blackcap Mtn., Mt. Abbot; Profiles 9, 5. Best mid or late season; 40.5 miles.

Grade	Trail/layover days	Total recommended days
Leisurely	7/3	10
Moderate	5/2	7
Strenuous	4/2	6

HILITES   Crossing the Le Conte Divide at Hell-for-Sure Pass, this fine shuttle trip tours the headwaters of two major Sierra drainages—North Fork of the Kings River and

— 72 —

South Fork of the San Joaquin. Unparalleled scenery and excellent angling earmark this trek for hiker and angler.

DESCRIPTION   *(Moderate trip)*

1st Hiking Day   (Courtright Reservoir to Post Corral Meadows, 8 miles): See 1st hiking day, trip 27.

2nd Hiking Day   (Post Corral Meadows to Rae Lake, 6 miles): See 2nd hiking day, trip 29.

3rd Hiking Day   (Rae Lake to Lower Goddard Canyon, 11 miles): Proceed to the Devils Punchbowl trail junction as described 3rd hiking day, trip 30. From this junction, our trail ascends steadily above the meadowed basin to the barren granite bench north of Disappointment Lake. Far from being a disappointment, anglers will find the brook trout fishing in this lake to be good to excellent (to 15").

The trail winds across slab granite, talus and turfy patches to the east end of the bench, and then ascends steeply to the north end of barren Hell-for-Sure Lake. This large (58-acre) lake with its narrow northern meadow fringe is a long-time favorite of people using this three-quarters of a century old sheep trail. A fine fishing spot for brook trout (to 10"), this lake takes up the largest part of the upper cirque of Red Mountain Basin. Smoothed and polished slab granite issues from the lake's waters, broken only by an occasional glacial erratic or a lonesome, dwarfed lodgepole. Just beyond the slab granite the broken slopes of talus and scree lead up to the abrupt, metavolcanic-topped Le Conte Divide. The notch to the northeast of Hell-for-Sure Lake marks Hell-for-Sure Pass (11297'), and the climb to this saddle is a steep, switchbacking, rocky slog. The traveler arriving at the summit of Hell-for-Sure Pass inevitably agrees with the thousands who have gone before who pantingly said, "Ain't it though?" From the pass, Hell-for-Sure Lake takes up most of the immediate scenery to the southwest, but one can see a good part of the way down the Fleming Creek drainage. The most impressive view, however, is that of Goddard Canyon, Emerald Peak, Peter Peak and Mt. McGee to the east and northeast. Virtually naked of vegetation, the incredibly steep canyon walls plunge uninterrupted to the valley floor nearly 2500' below. This breathtaking view lasts most of the switchbacking way down to the ford of the first unnamed tributary feeding the South Fork of the San Joaquin. From this ford (about half way down the vertical distance) the trail traverses the west canyon wall on a long steady descent that crosses two more tributaries, and then doubles back along the South Fork of the San Joaquin. The subsequent steady-to-moderate descent stays on the west side of the river and refords the tributaries cited above. The trail crosses over mostly rock, some talus and scree, and occasional meadowy sections. Willow clumps along the river always indicate the presence of birdlife, and the passerby is sure to encounter Brewer blackbirds, hummingbirds, flycatchers, fox sparrow, Lincoln sparrow, nuthatches, robins, and an occasional finch. Among the flowers and shrubs seen along this section of trail are sagebrush, Labrador tea, monkey flower, yellow cinquefoil, shooting star, milfoil, tiger lily, red columbine, buckwheat, pentstemon, western mountain aster, camas, red heather, and the ubiquitous lupine. This descent, leveling near the confluence with Evolution Creek re-enters forest cover with the appearance of lodgepole and aspen. The trail then passes the drift fence a short way upstream from the John Muir Trail junction, and arrives at the fair-to-good campsites (both packer and primitive) south of the bridge (8600'). Fishing for brook and some rainbow on the river remains fair-to-good despite heavy angling pressure. Wood is somewhat scarce.

4th Hiking Day (Lower Goddard Canyon to Lower Blaney Meadows Campground, 8 miles): The trail descends to the junction with the John Muir Trail, and turns left onto that trail. This is a steady descent over a dusty trail through stands of quaking aspen, lodgepole and some juniper. Underfoot, wildflowers line the trail, including sneezeweed, pentstemon, yellow cinquefoil, pennyroyal, Mariposa lily and lupine. As the trail approaches the suspension bridge ford of the South Fork of the San Joaquin River, the canyon walls narrow and rise V-shaped from the canyon floor. On the north wall one can make out the unmistakable striations carved there by ice-driven rocks in the last glacial stage. Our route passes by several more campsites just before crossing the bridge, and then descends a rocky stretch over morainal debris. This steady descent levels out through a densely forested flat that is made up of post-glacial alluvial deposits. An occasional Jeffrey and juniper add variety to the forest cover as the trail leaves the flat and descends steeply on a rocky, dusty trail. Looking back, one has a last look at Emerald Peak, Veed by the steep canyon walls, and ahead one catches his first glimpse of imposing Ward Mountain. Our route fords Piute Creek and passes the Hutchinson Meadow trail that branches to the right. From this junction one has good views of the domes to the east, the most notable being Pavilion Dome. Passing several campsites, this route continues as described in 3rd hiking day, trip 26.

5th Hiking Day (Lower Blaney Meadows Campground to Florence Lake Roadend, 7.5 miles): See 4th hiking day, trip 8.

 36

TRIP   From COURTRIGHT RESERVOIR to PINE CREEK ROADEND via Post Corral Meadows, Rae Lake, Hell-for-Sure Pass, Goddard Canyon, John Muir Trail, Hutchinson Meadow, Pine Creek Pass, Upper Pine Lake (shuttle trip). Topo maps (15') Blackcap Mtn., Mt. Abbot, Mt. Tom; Profiles 9, 5, 4. Best mid or late season: 47.5 miles.

	Trail/layover	Total recom-
Grade	days	mended days
Leisurely	8/3	11
Moderate	6/3	9
Strenuous	5/2	7

HILITES Every route that crosses the Sierra crest offers, at its completion, a sense of accomplishment to the traveler. This S-shaped route boasts two for the price of one in that it crosses two major passes, Hell-for-Sure and Pine Creek Pass. For the most part, this trans-Sierra route plan is one of the lesser used. The trail is well maintained; the fishing is excellent; and the scenery is regal.

DESCRIPTION   (Moderate trip)

1st Hiking Day (Courtright Reservoir to Post Corral Meadows, 8 miles): See 1st hiking day, trip 27.

2nd Hiking Day (Post Corral Meadows to Rae Lake, 6 miles): See 2nd hiking day, trip 29.

3rd Hiking Day (Rae Lake to Lower Goddard Canyon, 11 miles): See 3rd hiking day, trip 35.

4th Hiking Day (Lower Goddard Canyon to Hutchinson Meadow, 8.5 miles): Proceed to the John Muir Trail/Hutchinson Meadow trail junction as described in 4th hiking day, trip 35; where our route turns right onto the Hutchinson Meadow trail and continues as described in 5th hiking day, trip 22.

5th Hiking Day (Hutchinson Meadow to Upper Pine Lake, 9 miles): See 6th hiking day, trip 22.

6th Hiking Day (Upper Pine Lake to Pine Creek Roadend, 5 miles): See 1st hiking day, trip 17.

TRIP From COURTRIGHT RESERVOIR to WISHON RESERVOIR ROADEND via Post Corral Meadows, North Fork Kings River, Portal Lake (Blackcap Basin), cross country to Blue Canyon, then by trail over Kettle Ridge to Cabin Creek (shuttle trip). Topo maps (15′) Blackcap Mtn., Mt. Goddard, Marion Peak, Tehipite Dome; Profiles 9, 8. Best mid or late season; 50 miles.

Grade	Trail/layover days	Total recommended days
Leisurely	8/4	12
Moderate	7/3	10
Strenuous	5/3	8

HILITES   Employing a challenging cross-country route (for intermediate and experienced knapsackers only), this trip joins Blackcap Basin with Blue Canyon. Where it crosses the Le Conte Divide, it traverses the spine of that divide, offering breathtaking views to either side. The trailed segments of this trip touch a full range of flora and fauna representative of the exciting west slopes.

DESCRIPTION   (Moderate trip)

1st Hiking Day   (Courtright Reservoir to Post Corral Meadows, 8 miles): See 1st hiking day, trip 27.

2nd Hiking Day   (Post Corral Meadows to Big Maxson Meadow, 8 miles): See 2nd hiking day, trip 34.

3rd Hiking Day   (Big Maxson Meadow to Portal Lake, 7.5 miles): See 3rd hiking day, trip 34.

4th Hiking Day   (Portal Lake to Blue Canyon Cabinsite, 7 miles cross country): Staying on the north side of the inlet stream from Portal Lake (10300'), our route ascends the steep fractured granite slope to granitoid Midway Lake (poor fishing). Then, on a gentler ascent, this route follows up that lake's inlet stream past several rocky tarns to large (30-acre) Cathedral Lake. Fair fishing for rainbow and some brook trout (to 10") is available here. This high, alpine lake is typical of the lakes of Blackcap Basin. Situated in a granite pocket, ringed by cirque walls on three sides, characterized by deep, cold waters, and relieved only by an occasional clump of willow, heather or stunted lodgepole, the lake hugs the White Divide. Our route skirts the north side of the lake, then turns southeast and climbs the talus and steep granite slabs to the crest of the White Divide just north of distinctive Finger Peak. After contouring beneath the steep north face of Finger Peak, this route crosses the saddle between Finger and Blue Canyon peaks. Views from this saddle are superlative of the White Divide, Goddard Divide, and Ragged Spur, and down into the Blue Canyon Creek drainage. Thence, our route descends by chutes to the northernmost, unnamed lakes of the Blue Canyon Creek drainage, and follows the southwest course of this drainage over slab granite that is broken by welcome grassy pockets. The route veers left and drops down to the west side of granitoid lake 10364. At the outlet of this lake, our route crosses the stream and descends steeply to the moderately forested (lodgepole, quaking aspen, some hemlock) flats at the head of Blue Canyon. Staying on the south side of the creek, this route meets the fisherman's trail that descends steadily over a jumbled, rocky slope. From the slopes on the left, the hiker is very apt to hear the piping of a marmot as he rounds the turn in the canyon that gives him the view of the lovely, open meadows below. This trail scrambles down to the head of these meadows, skirting the eastern fringe, and arrives at the log ford leading to the good campsites up and downstream from the landmark cabinsite. Fishing for brook (to 10″) on Blue Canyon Creek is good, and firewood is plentiful.

5th Hiking Day (Blue Canyon Cabinsite to Kettle Dome Campsite, 3.5 miles): See 4th hiking day, trip 39.

6th Hiking Day (Kettle Dome Campsite to Cabin Creek, 10.5 miles): See 3rd and 2nd hiking days, trip 39.

7th Hiking Day (Cabin Creek to Wishon Reservoir Roadend, 5.5 miles): See 1st hiking day, trip 39.

TRIP		From COURTRIGHT RESERVOIR to SOUTH LAKE via Post Corral Meadows, Big Maxson Meadow, Portal Lake, Blue Canyon, cross country on the Tunemah Trail to Simpson Meadow, trail to Palisade Creek, Dusy Basin, Bishop Pass (shuttle trip). Topo maps (15′) Blackcap Mtn., Mt. Goddard, Marion Peak; Profiles 9, 8, 7, 10. Best mid or late season; 68 miles.

Grade	Trail/layover days	Total recommended days
Leisurely	11/3	14
Moderate	10/3	13
Strenuous	9/3	12

HILITES	Experienced hikers should find this long, and sometimes difficult, route to their liking. Crossing the Le Conte Divide from Blackcap Basin, this route follows the seldom used Tunemah Trail (via cross country) to Simpson Meadow, and after ascending the Middle Fork Kings River to Dusy Basin, crosses the Sierra Crest at Bishop Pass. The magnificent scenery of four divides (photographers should take color film) and excellent fishing on the lakes and streams of their watersheds make this trip a provocative choice.

DESCRIPTION (Strenuous trip)

1st Hiking Day (Courtright Reservoir to Post Corral Meadows, 8 miles): See 1st hiking day, trip 28.

2nd Hiking Day (Post Corral Meadows to Big Maxson Meadow, 8 miles): See 2nd hiking day, trip 34.

3rd Hiking Day (Big Maxson Meadow to Portal Lake, 7.5 miles): See 3rd hiking day, trip 34.

4th Hiking Day (Portal Lake to Blue Canyon Cabinsite, 7 miles cross country): See 4th hiking day, trip 37.

5th Hiking Day (Blue Canyon Cabinsite to Upper Alpine Creek, 4 miles cross country): See 5th hiking day, trip 40.

6th Hiking Day (Upper Alpine Creek to Simpson Meadow, 9 miles cross country): See 6th hiking day, trip 42.

7th Hiking Day (Simpson Meadow to Grouse Meadows, 10 miles): See 4th hiking day, trip 58.

8th Hiking Day (Grouse Meadows to Dusy Basin, 8 miles): See 5th hiking day, trip 58.

9th Hiking Day (Dusy Basin to South Lake, 6.5 miles): See 1st hiking day, trip 45.

TRIP   From WISHON RESERVOIR ROADEND to BLUE CANYON via Cabin Creek, Crown Creek, Kettle Ridge (round trip). Topo maps (15') Tehipite Dome, Marion Peak, Mt. Goddard; Profile 8. Best mid or late season; 39 miles.

Grade	Trail/layover days	Total recommended days
Leisurely	8/2	10
Moderate	6/2	8
Strenuous	4/2	6

HILITES   This trip winds through magnificent stands of fir and lodgepole before crossing lofty Kettle Ridge to Blue Canyon. Naturalists will find that the ecological contrast between the west and east slopes of Kettle Ridge almost coincides with that found when crossing the Sierra Crest. Wildflowers abound around the many tributary crossings, and fishing is excellent.

DESCRIPTION (Leisurely trip)

1st Hiking Day (Wishon Reservoir Roadend to Cabin Creek, 5.5 miles): From the end (6740') of the passenger-car road (marked "jeep road"), our route follows the jeep road for approximately 1 mile, then our trail branches left (unsigned). Crossing an easy rise to the east, the trail passes through a magnificent forest of sugar, lodgepole, Jeffrey, white fir and incense cedar. Mostly duff, the trail becomes very dusty owing to heavy stock usage as the summer progresses. The trail then fords Little Rancheria Creek, and continues its gentle ascent past the Spanish Lake trail, where the ascent becomes steeper. Short switchbacks bring one to the lush, wildflower-filled seepage area surrounding Three Springs. Here, fresh, cold water gushes from the ground in a dainty meadow. A dense fir forest pushes against the edges of the lush meadow, and wildlife tracks abound in the vicinity of the spring. Among the tracks one is very apt to find those of the mule deer, porcupine, black bear, meadow mouse, skunk, squirrel, and any number of a variety of birds including pygmy nuthatch, robin, bluejay, junco, horned owl and woodpecker. After leaving the springs, the ascent levels off gradually until it reaches the top of the ridge, and it passes the first of three laterals to Hoffman Mtn. Tiny tributaries repeatedly cross the trail, making the top of this climb a lovely wildflower garden that includes lupine, monkey flower, golden brodiaea, currant, gooseberry and larkspur. As the trail turns somewhat southerly, it begins to descend, and, through the trees, one has limited views to the southeast of Spanish Mountain, Rodgers Ridge and the Obelisk. The duff trail then descends through a moderate-to-dense forest cover of lodgepole, red fir, and some Jeffrey to a ford of a tributary of Cabin Creek. About ¼ mile beyond, the trail dips to the good campsites at Cabin Creek (8240′). The creek is a tiny stream of water, but its diminutive size does not hide its irrepressible nature as it tumbles down with a riot of sound. Brook trout abound in this little creek, but fishermen will find them generally very small. The better campsites are located just upstream, and they are of the intimate, primitive kind, close to the red columbine, shooting star, western mountain aster, and Mariposa lily that line the banks of the stream. Wood is plentiful.

2nd Hiking Day (Cabin Creek to Crown Creek, 6 miles): Leaving Cabin Creek the trail continues easterly and passes the second lateral to Hoffman Mountain branching off to the left. Gradually ascending over a rock and duff surface, the trail tops an easy saddle that is distinguished by its stands of the smooth, pale-barked quaking aspen. From the saddle the trail descends gently through a dense forest cover of red fir and lodgepole past the last trail lateral to Hoffman Mountain (not shown on the topo map). (Most of the signing in Woodchuck Country is long out of date, and, except for indicating general directions, is dangerously misleading.) A few yards beyond, our route passes the Statum Meadow trail branching right, and continues on past Cow Meadow to Summit Meadow (incorrectly labeled as "Wet Meadow" on the topo map). Views on the left include the jumbled granite landmark of Crown Rock, and a few yards farther on our trail passes another trail lateral to Spanish Lake. The duff-and-sand trail winds through a dense timber cover on a gentle descent to the uniquely constructed Crown Valley Guard Station, where emergency services are available when it is manned. Turning somewhat northerly, the trail descends to the willow-infested and ghost-snagged west end of the Crown Valley meadows, and in the course of this descent passes several primitive campsites situated next to the small stream on the right. The trail fords this tributary at the head of the meadow, and winds around the fenced southern edge of the grasslands. The dozen or so buildings of the Crown Valley Ranch, a recently active "guest ranch," come into view as the trail winds the length of the valley. Just beyond the ranch clearing our trail passes the Tehipite Valley trail and the John Muir Wilderness Area boundary sign, and then winds through a dense forest of red fir, white fir, lodgepole and Jeffrey. Descending gently, the trail affords occasional, tree-shrouded views of the Monarch Divide, and in the more open sections one can see Spanish Mountain and the Obelisk to the southwest. Increasing amounts of manzanita, snowbrush and willow can be seen from the trail as it descends more steeply into the tributary drainages of Crown Creek, and the trail surface becomes very sandy as it traverses a long slope to Crown Creek itself. A few yards above the creek bed, a sign reading "campsite" points along a trail lateral branching left. This lateral ascends the Crown Creek drainage for about one mile, and then descends to a long, wade-across (dangerous in high water) ford. On the east side of the creek, the lateral terminates at several excellent meadowed campsites (7040') where firewood is abundant. Anglers will delight in the excellent rainbow fishing (to 16") to be found along the creek, and naturalists will find the natural salt lick at the creek ford a superlative spot for quiet wildlife watching.

3rd Hiking Day (Crown Creek to Kettle Dome Campsite, 4.5 miles): Retrace steps to the main trail, and turn left toward Crown Creek. A few descending steps from this junction, the trail fords Crown Creek and continues eastward in fairly level fashion. As the trail nears the foot of Kettle Ridge, Kettle Dome comes into view as a two-pronged granite finger. The topo map incorrectly shows the dome to be forested (green). It is not. The trail crosses several small run-off streams (not all are indicated on the topo), and at the Kings Canyon National Park boundary begins a steady climb. For those who are interested, the 7500' contour marks the best place to begin a side excursion to ascend Tehipite Dome. It is an interesting historical sidelight that Frank Dusy, a local sheepherder, around the turn of the century pursued a wounded grizzly bear approximately along this route. Further exploration by Dusy for grazing areas resulted in the blazing of this crossing of Kettle Ridge and the old Tunemah Trail (leading to Simpson Meadow). It is interesting to note that the lower slopes have some sugar pine, John Muir's favorite Sierra tree. The trail soon becomes very steep, with exceptionally few switchbacks, and this poor trail construction results in the trail's being heavily washed—a condition not helped by the heavy stock traffic it suffers. As the trail ascends, the forest cover thins somewhat, but still includes sugar pine, red fir, lodgepole and Jeffrey. The underbrush, for the most part, is manzanita and snowbrush. At the top of the ridge, it is time well spent to detour off to the right of the trail for the unsurpassed views of Monarch Divide and the Middle Fork Kings River watershed. The panorama of the Monarch Divide encompasses Goat Crest, Slide Peak, Kennedy Mountain and Hogback Peak. Slide Peak, with its clearly defined avalanche chutes, is particularly interesting, and above the canyon's blue haze one can trace the glacial paths on the far side that left the remarkable, unnamed,

finlike ridge to the east-southeast. The trail cross a tiny, incongru-
ous stream right on top of the ridge, and then descends steeply.
This descent offers a different set of views, including Tunemah
Peak, Burnt Mountain, Blue Canyon, Marion Peak, parts of Cirque
Crest, Goat Crest and the rest of the Monarch Divide. The initial
descent levels off in a meadowed bench containing a good tributary stream (unnamed) and several excellent campsites (8200').
These campsites are due east of Kettle Dome, and approximately
1000' above the Blue Canyon floor. Firewood is abundant.

4th Hiking Day   (Kettle Dome Campsite to Blue Canyon Cabinsite,
3.5 miles): The dusty and rocky trail descends by steady, steep
switchbacks the remaining 1000' to the canyon floor. This descent
parallels the tributary on which the campsites for the previous hiking day were situated until it nears Blue Canyon Creek. The flora
of Blue Canyon differs markedly from that of Crown Creek, and the
combination of sagebrush, quaking aspen, and rushing creek gives
the impression of being alongside one of the plummeting streams
on the east side of the Sierra. Ascending the rocky slopes of Blue
Canyon, the trail alternates between steady and steep climbing
through a sparse-to-moderate forest cover that includes lodgepole,
aspen and some juniper. Looking back down Blue Canyon, one has
Veed views across the Middle Fork Kings River to the Monarch
Divide and the pinnacle formations that constitute Kennedy Peak.
Flowers along this ascent include Indian paintbrush, pennyroyal,
Mariposa lily, pussy paws, scarlet gilia and larkspur. Just north
of the large packer site, the trail crosses to the east side of the
creek via a deep wade-across ford, and then continues its steady
climb. Above this ford, Blue Canyon Creek exhibits some of the
most spectacular granite-bottomed chutes in the Sierra. The water
shoots at an incredible velocity down these chutes, which are
sometimes ¼ mile long. They are marked at either end by cascades and waterfalls. At the head of one of these series, the trail
emerges at Blue Canyon meadows. Here, in contrast to the white-
water maelstrom below, Blue Canyon Creek winds docilely in
typical meadow-meandering fashion, and immediately on the left
one can see the old notched-log sheepherder cabin across the
creek. Access to the good campsites just south of the cabin is
achieved by a footlog just downstream from the cabin. Firewood is
ample, and angling for brook and rainbow (to 10") on Blue Canyon
Creek is good. These campsites make a good base camp for angling and discovery side trips to the head of Blue Canyon basin,
and to the adjoining watershed of Alpine Creek (to the east—
see trip 40).

5th Hiking Day   (Blue Canyon Cabinsite to Kettle Dome Campsite,
3.5 miles): Retrace steps of 4th hiking day.

6th Hiking Day   (Kettle Dome Campsite to Crown Creek, 4.5
miles): Retrace steps of 3rd hiking day.

7th Hiking Day   (Crown Creek to Cabin Creek, 6 miles): Retrace
steps of 2nd hiking day.

8th Hiking Day   (Cabin Creek to Wishon Reservoir Roadend, 5.5
miles): Retrace steps of 1st hiking day.

40

TRIP   From WISHON RESERVOIR ROADEND to TUNE-
MAH LAKE via Cabin Creek, Crown Creek, Kettle
Ridge, Blue Canyon, Tunemah Trail (round trip). Topo
maps (15') Tehipite Dome, Marion Peak; Profile 8.
Best mid or late season; 47 miles.

Grade	Trail/layover days	Total recom-mended days
Leisurely	10/3	13
Moderate	8/3	11
Strenuous	5/2	7

HILITES   Traversing mostly wooded slopes, this trip crosses
Kettle Ridge and descends to captivating Blue Canyon. The excellent fishing on Crown and Blue Canyon
creeks might understandably warrant making this trip,
but the subsequent cross-country travel to Tunemah
Lake adds a dash of spice that makes this a must for
intermediate hikers.

DESCRIPTION   (Leisurely trip)

1st Hiking Day   (Wishon Reservoir Roadend to Cabin Creek, 5.5
miles): See 1st hiking day, trip 39.

2nd Hiking Day   (Cabin Creek to Crown Creek, 6 miles): See 2nd
hiking day, trip 39.

3rd Hiking Day   (Crown Creek to Kettle Dome Campsite, 4.5
miles): See 3rd hiking day, trip 39.

4th Hiking Day   (Kettle Dome Campsite to Blue Canyon Cabinsite,
3.5 miles): See 4th hiking day, trip 39.

5th Hiking Day   (Blue Canyon Cabinsite to Upper Alpine Creek,
4 miles cross country): This hiking day's route follows the old
Tunemah trail. Originally a sheepherder's route to Simpson Meadow, this route then became a heavily used stock trail, but with the
advent of Kings Canyon National Park and the subsequent exclu-
sion of grazing rights, the trail fell into disuse. Today the only
mark, other than that of the abundant wildlife, which one sees on
this trail is the boottrack of the adventurous knapsacker. The derivation of the name "Tunemah," as described in an old magazine
article, is: "a Chinese 'cuss-word' of very vivacious connotation."*

*"Unexplored Regions of the High Sierras," T. S. Solomons, *Over-
land,* Nov. 1896.

The point where the Tunemah trail branches east from Blue Canyon is due east of the cabinsite described in the previous hiking day. Unsigned, this trail is marked only by two ancient blazes. The old Tunemah Trail left the canyon about 1½ miles down canyon. Once found, however, the trail remains remarkably clear as it ascends the east wall of the canyon. The initial section is ducked, but it soon resolves into a long, steady traverse that parallels a stream not shown on the topo map. This first rise terminates at a small meadow where the hiker can see a marked change in the forest cover, as dense stands of lodgepole, silver pine and some juniper line the wild pasture. The trail then continues to climb steadily. This well-ducked ascent keeps to the left of the stream that empties this long, timbered cirque, and as the hiker rises above the cirque floor, he has fine views southwest to Tehipite Dome, Tombstone ridge, and the timbered east face of Kettle Dome. This steady ascent terminates at the moderately timbered saddle just north of Burnt Mountain. On the east side of that saddle, one has fine views ranging from the northeast to the southeast of White Divide, Tunemah Peak, Observation Peak, Red Point, Marion Peak, State Peak, Dougherty Peak, Dead Pine Ridge and Kennedy Mountain. From this saddle our route descends past the wet-meadowed site of a snow survey tower and contours around the upper Rattlesnake Creek drainage. All vestiges of the trail disappear in this drainage, but finding the route is no problem, as it continues due east across the moderately timbered divide separating the Rattlesnake and Alpine Creek drainages. Contouring around the head of the steep west wall of the Alpine Creek drainage entails some bouldering and traversing of granite slabs to the creek, where our route fords. This ford is best made above the picturesque waterfall and chute. Staying on the east side of Alpine Creek, a faint trail ascends to open, alpine tundra-meadows and the excellent campsites (10400') just west of Tunemah Peak. Those interested in these fragile, high-country meadows will find the typical red-flowered primrose and the clustered, much-tufted, white-flowered alpine saxifrage underfoot. Good fishing for brook trout (to 10") is available on Alpine Creek, and firewood is ample. These campsites provide a splendid alpine setting for further excursions to Tunemah Lake and ascents of nearby Tunemah, Blue Canyon and Finger peaks.

6th Hiking Day (Upper Alpine Creek to Blue Canyon Cabinsite, 4 miles cross country): Retrace steps of 5th hiking day, or ascend the Alpine Creek drainage ½ mile and cross the divide between the Alpine and Blue Canyon Creek drainages at saddle 11046. Because this route is frequently touched with snow until late in the season, care should be exercised. This route descends via chutes to the wooded head of Blue Canyon Creek, and then proceeds as described in 4th hiking day, trip 37.

7th Hiking Day (Blue Canyon Cabinsite to Kettle Dome Campsite, 3.5 miles): Retrace steps of 4th hiking day.

8th Hiking Day (Kettle Dome Campsite to Crown Creek, 4.5 miles): Retrace steps of 3rd hiking day.

9th Hiking Day (Crown Creek to Cabin Creek, 6 miles): Retrace steps of 2nd hiking day.

10th Hiking Day (Cabin Creek to Wishon Reservoir Roadend, 5.5 miles): Retrace steps of 1st hiking day.

41

TRIP From WISHON RESERVOIR to COURTRIGHT RESERVOIR via Crown Valley, Blue Canyon, Blackcap Basin, North Fork Kings River, Bench Valley, cross country to Devils Punchbowl, trail to Fleming Lake, Post Corral Meadows (shuttle trip). Topo maps (15′) Tehipite Dome, Marion Peak, Mt. Goddard, Blackcap Mtn.; Profiles 8, 9. Best mid or late season; 66 miles.

Grade	Trail/layover days	Total recommended days
Leisurely	11/3	14
Moderate	9/3	12
Strenuous	7/3	10

HILITES This long trip is broken with difficult cross-country stretches, and should be considered only by experienced knapsackers. Touring the west side of volcanic-topped Le Conte Divide, this route visits its three major basins. Excellent fishing, grand scenery, and memorable campsites make this a fine choice for the old-timer, and a trip to which beginning and intermediate backpackers can some day aspire.

DESCRIPTION (Leisurely trip)

1st Hiking Day (Wishon Reservoir Roadend to Cabin Creek, 5.5 miles): See 1st hiking day, trip 39.

2nd Hiking Day (Cabin Creek to Crown Creek, 6 miles): See 2nd hiking day, trip 39.

3rd Hiking Day (Crown Creek to Kettle Dome Campsite, 4.5 miles): See 3rd hiking day, trip 39.

4th Hiking Day (Kettle Dome Campsite to Blue Canyon Cabinsite, 3.5 miles): See 4th hiking day, trip 39.

5th Hiking Day (Blue Canyon Cabinsite to Portal Lake, 7 miles cross country): See 4th hiking day, trip 37.

6th Hiking Day (Portal Lake to Big Maxson Meadow, 7.5 miles): See 3rd hiking day, trip 34.

7th Hiking Day (Big Maxson Meadow to Guest Lake, 6 miles): The trail stays on the northeast side of Big Maxson Meadow as it descends moderately. Hugging the east canyon wall, it parallels the cascading flow of the North Fork Kings River to the Bench Valley trail junction. Our route branches right onto this trail and continues as described in 3rd hiking day, trip 31. This trail lateral is not maintained by the Forest Service.

8th Hiking Day (Guest Lake to Devils Punchbowl, 6.5 miles cross country): See 4th hiking day, trip 32.

9th Hiking Day (Devils Punchbowl to Rae Lake, 5.5 miles): See 3rd hiking day, trip 30.

10th Hiking Day (Rae Lake to Post Corral Meadows, 6 miles): See 2nd hiking day, trip 29.

11th Hiking Day (Post Corral Meadows to Courtright Reservoir, 8 miles): See 1st hiking day, trip 27.

 42

TRIP

From WISHON RESERVOIR ROADEND to SOUTH LAKE via Crown Valley, Blue Canyon, Tunemah Trail, Simpson Meadow, Middle Fork Kings River, Dusy Basin, Bishop Pass (shuttle trip). Topo maps (15′) Tehipite Dome, Marion Peak, Mt. Goddard; Profiles 8, 7, 10. Best mid or late season; 57 miles.

Grade	Trail/layover days	Total recommended days
Leisurely	11/4	15
Moderate	9/3	12
Strenuous	6/3	9

HILITES

Experienced backpackers who like their country "high and wild" will find this remote trans-Sierra route to their liking. The fine fishing at the beginning and end of this long trip justifies taking a rod along, and the photographer will find ample cause to use several rolls of film on the abundant wildlife and landscape focus opportunities he will encounter. The cross country composing the midsection of this trip employs the abandoned Tunemah Trail.

DESCRIPTION (Moderate trip)

1st Hiking Day (Wishon Reservoir Roadend to Cabin Creek, 5.5 miles): See 1st hiking day, trip 39.

2nd Hiking Day (Cabin Creek to Crown Creek, 6 miles): See 2nd hiking day, trip 39.

3rd Hiking Day (Crown Creek to Kettle Dome Campsite, 4.5 miles): See 3rd hiking day, trip 39.

4th Hiking Day (Kettle Dome Campsite to Blue Canyon Cabinsite, 3.5 miles): See 4th hiking day, trip 39.

5th Hiking Day (Blue Canyon Cabinsite to Upper Alpine Creek, 4 miles cross country): See 5th hiking day, trip 40.

6th Hiking Day (Upper Alpine Creek to Simpson Meadow, 9 miles cross country): Descending along the east side of Alpine Creek, the route starts to contour along the Alpine Creek drainage just below the chutes and waterfalls cited in the previous hiking day. This contouring traverse fords the tiny East Fork of Alpine Creek amid a moderate forest cover of lodgepole and red fir, and then rounds the rocky nose of the watershed divide above Bunchgrass Flat. After fording Dog Creek, the route ascends steeply to a timbered depression just south of point 10985, from which one obtains sweeping views northward of the Goddard Creek drainage, including Ragged Spur and portions of the Black Divide. Directly east-northeast, towering Mt. Woodworth tops the horizon, and the barren heights of the Monarch Divide and Cirque Crest dominate the south and southeast, with the impressive avalanche-chute-scarred Windy Peak in the foreground. From this point, the route is a problem of steep, rocky boulder-hopping eastward down a steep slope to the alluvial flats of Simpson Meadow at the confluence of Goddard Creek. The ford of the Middle Fork Kings River can be accomplished via several fallen logs that span the river just below stream junction. A few yards southwest of this ford, the hiker will find several fair-to-good campsites (including several packer sites). The timber cover on this flat includes lodgepole, fir, Jeffrey and quaking aspen; and the predominant shrub is sagebrush. Firewood is plentiful, and the brook and rainbow fishing (to 16") in the Middle Fork is good to excellent. For those interested in reliving bits of history, this meadow site and the flats of Tehipite Valley were a favorite campsite of the Indian tribe of the Monache (the mountain men of the Yokuts tribe). A little casting around on the granite slopes above the trail will reveal several examples of bedrock mortars in which the Indians ground seeds and tanned hides.

7th Hiking Day (Simpson Meadow to Grouse Meadows, 10 miles): See 4th hiking day, trip 58.

8th Hiking Day (Grouse Meadows to Dusy Basin, 8 miles): See 5th hiking day, trip 58.

9th Hiking Day (Dusy Basin to South Lake, 6.5 miles): See 1st hiking day, trip 45.

43

TRIP   From SOUTH LAKE to TREASURE LAKES (round
        trip). Topo map (15') Mt. Goddard; Profile 10. Best
        mid or late season; 5 miles.

Grade	Trail/layover days	Total recom- mended days
Leisurely	2/0	2
Moderate	- - -	- - -
Strenuous	- - -	- - -

HILITES This short trip is a fine "weekender." Touching the
        upper reaches of the South Fork of Bishop Creek, it
        exposes the traveler to three life zones with a very
        limited expenditure of energy and time.

DESCRIPTION (Leisurely trip)

1st Hiking Day   (South Lake to Treasure Lakes, 2.5 miles): From
the roadend (9800') the trail climbs steadily along the east side
of South Lake. A moderate-to-dense forest cover of lodgepole pine
and fir lines the rocky trail as it meets and turns onto the Treasure
Lakes trail. Mostly over duff and sand, the trail descends, fording Bishop Creek's South Fork and a tributary. This descent, mostly
moderate, affords good views of Hurd Peak and the backgrounding, glacially topped Sierra crest. The trail then fords another
tributary and the outlet from the largest of the Treasure Lakes.
(The topo map incorrectly shows the inlet and outlet streams as
connecting through the lake ¼ mile east of lake 10646.) After
this ford, the trail begins a moderate-to-steep ascent on a duff-
and-sand trail that swerves somewhat northerly before doubling
back and continuing the ascent in a southerly direction. In the
higher elevations, the forest cover shows increasing whitebark
pine mixed with the lodgepole, and there is an abundance of wildflowers lining the trail and clustered in the grassy sections that
seam the granite. Although this trail does see some stock traffic,
it is, for the most part, a hiker's trail. The ascent steepens, crosses
over an area of smoothed granite slabs dotted with glacial erratics, and after fording the outlet stream from lake 10646, the
trail arrives at the good campsites on the northeast side of that
lake. This lake is the largest in the Treasure Lakes basin (12 acres)
and affords fair-to-good fishing for golden (to 12"). Anglers who
wish to spend a layover day here will find that, contrary to the
usual rule of thumb, the fishing gets better as one tries the lakes
of the upper basin. Firewood is ample.

2nd Hiking Day   (Treasure Lakes to South Lake, 2.5 miles): Retrace steps of 1st hiking day.

TRIP   From SOUTH LAKE to TREASURE LAKES, return via
            cross country route to Long Lake (loop trip). Topo
            map (15′) Mt. Goddard; Profile 10. Best mid or late
            season; 8 miles.

	Trail/layover days	Total recom- mended days
Grade		
Leisurely	2/0	2
Moderate	- - -	- - -
Strenuous	- - -	- - -

HILITES   Like the previous trip, this two-day trek explores the
            Treasure Lakes chain, but, unlike the previous trip, it
            returns by an easy cross-country route to the Bishop
            Pass trail. Thus it makes a fine, easy semiloop that
            should be investigated by all, regardless of experi-
            ence.

DESCRIPTION (Leisurely trip)

1st Hiking Day (South Lake to Treasure Lakes, 2.5 miles): See
1st hiking day, trip 43.

2nd Hiking Day (Treasure Lakes to South Lake via Long Lake,
5.5 miles part cross country): Following the faint fisherman's trail
that ascends from the south end of the largest of the Treasure
Lakes (10646′), one follows the intervening stream to the cirque-
basined three upper lakes. This ascent sees the timber cover thinning until, at the upper triad, all that remains is low-lying whitebark pine. Like the lower Treasure Lakes, these three lakes
contain a good population of golden trout (to 15″). These trout
were originally backpacked in by A. Parcher, son of the pioneer
resort owner W. C. Parcher, and the spawn of that initial plant
provide good fishing for today's anglers. From the upper lake,
our route crosses the outlet and ascends the moderate slopes to
the saddle just east of the lake. This ascent crosses easy ledges
and some loose rock just south of the grey fractured slopes of
Hurd Peak. Grand views from this saddle include Mts. Gilbert,
Johnson and Goode to the south and southwest; and the spectacular comb ridge of the Inconsolable Range lining the South
Fork Bishop Creek drainage to the east. Our route then follows
the natural, moderate-sloped descent to lovely Margaret Lake
(brook, to 8″). Thence it descends along the tarn-dotted slopes
northeast of Margaret Lake, and, after fording tumbling South
Fork Bishop Creek just north of Spearhead Lake (rainbow, to 16″),
meets and turns left onto the South Lake/Bishop Pass trail. Ford-

ing the willow infested outlet of Ruwau Lake, it passes the trail lateral to that lake, and circles very close along the east shore of Long Lake (brook, rainbow, brown, to 17"). At the tail of Long Lake, the trail refords the South Fork Bishop Creek. Our route then passes the Bull and Chocolate Lakes trail lateral. The moderate descent changes to a steep switchbacking downgrade before recrossing the South Fork of Bishop Creek for the last time. As it levels out, it passes the Treasure Lakes spur trail, and retraces a portion of the 1st hiking day's route to South Lake.

TRIP   From SOUTH LAKE to DUSY BASIN via Bishop Pass (round trip). Topo map (15') Mt. Goddard; Profile 10. Best mid or late season; 13 miles.

Grade	Trail/layover days	Total recommended days
Leisurely	2/1	3
Moderate	- - -	- - -
Strenuous	- - -	- - -

HILITES   A popular route, the Bishop Pass trail climbs the scenic course of the South Fork of Bishop Creek. At Bishop Pass, the trail enters Kings Canyon National Park, but, more cogently, it begins the adventure of the high, barren, granitoid country of Dusy Basin. Grand side-trip possibilities are sufficient reason for planning layover days on this trip.

DESCRIPTION (Leisurely trip)

1st Hiking Day (South Lake to Dusy Basin, 6.5 miles): Starting from the roadend (9800') — about ¼ mile above the South Lake dam — the trail ascends through a moderate-to-dense forest cover of lodgepole and fir on a somewhat rocky trail. This ascent traverses the morainal slope on the east side of South Lake, bearing toward Hurd Peak, and then passes the junction with the Treasure Lakes trail. The trail shifts direction somewhat easterly as it slopes upward along the South Fork Bishop Creek, and passes the Bull and Chocolate Lakes trail junction. Frequent patches of lupine, forget-me-nots, wallflowers, and swamp onions delight the traveler as he fords tributaries and crosses swampy sections. The trail then fords the South Fork Bishop Creek and switchbacks up to the islet-dotted north end of Long Lake. Recrossing South Fork Bishop Creek, it undulates along the east side of beautiful Long Lake (brook, rainbow, brown, to 17") and passes the junction with the Chocolate and Ruwau lakes trail. The memorable vistas of the wooded and meadowed shores of Long Lake stay with the visitor as he crosses the cascading Ruwau Lake outlet stream and ascends through sporadic subalpine, tarn-dotted meadows. Sometimes steep, this steadily ascending trail climbs past spectacular Saddlerock Lake (rainbow to 10″), and the unmarked fishermen's trail spur to Bishop Lake (brook to 14″). Beyond Saddlerock Lake, the trail passes timberline and begins a series of steep switchbacks at the head of a spectacular cirque basin. Excellent views of Mt. Goode appear on the right, and the incredible comb spires of the Inconsolable Range on the left accompany the panting climber, making his breather stops unforgettable occasions. Glacially smoothed ledge granite and quarried blocks on every hand line this well-maintained trail as it passes the unmarked and unmaintained Jigsaw Pass route, visible as a steep, nearby, talus-bottomed col at the head of the Inconsolable Range. Occasional pockets of snow sometimes blanket the approach to Bishop Pass (11989′) late into the season, and care should be exercised in the final ascent to the summit. Views from the pass are excellent of the Inconsolable Range to the north; the Palisades to the southeast; Dusy Basin immediately to the south, flanked by Columbine and Giraud peaks; and the Black Divide on the distant western skyline. From the pass our route descends on a sometimes switchbacking southwestern traverse. This rocky descent contours over rock-bench systems some distance north of the basin's northernmost lake (11,300′), fording its inlet stream. Just below this stream ford, our route branches left, leaving the trail and crossing smooth granite and tundra to the good campsites at the west end of this lake. Other good campsites can be found a few yards to the southeast, along the outlet stream. Fishing for golden and brook trout on this northernmost lake is fair, but anglers should try the good-to-excellent golden and brook angling (to 22″) at lake 11393 and the lake just west, along with the connecting stream. Alpine scenery from the above campsites is breathtaking in its vastness. One can see the Inconsolable Range as it rises behind Bishop Pass, and the climber's Mecca, the Palisades crest, fills the eastern skyline. Also to the east towers symmetrical Isosceles Peak. A very sparse forest cover of gnarled whitebark pine dots the granite landscape on all sides, and the fractures in the granite are filled with grassy, heather-lined pockets. Firewood is scarce, owing to the sparseness of the timber cover and the heavy visitor use to which the Dusy Basin is subjected. This use factor has forced the Kings Canyon National Park officials to consider the possibility of restricting the human use of this fine basin in the interests of preserving its wilderness characteristics. Grazing of stock is currently restricted — check with National Park officials before planning a trip using stock.

2nd Hiking Day (Dusy Basin to South Lake, 6.5 miles): Retrace steps of 1st hiking day.

46

TRIP	From SOUTH LAKE to BIG PINE CREEK ROADEND via Treasure Lakes, Dusy Basin, cross country to Jigsaw Pass, Fourth Lake (shuttle trip). Topo maps (15') Mt. Goddard, Big Pine; Profile 10. Best mid or late season; 21 miles.

Grade	Trail/layover days	Total recommended days
Leisurely	- - -	- - -
Moderate	4/1	5
Strenuous	- - -	- - -

HILITES	This unusual route is a fine selection for the novice or intermediate backpacker who is looking for an interesting and challenging route with some cross-country work. The scenery en route is claimed by many to be the most impressive in the Sierra, and the angling varies from good to excellent, mostly on lakes. Camera buffs who neglect to bring along color film will regret it.

DESCRIPTION   (Moderate trip)

1st Hiking Day   (South Lake to Treasure Lakes, 2.5 miles): See 1st hiking day, trip 43.

2nd Hiking Day   (Treasure Lakes to Dusy Basin, 6 miles part cross country): Proceed cross country to the South Lake/Bishop Pass trail as described in 2nd hiking day, trip 44, where our route turns right onto the South Lake/Bishop Pass trail and continues as described in 1st hiking day, trip 45.

3rd Hiking Day   (Dusy Basin to Fourth Lake, 6.5 miles cross country): Retrace steps of the 2nd hiking day to Bishop Pass. As the trail descends easterly from the pass, it levels out somewhat and then swings north. Where the trail changes direction, our route branches right (unsigned) over granite ledges and boulders to the heavy talus pile that marks the foot of the Jigsaw Pass col. This cross-country boulder hopping requires concentration, but the most absorbed hiker will hear the underground tributary stream flowing several feet beneath the rock underfooting. Occasionally, between the large boulders, the beautifully built, now-landslide-covered Jigsaw Pass trail, can be seen. This old trail once was traveled by stock (believe it or not!). The top of the col is cairned (12622'), and taking a breather stop at this cairn affords excellent views west to Mt. Goode and the upper South Fork Bishop Creek drainage. Views to the south and north are restricted, but one can see down the steep North Fork Big Pine Creek tributary drainage occupying the precipitous canyon to the east. Our route descends from the pass over talus and scree, and, keeping to the right, climbs down over stepladdering bench systems of fractured granite. Some sections of this steep downgrade entail difficult route-picking over huge boulders and "greasy rock," and care in one's footing is a must. Spectacular, knife-edged ridges line this descent on either side, but the steep watershed opens as it approaches the final, stiff climb down to the sparse-to-moderate forest cover at the southeast end of Fifth Lake. The best route keeps to the right to avoid the final steep bluffs above (immediately south of) Fifth Lake. Excellent campsites can be found near the outlet and along the east side of this fine lake, and firewood is ample. Fishing for rainbow, brook and brown (to 18") is good to excellent.

4th Hiking Day (Fourth Lake to Big Pine Creek Roadend, 6 miles): At the outlet of Fifth Lake a faint fisherman's trail descends along the east side of the stream, turns east and, near the west side of Fourth Lake, strikes the Sixth Lake trail, branching left, and the Black Lake trail, continuing east. Our trail route turns right and descends along the east side of North Fork Big Pine Creek toward Third Lake. An interesting side trip that requires an extra hiking day can be taken to Palisade Glacier. (This cross-country route fords North Fork Big Pine Creek and ascends the Sam Mack Lake outlet stream. Keeping left of the stream, the route veers away from the lake on an easy ascent over granite and wildflower-filled grassy pockets to the foot of this algae-reddened ice mass.) Our trail route continues down the North Fork Big Pine Creek drainage through a moderate forest cover of whitebark pine and lodgepole. The trail is frequently rocky, particularly in the steeper stretches, as it switchbacks down the slope above Third Lake. Geologically interesting views to the south and east, of the differing granites of Temple Crag and Mt. Alice, make the traveler's rest breaks pleasurable as well as educational. Fair fishing for rainbow (to 12") characterizes the waters of Third Lake, and this description holds for Second and First lakes as well. Wildflowers seen along this descent include Indian paintbrush, pussy paws, red columbine, wallflower, lupine, fireweed, tiger lily and shooting star. Passing man-enlarged Second and natural First lakes, the trail fords the North Fork Big Pine Creek and passes the trail lateral to Black Lake branching left. From that junction the trail continues to descend on a rocky slope, staying close to the north side of the North Fork Big Pine Creek. The decrease in altitude is reflected in the changing forest cover, which includes the lower altitude loving Jeffrey and fir, mixed with lodgepole, as it passes the large stone cabin marking Cienega Mirth flats. Descending past dashing Second Falls, the trail makes several long traverses, and enroute passes the High Meadows trail (branching left). A few yards past that junction our route meets the Big Pine Creek Roadend (8400'), about 1 mile above the confluence of the North and South Forks of Big Pine Creek.

47

TRIP | From SOUTH LAKE to CHOCOLATE LAKES (round trip). Topo map (15') Mt. Goddard; Profile 10. Best mid season; 6 miles.

Grade	Trail/layover days	Total recommended days
Leisurely	2/0	2
Moderate	- - -	- - -
Strenuous	- - -	- - -

HILITES | The barren heights of the Inconsolable Range mirrored in the lakes of the Chocolate chain make this trip one to be remembered. The good fishing on the lakes is a bonus, and the package ties up as a grand "warm-up" trip for the hiker starting his season a little late.

DESCRIPTION *(Leisurely trip)*

1st Hiking Day (South Lake to Chocolate Lakes, 3 miles): Proceed to the Bull Lake trail junction as described in 1st hiking day, trip 45. Here our route turns left, away from the South Lake/Bishop Pass trail. Ascending moderately, the trail refords the South Fork Bishop Creek, and arrives at sparsely timbered, moderate-sized (10-acre) Bull Lake. Rock-encircled clumps of willows alternate with grassy sections as the trail skirts the north side of the lake. Fishermen may wish to sample this lake's fair brook trout fishing (to 9″) before continuing up the lake's inlet stream to the lower Chocolate Lakes. This ascent crosses rocky talus stretches as it fords and refords the stream. Breather stops offer sweeping views back across the South Fork Bishop Creek drainage to Mts. Goode, Johnson, Gilbert and Thompson. Dominating all views to the east are the barren, pinnacle-comb formations of the sombre Inconsolable Range. The granitoid Chocolate Lakes chain consists of three lakes that become progressively larger as one ascends the basin. Necklaced together, they hang like sapphire jewels around the northeast side of red-rocked Chocolate Peak. The trail passes several good campsites at lower Chocolate Lake, where the camper will find ample firewood. All these lakes have a fair fishery of brook (to 10″), and the upper, larger lake (11100') affords good campsites on the sparsely timbered west shore. Firewood here is somewhat scarce.

2nd Hiking Day (Chocolate Lakes to South Lake, 3 miles): Retrace steps of 1st hiking day.

48

TRIP   From SOUTH LAKE to CHOCOLATE LAKES return
cross country to Treasure Lakes (loop trip). Topo map
(15') Mt. Goddard; Profile 10. Best mid or late season;
9.5 miles.

Grade	Trail/layover days	Total recommended days
Leisurely	3/1	4
Moderate	2/1	3
Strenuous	- - -	- - -

HILITES A premium added to the previous trip, this route returns via Ruwau Lake and Treasure Lakes. The short
cross-country stretch of the second hiking day is a
good test for novices who want to try their skills.

DESCRIPTION (Leisurely trip)

1st Hiking Day (South Lake to Chocolate Lakes, 3 miles): See
1st hiking day, trip 47.

2nd Hiking Day (Chocolate Lakes to Treasure Lakes, 4 miles part
cross country): From the upper Chocolate Lake (11100'), the trail
ascends southward up the easy ridge joining Chocolate Peak with
the main crest of the Inconsolable Range. This rocky, sometimes
faint trail then turns westerly as it descends steeply to the north
shore of large (15-acre), deep Ruwau Lake. Fishing on this lake
is fair to good for rainbow (to 16"). The trail then turns northerly
and switchbacks down the steep, rocky valley wall to the South
Lake/Bishop Pass trail. Our route turns left onto this trail, fords
the outlet creek from Ruwau Lake and around the south end of
Long Lake, fording the South Fork Bishop Creek. Then it climbs
southwest, up the easy sloping basin to Margaret Lake (brook, to
8"). Above Margaret Lake, the obvious route ascends the rocky
talus basin to the southwest, and crosses the divide south of
Hurd Peak. Barren except for occasional whitebark, this cross-
country route-course ascends by glaciated granite ledge systems
to the rock-ribbed saddle. Views from this saddle are good of Mts.
Goode, Johnson and Gilbert to the south and west, and the Inconsolable Range to the east. In addition to the boot track of the occasional cross-country walker, this saddle also sees the track of deer,
fox, marmot and cony. The steep descent route from this saddle
to the Treasure Lakes chain is easily ascertained, and the traveler
meets a faint fisherman's trail at the east side of the upper of
these lakes. This trail crosses talus and ledges around the east
side, fords the outlet, and follows the stream down through mod-

erate stands of whitebark pine to lake 10646, the largest of the Treasure Lakes chain. The hiker will find good campsites on the northeast side of this lake, and firewood is ample. Fishing on this lake is fair-to-good for golden (to 12″), and anglers investigating the fishing on the upper Treasure Lakes will find good-to-excellent angling for golden ranging in length from 8″ to 15″.

3rd Hiking Day (Treasure Lakes to South Lake, 2.5 miles): See 1st hiking day, trip 43.

TRIP   From SOUTH LAKE to DUSY BASIN return via Palisade Basin, Deer Meadow, Middle Fork Kings River, Bishop Pass (semiloop trip). Topo maps (15′) Mt. Goddard, Big Pine; Profiles 10, 9. Best mid or late season; 38 miles.

Grade	Trail/layover days	Total recommended days
Leisurely	7/3	10
Moderate	6/2	8
Strenuous	4/2	6

HILITES   Those who yearn to go "high and light" will find this rugged route to their liking. For scenery the incomparable Palisades crest dominates the route, excepting along the short looping section (John Muir Trail) down Palisades Creek and up Le Conte Canyon.

DESCRIPTION (Moderate trip)

1st Hiking Day (South Lake to Dusy Basin, 6.5 miles): See 1st hiking day, trip 45.

2nd Hiking Day (Dusy Basin to Glacier Creek, 7 miles cross country): The backpacker can contemplate crossing to Palisade Basin via any one of three foot-walkers' passes: Knapsack Pass; the unnamed pass between Columbine Peak and Isosceles Peak; and what has come to be known as "Thunderbolt Pass," just southwest of Thunderbolt Peak. Our route uses Knapsack Pass (11673′). Leaving our campsite at the northernmost lake of Dusy Basin, one follows the trail descending into the basin. The best cross-country route fords Dusy Branch Creek at 10900′, just above (north of) the lowest lakes of the basin, and boulder-hops southeastward on a steady ascent. The footing is mostly rock, broken by occasional pockets of granite sand, and the forest cover consists of very sparse clumps of the five-needled, stunted whitebark pine.

These lower lakes contain golden and brook trout (to 12"). The steady ascent over heavily fractured rock becomes steeper on the final climb to the pass. Impossible as it may sound, there are recorded visits to Palisades Basin via this pass with stock! Views from the pass include Black Giant, Mts. Powell and Thompson to the northwest; and the Palisades Basin and Crest to the east. From this vantage point, the vast expanses of Palisades Basin appear totally barren of life except for an isolated whitebark or a spiring snag, but a closer examination later in this hiking day will reveal that this is certainly not the case. The continuing bracing views of the Palisades Crest, as our route descends from Knapsack Pass, stir the most blasé non-mountain-climber. These peaks look, as one climber expressed it, "like mountain peaks are supposed to look." Precipitous faces composed of relatively unfractured granite, couloirs, buttresses and residual glaciers combine to make this range one of the finer (many climbers claim it to be the finest) climbing areas in the Sierra Nevada. Our route keeps to the left as it descends over a moderate-to-steep ledge system to the westernmost lake of the Barrett chain. Routing around the south end of this rockbound lake, this route crosses the easy saddle east of the lake to the largest lake of the chain, and follows a fisherman's trail around the north end. From this lake the sheer cliffs of the west face of North Palisade dominate the skyline, and our route continues eastward past several tiny, rockbound lakelets. Unlike the granite of lower Dusy Basin, this granite is "newer," and it shows much less fracturing and exfoliation. Contouring around the head of the drainage at the southeast end of Palisade Basin, our route crosses the definite saddle between point 12692 and the main Palisade Crest. Among climbers this saddle is known as "Potluck Pass." Along with the continuing views of the Palisades, this vantage point also looks across the Palisade Creek watershed to Amphitheater Lake. To the southwest the glacially sculpted terrain has a sun-cup appearance similar to the top of a meringue pie. The descent from Potluck is a scramble over a steep, smoothed granite ledge system, keeping to the right. This downgrade continues over scree and then levels out at Lake 11672, and our route follows the west shore of the lake to the good campsites on that edge of the lake and along the outlet creek just below the lake. There is virtually no wood around these sites, and hikers using this trip should anticipate this fact. Fishing at this lake is poor-to-fair for golden (to 8"). Grassy sections around the sandy-bottomed lake provide a foothold for colorful alpine wildflowers, including yellow columbine, sturdy white heather, and the blue sky pilot.

3rd Hiking Day (Glacier Creek to Deer Meadow, 5 miles part cross country): Fording Glacier Creek, our route ascends the sloping basin to the southeast to the saddle overlooking the Palisade Lakes basin. Views from this saddle are good of Devils Crags and Mt. McDuffie to the west, North Palisade to the north and Middle Palisade to the east. Sometimes over snow, this route descends past several tiny glacial tarns, across fractured granite as it veers westward. Part way down this moderate-to-steep grade, Palisade Lakes and the glacially smoothed bowl-like cirque surrounding the lakes come into view. Then, by route-finding down a ledge system, this route encounters sparse whitebark just before it meets the John Muir Trail just west of Palisade Lakes. Anglers, and those wishing to view the lovely Palisade Lakes cirque basin, should walk the short distance northeast to the northernmost of these lakes. Angling on these large lakes is fair-to-good for rainbow and golden (to 15"). Continuing west on the John Muir Trail, the route descends by zigzagging switchbacks along the north side of Palisade Creek. Wildflowers seen along the creek include wallflower, shooting star, white cinquefoil, Indian paintbrush and pentstemon. The head of these switchbacks is an excellent vantage point from which one can see the crest of Middle Palisade peak to the northeast, and, above Deer Meadow lying immediately below, Devils Crags, Wheel Mountain, and Mt. McDuffie to the west. Slopes on both sides of this steep descent are dramatically glacially smoothed. As the trail reaches the head of the flats above Deer Meadow, it enters a moderate stand of lodgepole and silver pine. Abundant wildflowers, including western mountain aster, Douglas phlox, pennyroyal, red columbine and tiger lily, appear as the trail comes close to the creek, and red fir, juniper and aspen occasionally mingle with the predominant lodgepole forest cover. The trail then passes several good campsites before refording Glacier Creek via several step-across branchlets. There are excellent views across the Palisade Creek canyon to the cascading falls of Cataract Creek as they tumble down the steep south wall. Through a heavily ferned area, the trail reaches the Amphitheater Lake trail junction (unmarked except for a sign reading, "Deer Meadow, John Muir Trail"). Here amid a dense grove of lodgepole are several excellent campsites (8800'), where firewood is abundant, and fishing for golden and brook is excellent (to 12"). Hikers having a layover day here will find the steep climb up the unmaintained trail to Amphitheater Lake a rewarding one. Fine views, excellent angling for brook and golden, and evidence of abandoned mining ventures make this side trip an intriguing one.

4th Hiking Day (Deer Meadow to Grouse Meadows, 5 miles): About 100 yards below these campsites, the trail fords the un-named drainage creek (multi-branched) of Palisade Basin, and then descends moderately through a moderate-to-dense forest cover of lodgepole, aspen, red fir, and some juniper and Jeffrey. This descent passes a packers' campsite and a drift fence about 1.5 miles farther on, and then more campsites a short distance beyond that. Concentrations of wildflowers include Indian paintbrush, pentstemon, white cinquefoil, Mariposa lily and goldenrod. Underfooting is mostly duff and sand, through an alternating forest-to-meadow setting. The trail veers away from Palisade Creek, only to return, and, keeping to the north side of the creek, descends steadily over morainal debris to the Middle Fork Kings River trail. This junction is preceded by a drift fence at a meadow signed as "Stillwater Meadow." Our route turns right, up the Middle Fork Kings River, and proceeds as described in 4th hiking day, trip 58.

5th Hiking Day (Grouse Meadows to Dusy Basin, 8 miles): See 5th hiking day, trip 58.

6th Hiking Day (Dusy Basin to South Lake, 6.5 miles): Retrace steps of 1st hiking day.

50

TRIP   From SOUTH LAKE to COURTRIGHT RESERVOIR,
via Bishop Pass, Dusy Basin, John Muir Trail, Muir
Pass, Evolution Valley, Goddard Canyon, Hell-for-Sure
Pass, Rae Lake, Post Corral Meadows (shuttle trip).
Topo maps (15′) Mt. Goddard, Blackcap Mtn.; Pro-
files 10, 9, 5, 7. Best mid or late season; 60 miles.

Grade	Trail/layover days	Total recom- mended days
Leisurely	11/5	16
Moderate	9/4	13
Strenuous	7/3	10

HILITES   So much laudatory prose has been written about the
famous Muir Trail that it seems redundant to add to
it. Suffice it to say that this section of trail tours the
essence of high country, and has the added fillip of
finishing via the elegant forest stretches found west
of Hell-for-Sure Pass.

DESCRIPTION   (Moderate trip)
1st Hiking Day (South Lake to Dusy Basin, 6.5 miles): See 1st
hiking day, trip 45.

2nd Hiking Day (Dusy Basin to Little Pete Meadow, 6 miles):
The trail from the northernmost lake of the Dusy Basin descends
over smooth granite ledges and tundra sections. Occasional
clumps of the flaky-barked, five-needled whitebark pine dot the
otherwise barren, glacially carved basin, and impressive views
of Mts. Agassiz and Winchell and Thunderbolt Peak background
Isosceles Peak to the east. To the south the heavily fractured
and less well defined summits of Columbine and Giraud peaks
occupy the skyline. This moderate descent swings westward above
the lowest lakes of the Dusy Basin, and begins a series of steady
switchbacks along the north side of Dusy Branch Creek. Wildflowers seen during this descent include Indian paintbrush, pennyroyal, lupine, white cinquefoil, pentstemon, shooting star and
some yellow columbine. Views of the U-shaped Middle Fork Kings
River are seen constantly during the zigzagging downgrade, and
on the far side of the valley one can see the major peaks of the
Black Divide, flanked, in the foreground, by The Citadel and
Langille Peak. As the trail descends, the very sparse forest cover
of stunted whitebark seen in most of Dusy Basin gives way to
the trees of lower altitudes, including silver pine, juniper, lodgepole, aspen and some red fir near the foot of the switchbacks.

Naturalists will be interested in the record girth of the old juniper marking the "elbow" of the final switchback before fording Dusy Branch Creek just above that stream's confluence with the outlet stream from Rainbow Lakes. The chutes and cascades of Dusy Branch Creek are dramatic examples of High Sierra streams, and are time-honored favorites of the photographer. The trail refords Dusy Branch Creek at the head of a stepladdering bench, and then makes the final switchbacking descent to the junction with the John Muir Trail in Le Conte Canyon. Emergency services are available from the ranger station just a few yards northwest of the junction. Our route turns right, onto the famous Muir Trail, and ascends moderately over a duff trail through moderate-to-dense stands of lodgepole. Langille Peak dominates the views to the left, and its striking white, exfoliated granite face is a constant reminder of the massive forces expended by the river of ice that once filled this canyon. Abundant fields of wildflowers color the trailside, including corn lily, white mariposa, tiger lily, buckwheat, fireweed, larkspur, red heather, shooting star, Indian paintbrush, white cinquefoil, monkey flower, pennyroyal, pentstemon, western mountain aster, gooseberry, currant, goldenrod and wallflower. As the trail approaches the south end of Little Pete Meadow, occasional hemlock will be found mixed with the lodgepole, and the view north at the edge of the meadow includes Mts. Powell and Thompson. There are excellent streamside campsites at Little Pete Meadow, but heavy use has made firewood somewhat scarce. Fishing for rainbow, golden and brook is good (to 13").

3rd Hiking Day   (Little Pete Meadow to Campsites, Upper Middle Fork Kings River, 3.5 miles): The trail from Little Pete to Big Pete Meadow is a moderate ascent on rock and sand through a sparse-to-moderate forest cover of lodgepole and occasional hemlock. Looking back over one's shoulder rewards the traveler with fine views of Le Conte Canyon, while ahead the granite walls where the canyon veers west show glacially smoothed, unfractured faces. Some quaking aspen can be seen as the trail ascends through Big Pete Meadow and passes the large area of campsites. As the trail turns westward, one has his first, excellent views of the darker rock of Black Giant, and a few yards beyond the turn the trail fords the tributary stream draining the slopes of Mts. Johnson and Gilbert. Passing more campsites, the trail continues west on an easy-to-moderate ascent through grassy extensions of Big Pete Meadow. Most of the rock underfooting encountered to this point has been of the rounded morainal variety, but as soon as the trail leaves the westernmost fringes of Big Pete Meadow, the rock's sharp, fractured edges reflect its weathering origins. Over this talus, the trail ascends more steeply through a moderate forest cover of silver, lodgepole, whitebark and some hemlock. The brush is mostly chinquapin and manzanita. Flowers encountered along the trail and clumped in the wetter stretches include Indian paintbrush, pentstemon, pennyroyal, wallflower, red heather, swamp onion, white cinquefoil, buckwheat, labrador tea, milfoil, fleabane and shooting star. Canyon ecologies, such as the one encountered in Le Conte Canyon, are of scientific interest to the naturalist, but they hold an equal fascination for laymen who simply appreciate natural beauty. The two natural features that usually claim the traveler's attention are the canyon walls and the watercourse. In Le Conte Canyon both are worthy of study because they are dramatic and exciting, but equally deserving of scrutiny is the geologic history of the meadowed and forested flats encountered on the trail. On the canyon floor, accumulations of sand — usually of granitic origin, weathered or chemically eroded from the canyon walls — combine with silt to make an environment suitable for dense stands of evergreens and wildflowers. These alluvial deposits occur as a result of both glacial and subsequent river erosion. Canyon flats, frequently meadowed, that owe their birth to glacial cutting, occur where the glacier "ground down on its heel." After the ice had melted, what was left was a step-laddering canyon. The flats, which were first covered by lakes, later filled with sediment, and the sediment provided a foothold for grasses and trees. As one ascends to timberline above Big Pete Meadow, he bcomes increasingly aware of this evolutionary process, and of the complicating factors of the harsher climatic environment affecting the process at higher elevations. The meadowed flat where the trail jogs north toward the tiny, unnamed lake east of Helen Lake is an earlier stage of the process, and supports a sparse forest fringe of lodgepole, silver and some whitebark. This hiking day ends at the fair-to-good campsites just above the meadow (10400'). Firewood is scarce.

4th Hiking Day (Campsites, Upper Middle Fork Kings River to Wanda Lake, 6 miles): An early start for crossing Muir Pass is both expedient and rewarding. Steep climbs, even over snow, are best achieved in the cool of the morning. But arriving at the summit of Muir Pass in the early hours has compensations greater than those of physical comfort, for, with early light, one is treated to a rare and beautiful panorama unmatched anywhere. The ascent to the pass starts with a steady climb over sand and rock through a sparse timber cover of whitebark. That timber cover soon disappears, giving way to low-lying heather. At the talus-bound, round, unnamed lake east of Helen Lake, the trail veers westerly, crossing and recrossing the trickling headwaters of the Middle Fork Kings River. Excellent views to the southeast of the Palisades and Langille, Giraud and Columbine peaks make the breather stops welcome occasions. The trail becomes rocky and the slope more moderate as it passes the next unnamed lake and winds over the terminal shoulder of the Black Divide to Helen Lake. Rock in colorful reds, yellows, blacks and whites that characterize this metamorphic divide are on every hand. The trail rounds the loose-rocked south end of this barren lake, and ascends steadily over a rocky trail that is often covered with snow throughout the season. Looking back, one can see the striking meeting of the black metamorphic rock of the Black Divide and the white granite just east of Helen Lake. Muir Pass (12059') is marked by a sign and a unique stone shelter. This hut, erected by the Sierra Club in memoriam to John Muir, the Sierra's best-known and most-loved mountaineer, stands as a shelter for storm-bound travelers. In a sense, it is a wilderness monument, and should be treated as such — leave nothing but your boottracks and firewood for those who follow. Both will be appreciated. From this pass the views are magnificent. In the morning light, the sombre crags to the north and south relieve the intense whites of the lighter granite to the east. Situated in a gigantic rock bowl, Wanda Lake's emerald blue waters contrast sharply with its lower white sides, which, on the south side, disappear into the darker rock of the Goddard Divide. The descent from the pass is moderate and then steady over crushed rock, and then it levels out, passing the south end of the smaller lake at the head of the cirque. Skirting the east side of Wanda Lake, the trail affords excellent views of snow- and ice-necklaced Mt. Goddard, and then arrives at the fair-to-good campsites near the lake's outlet. No firewood. Views from these campsites include Mt. Goddard and the Goddard Divide to the south, and Mts. Huxley, Spencer, Darwin and Mendel to the north.

5th Hiking Day (Wanda Lake to Colby Meadow, 7 miles): Occasional wildflowers, including heather, wallflower and pentstemon, can be seen as the trail descends over rock and sand. The trail crosses Evolution Creek and stays on the west bank on a moderate descent that becomes switchbacks above Sapphire Lake. Fine views of the Sierra crest to the east make watching one's footing a difficult task. Sapphire Lake is indeed a high-country gem, fringed with green, marshy grass, and situated on a large glacial step. Our route traverses its steeper west side, and, after a steady descent, refords Evolution Creek about a mile below, just above Evolution Lake. The trail crosses a meadowy section before winding the length of the east shore. Glacial smoothing and some polish can be seen in the granite surrounding the lake, and on the abrupt walls on either side of the lake. Passing several campsites at the lower end of the lake, the trail makes a brief northward swing before switchbacking down to Evolution Valley. This northward swing passes the unsigned, ducked trail ascending to Darwin Canyon, and the route to the Darwin Glacier. The zigzagging downgrade over morainal debris re-enters forest cover (lodgepole and whitebark) and passes clumps of wildflowers that include pentstemon, Indian paintbrush, swamp onion, lupine, forget-me-not, yellow cinquefoil, buckwheat, heather and tiger lily. At the foot of the grade, where the trail fords the stream emptying Darwin Canyon, our route passes more campsites, and then continues on a relatively level course through moderate stands of lodgepole to the good campsites at Colby Meadow. Firewood is ample, and fishing for golden is fair (to 9″) in nearby Evolution Creek.

6th Hiking Day (Colby Meadow to Campsites, Lower Goddard Canyon, 6 miles): From Colby Meadow the trail continues westward, and, unlike the topo, does not ford Evolution Creek before passing the McGee Lakes trail. The Evolution Valley meadow complex consists of three charming, subalpine grasslands: Colby, McClure and Evolution meadows. The trail joining these meadows is a winding pathway that wends its way through moderate and dense stands of lodgepole, and, in the midst of McClure Meadow, passes a ranger station (emergency services available here). The friendly intimacy of the meadows has, over the past sixty years, made this valley a favorite camping site for back-country travelers, and one which, with the subsequent establishment of the John Muir Trail, has subjected these delicate wild pastures to serious overuse. As our route winds past the campsites in McClure Meadow, the largest of the Evolution group, the traveler can see for himself the toll taken by the heavy traffic, both human and stock. Before controls were exerted upon grazing stock of large pack-train parties, the foraging animals trampled tender, young spring shoots of grass in such quantities as to change the meadow to a patchwork of barren hillocks. In the absence of grasses to hold back the water, serious erosion became a matter of concern, and today, to preserve these meadows, stock forage is necessarily limited. Human impact in the form of ugly scars around smoke-blackened fireplaces, plastic remnants and tin cans is all too evi-dent, and it is proper for the passerby to pause, reflect, and re-solve to keep his presence here confined to memories — not to blight. The duff trail passes the drift fence below McClure Meadow on a moderate-to-steady descent that fords several tributaries draining the Glacier Divide. These fords are usually accomplished via footlogs or easy rock-hopping. At Evolution Meadow the trail fords Evolution Creek (shallow wade-across) for the last time, and then continues west to the head of the switchbacks that drop down to the South Fork San Joaquin River. Views before the descent are excellent of the cascades of the stream draining Emerald Peak (southeast), the falls and cascades of Evolution Creek below the ford, and the South Fork San Joaquin River drainage (northwest). Midway down the switchbacks, one has impressive views of God-dard Canyon, part of the route for the 7th hiking day. The forest cover along the zigzags is sparse-to-moderate lodgepole, juniper and some aspen, and flowers seen along the trail include penny-royal, larkspur, pentstemon, white cinquefoil, currant, monkey flower, buckwheat and Indian paintbrush. The switchbacking trail crosses glacial polish exhibiting some striations, and, at the foot, passes a packer campsite and several good primitive sites as it passes through a heavy stand of lodgepole. Just beyond these campsites, our trail crosses the footbridge, meets the Goddard Canyon/Hell-for-Sure Pass trail, and branches left. The forest cover of lodgepole, with large concentrations of quaking aspen, continues as the trail ascends moderately past the drift fence. About ½ mile above the drift fence, near a small meadow, the trail reaches several good-to-excellent campsites where firewood is ample. Fishing on nearby South Fork San Joaquin is fair for rain-bow, some golden and brook (to 10″).

7th Hiking Day (Lower Goddard Canyon to Rae Lake, 11 miles): See 3rd hiking day, trip 35.

8th Hiking Day (Rae Lake to Post Corral Meadows, 6 miles): See 2nd hiking day, trip 29.

9th Hiking Day (Post Corral Meadows to Courtright Reservoir, 8 miles): See 1st hiking day, trip 27.

51

TRIP   From SOUTH LAKE to BEAR DIVERSION DAM via Bishop Pass, Dusy Basin, John Muir Trail, Muir Pass, Evolution Valley, Selden Pass, Sandpiper Lake, Kip Camp (shuttle trip). Topo maps (15′) Mt. Goddard, Blackcap Mtn., Mt. Abbot; Profiles 10, 9, 5, 2, 1. Best mid or late season; 68 miles.

Grade	Trail/layover days	Total recom-mended days
Leisurely	12/4	16
Moderate	10/4	14
Strenuous	8/3	11

HILITES   Best traveled in midsummer, this long, choice route tours high alpine country and winds through dramatic, glacially scoured canyons. The renowned Muir Trail, over which most of this route passes, retains its primitive appeal despite its heavy use, and anyone who would "know" the Sierra owes it to himself to travel it.

DESCRIPTION   (Moderate trip)

1st Hiking Day   (South Lake to Dusy Basin, 6.5 miles): See 1st hiking day, trip 45.

2nd Hiking Day   (Dusy Basin to Little Pete Meadow, 6 miles): See 2nd hiking day, trip 50.

3rd Hiking Day   (Little Pete Meadow to Campsites, Upper Middle Fork Kings River, 3.5 miles): See 3rd hiking day, trip 50.

4th Hiking Day   (Campsites, Upper Middle Fork Kings River to Wanda Lake, 6 miles): See 4th hiking day, trip 50.

5th Hiking Day   (Wanda Lake to Colby Meadow, 7 miles): See 5th hiking day, trip 50.

6th Hiking Day   (Colby Meadow to Campsites, Hutchinson Meadow Trail Junction, 8.5 miles): Proceed to the Goddard Canyon/Hell-for-Sure Pass trail junction as described in 6th hiking day, trip 50, where our route continues right on the John Muir Trail. After the bridge crossing of the South Fork San Joaquin River, the trail passes more packer and primitive campsites situated in aspen groves, and descends steadily past a drift fence. This stretch boasts many wildflowers, including pentstemon, Bigelow sneezeweed, yellow cinquefoil, groundsel and Indian paintbrush. Just beyond the drift fence, the trail crosses another bridge over the river (steel suspension), and continues to descend steadily over underfooting of morainal outflow. The narrow canyon walls open briefly at Aspen Flat, where the forest cover thickens (lodgepole, aspen and some Jeffrey and juniper). Several good campsites on the river bank in the flats make this a good alternative camping site for this hiking day. The duff footing of Aspen Flat gives way to rock and dust as the trail becomes steeper, and the forest cover thinner. The trail crosses Piute Creek via a footbridge, and arrives at the good campsites near the Hutchinson Meadow trail junction. Firewood is ample, and fishing for rainbow, some golden and brook is fair (to 10″).

7th Hiking Day (Campsites, Hutchinson Meadow Trail Junction to Sally Keyes Lakes, 7.5 miles): See 5th hiking day, trip 22.

8th Hiking Day (Sally Keyes Lakes to Sandpiper Lake, 5 miles cross country): See 3rd hiking day, trip 8.

9th Hiking Day (Sandpiper Lake to Kip Camp, 8.5 miles): See 2nd hiking day, trip 6.

10th Hiking Day (Kip Camp to Bear Diversion Dam Jeep Road Junction, 9.5 miles): See 1st hiking day, trip 2.

 52

TRIP   From SOUTH LAKE to PINE CREEK ROADEND via Bishop Pass, Dusy Basin, John Muir Trail, Muir Pass, Evolution Valley, Hutchinson Meadow, Pine Creek Pass, Upper Pine Lake (shuttle trip). Topo maps (15′) Mt. Goddard, Blackcap Mtn., Mt. Abbot, Mt. Tom; Profiles 10, 9, 5, 4. Best mid or late season; 56.5 miles.

Grade	Trail/layover days	Total recommended days
Leisurely	9/3	12
Moderate	7/3	10
Strenuous	6/2	8

HILITES   Crossing the bulwark of the Sierra at Bishop and Pine Creek passes, this splendid trip treks the heart of Kings Canyon National Park via the Muir Trail.

DESCRIPTION (Leisurely trip)
1st Hiking Day (South Lake to Dusy Basin, 6.5 miles): See 1st hiking day, trip 45.

2nd Hiking Day (Dusy Basin to Little Pete Meadow, 6 miles): See 2nd hiking day, trip 50.

3rd Hiking Day (Little Pete Meadow to Campsites, Upper Middle Fork Kings River, 3.5 miles): See 3rd hiking day, trip 50.

4th Hiking Day (Campsites, Upper Middle Fork Kings River to Wanda Lake, 6 miles): See 4th hiking day, trip 50.

5th Hiking Day (Wanda Lake to Colby Meadow, 7 miles): See 5th hiking day, trip 50.

6th Hiking Day (Colby Meadow to Campsites, Hutchinson Meadow Trail Junction, 8.5 miles): See 6th hiking day, trip 50; 6th hiking day, trip 51.

7th Hiking Day (Campsites, Hutchinson Meadow Trail Junction to Hutchinson Meadow, 5 miles): See 5th hiking day, trip 22.

8th Hiking Day (Hutchinson Meadow to Upper Pine Lake, 9 miles): See 6th hiking day, trip 22.

9th Hiking Day (Upper Pine Lake to Pine Creek Roadend, 5 miles): See 1st hiking day, trip 17.

TRIP From SOUTH LAKE to NORTH LAKE via Bishop Pass, Dusy Basin, John Muir Trail, Muir Pass, Evolution Valley, Piute Canyon, Piute Pass (shuttle trip). Topo maps (15′) Mt. Goddard, Blackcap Mtn., Mt. Abbot, Mt. Tom; Profiles 10, 9, 5, 4, 6. Best mid or late season; 53.5 miles.

Grade	Trail/layover days	Total recommended days
Leisurely	9/3	12
Moderate	7/3	10
Strenuous	5/2	7

HILITES The proximity of the beginning and end of this trip makes it an easy shuttle. Like the previous trip this route crosses the Sierra crest at Bishop Pass and follows the eminent Muir Trail, but it exits via Piute Pass.

DESCRIPTION (Leisurely trip)
1st Hiking Day (South Lake to Dusy Basin, 6.5 miles): See 1st hiking day, trip 45.

2nd Hiking Day (Dusy Basin to Little Pete Meadow, 6 miles): See 2nd hiking day, trip 50.

3rd Hiking Day (Little Pete Meadow to Campsites, Upper Middle Fork Kings River, 3.5 miles): See 3rd hiking day, trip 50.

4th Hiking Day (Campsites, Upper Middle Fork Kings River to Wanda Lake, 6 miles): See 4th hiking day, trip 50.

5th Hiking Day (Wanda Lake to Colby Meadow, 7 miles): See 5th hiking day, trip 50.

6th Hiking Day (Colby Meadow to Campsites, Hutchinson Meadow Trail Junction, 8.5 miles): See 6th hiking day, trip 51.

7th Hiking Day (Campsites, Hutchinson Meadow Trail Junction to Hutchinson Meadow, 5 miles): See part of 5th hiking day, trip 22.

8th Hiking Day (Hutchinson Meadow to Piute Lake, 7.5 miles): See 2nd hiking day, trip 24.

9th Hiking Day (Piute Lake to North Lake Campground, 3.5 miles): See 1st hiking day, trip 23.

 54

TRIP From SOUTH LAKE to FLORENCE LAKE ROADEND via Bishop Pass, Dusy Basin, John Muir Trail, Muir Pass, Evolution Valley, Blaney Meadows (shuttle trip). Topo maps (15′) Mt. Goddard, Blackcap Mtn., Mt. Abbot; Profiles 10, 9, 5. Best mid or late season; 50.5 miles.

Grade	Trail/layover days	Total recommended days
Leisurely	8/3	11
Moderate	6/2	8
Strenuous	5/2	7

HILITES This long trans-Sierra crossing tours the drainages of the South Fork of Bishop Creek, the Middle Fork of the Kings River, and the South Fork of the San Joaquin River. Scenery at Dusy Basin and at the Goddard Divide is of the aloof alpine variety, while the intermediate canyon passages provide a warm forested country contrast.

DESCRIPTION (Leisurely trip)
1st Hiking Day (South Lake to Dusy Basin, 6.5 miles): See 1st hiking day, trip 45.

2nd Hiking Day (Dusy Basin to Little Pete Meadow, 6 miles): See 2nd hiking day, trip 50.

3rd Hiking Day (Little Pete Meadow to Campsites, Upper Middle Fork Kings River, 3.5 miles): See 3rd hiking day, trip 50.

4th Hiking Day (Campsites, Upper Middle Fork Kings River to Wanda Lake, 6 miles): See 4th hiking day, trip 50.

5th Hiking Day (Wanda Lake to Colby Meadow, 7 miles): See 5th hiking day, trip 50.

6th Hiking Day (Colby Meadow to Campsites, Hutchinson Meadow Trail Junction, 8.5 miles): See 6th hiking day, trip 51.

7th Hiking Day (Campsites, Hutchinson Meadow Trail Junction to Lower Blaney Meadows Campground, 5.5 miles): See part of 3rd hiking day, trip 26.

8th Hiking Day (Lower Blaney Meadows Campground to Florence Lake Roadend, 7.5 miles): See 4th hiking day, trip 8.

TRIP   From SOUTH LAKE to VERMILION CAMPGROUND (Lake Thomas A. Edison) via Bishop Pass, Dusy Basin, John Muir Trail, Muir Pass, Evolution Valley, Selden Pass, Kip Camp, Quail Meadows (shuttle trip). Topo maps (15′) Mt. Goddard, Blackcap Mtn., Mt. Abbot, Kaiser Peak; Profiles 10, 9, 5, 2, 1. Best mid or late season; 70.5 miles.

Grade	Trail/layover days	Total recommended days
Leisurely	11/4	15
Moderate	9/3	12
Strenuous	7/3	10

HILITES   Using the longest stretch of the Muir Trail found in these trip selections, this route traces representative sections of three major Sierra drainages, crosses three passes — all exceeding 11000′ in elevation — and tours some of the best trout-fishing country in the Sierra.

DESCRIPTION (Leisurely trip)

1st Hiking Day (South Lake to Dusy Basin, 6.5 miles): See 1st hiking day, trip 45.

2nd Hiking Day   (Dusy Basin to Little Pete Meadow, 6 miles): See 2nd hiking day, trip 50.

3rd Hiking Day   (Little Pete Meadow to Campsites, Upper Middle Fork Kings River, 3.5 miles): See 3rd hiking day, trip 50.

4th Hiking Day   (Campsites, Upper Middle Fork Kings River to Wanda Lake, 6 miles): See 4th hiking day, trip 50.

5th Hiking Day   (Wanda Lake to Colby Meadow, 7 miles): See 5th hiking day, trip 50.

6th Hiking Day   (Colby Meadow to Campsites, Hutchinson Meadow Trail Junction, 8.5 miles): See 6th hiking day, trip 51.

7th Hiking Day   (Campsites, Hutchinson Meadow Trail Junction to Lower Sally Keyes Lake, 8 miles): See part of 5th hiking day, trip 22.

8th Hiking Day   (Lower Sally Keyes Lake to Sandpiper Lake, 5 miles cross country): See part of 3rd hiking day, trip 8.

9th Hiking Day   (Sandpiper Lake to Kip Camp, 8.5 miles): See 2nd hiking day, trip 6.

10th Hiking Day   (Kip Camp to Quail Meadows, 6 miles): See 2nd hiking day, trip 3.

11th Hiking Day   (Quail Meadows to Vermilion Campground, 5.5 miles): See 3rd hiking day, trip 3.

 56

TRIP   From CEDAR GROVE ROADHEAD to GRANITE LAKE (round trip). Topo map (15′) Marion Peak; Profile 11. Best early or late season; 17 miles.

Grade	Trail/layover days	Total recommended days
Leisurely	- - -	- - -
Moderate	- - -	- - -
Strenuous	2/0	2

HILITES   "The first day is always the toughest" is an old adage to the backpacker. And this old saw added to the 5000′-plus elevation gain should warn the hiker that this "weekender" is one to be undertaken only after some conditioning. However, it should also be noted that the fine views and the good alpine campsite at the end of the trek compensate for the effort.

DESCRIPTION   (Strenuous trip)
1st Hiking Day   (Cedar Grove Roadend to Granite Lake, 8.5 miles):
The extreme elevation change encountered in the course of this trip
(over 5000'), necessarily removes it from the "Leisurely" grade,
but it makes a fine weekender for the person who has one or two
warm-up trips already under his belt. Starting at the north side of
the parking loop (5035'), the trail winds through a mature stand of
ponderosa, incense cedar, sugar pine and black oak. As the traveler begins this trip, it is interesting to contemplate the historic
usage of this trailhead. Evidence from archeological excavations
nearby indicate that Zumwalt Meadows was a permanent base camp
for Indian hunting parties for a period of time ranging from (in the
white man's terms) Magna Carta to the Declaration of Independence. Mortar rocks, pestles and manos found in the yard-deep
midden piles in this vicinity indicate that the acorn of the plentiful black oak was one of the main staples of the Indian's diet. It
is also possible that these grinding implements were used to grind
the pine nut (occasional pinon trees are found in the canyon). But
also found in the excavation sites were bones of deer and various
rodents, indicating that foraging parties took to the higher country
— and arrowheads found in the country of the Monarch Divide
indicate that these parties frequently used this same trail. The flats
of Zumwalt Meadows soon fall behind, and the trail ascends above
the dense forest cover to a moderate forest cover of scrub oak.
Turning northward, the trail begins the steadily rising switchbacks
through dense thickets of oak and manzanita. Views of glacially-
smoothed Grand Sentinel dominate the scenery of the canyon's
south wall. The first set of switchbacks terminates just east of
North Dome, and the trail levels off to a moderate-to-steady ascent
through a mixed forest cover of Douglas fir, sugar pine, Ponderosa,
incense cedar and black oak. Looking back over one's right
shoulder, to the southeast, one has a fine view of two beautifully
formed avalanche chutes on the northeast face of The Sphinx.
The trail then fords several trickling tributaries of Copper Creek,
and passes several campsites sheltered in a grove of white fir at
Lower Tent Meadow. Rising steeply, the trail leaves Lower Tent
Meadow and ascends a rocky slope to Upper Tent Meadow. Wildflowers seen along the trail include Mariposa lily, Clarkia, fleabane,
Collinsia, wallflower, pentstemon and shooting star. The switchbacks above Upper Tent Meadow are steep, and they bring the
traveler into the red-fir belt. However, the acquaintance with this
belt is brief as the trail soon climbs to an area mostly covered
with lodgepole, silver pine and quaking aspen (along the creek).
If it is of consolation, today's traveler can rest assured that the
noble red man who preceded him up this climb also paused to
pant and wonder. Leveling out, the trail fluctuates up and down
through properly named Granite Basin. Near the head of the
basin, the trail skirts a small, alpine meadow and strikes the
Granite Lake trail lateral. Our route turns left and ascends an easy
slope to the north side of scenic Granite Lake (10100'). Good campsites dot the outlet and east side of the lake, and firewood is
ample. Views of the Comb Spur are excellent, and the camper
will soon establish a vocal relationship with the many noisy marmots that share this private cirque. Fishing for brook trout is
fair-to-good (to 10").

2nd Hiking Day (Granite Lake to Cedar Grove Roadend, 8.5 miles): Retrace steps of 1st hiking day.

57

TRIP   From CEDAR GROVE ROADHEAD to STATE LAKES via Granite Basin, Granite Pass (round trip). Topo map (15') Marion Peak; Profile 11. Best early or late season; 31 miles.

Grade	Trail/layover days	Total recommended days
Leisurely	- - -	- - -
Moderate	- - -	- - -
Strenuous	4/2	6

HILITES   Once past the initial, tough 5000' climb, this exciting route has all the aspects of a glorious fishing trip. Beneath the peaks of the Monarch Divide, this trail visits the excellent fishing lakes of the State Lakes chain, and offers fine side trips for those who would linger.

DESCRIPTION   (Strenuous trip)

1st Hiking Day   (Cedar Grove Roadend to Granite Lake, 8.5 miles): See 1st hiking day, trip 56.

2nd Hiking Day (Granite Lake to State Lakes, 7 miles): This hiking day begins by retracing one's steps to the Granite Pass trail, where this day's route turns left toward Granite Pass. The ascent starts moderately, but soon steepens over rocky under-footing. Passing a tiny meadow with several campsites, the trail climbs again, and arrives at Granite Pass (10673'). This summit marks the divide between the Middle and South Forks of the Kings River. Views from the pass are fair of jumbled Goat Crest and the unnamed granite divide to the northwest. From the pass, the trail descends moderately over rock through an interesting, granite-walled ravine. Probably following a fault line, the ravine is deep-cut, and exhibits fine examples of mirrorlike glacial polish. Through a sparse cover of lodgepole, the trail passes over some marshy sections that in late season of a normal year dry up, and then passes a drift fence. There are several excellent campsites just south of the drift fence, in an alpine meadow setting. This descent resolves into steep switchbacks that drop down over a granite face to leveler going through a denser forest cover of lodgepole. Our route then passes by the Volcanic Lakes trail, and about ½ mile farther passes the unmarked and unmaintained spur to Lake of the Fallen Moon. As our trail begins the general descent toward the East Fork of Dougherty Creek, it turns easterly over undulating terrain to ford the outlet stream of Glacier Lakes. Although not abundant, the wildflowers along the trail are of many species. One is sure to encounter wallflower, shooting star, pentstemon, currant and white cinquefoil. In the vicinity of the ford mentioned above, there are excellent views up Glacier Valley to the Glacier Lakes cirque, and the sheer face of Goat Crest. After the ford, the trail ascends moderately to the excellent campsites on the north and northwest sides of the easternmost lake (10300') of the State Lakes complex. Here, fishing for golden (to 17") is excellent; firewood is abundant; and excursionary side-trip possibilities are magnificent. Anglers will want to try the waters of Glacier Lakes, the three other lakes in the State Lakes chain, and Horseshoe Lakes. Climbers looking for challenge will find the Cirque Crest peaks more than adequate.

3rd Hiking Day (State Lakes to Granite Lake, 7 miles): Retrace steps of 2nd hiking day.

4th Hiking Day (Granite Lake to Cedar Grove Roadend, 8.5 miles): Retrace steps of 1st hiking day.

TRIP   From CEDAR GROVE ROADHEAD to SOUTH LAKE via Granite Basin, Granite Pass, State Lakes, Simpson Meadow, Middle Fork Kings River, Dusy Basin, Bishop Pass (shuttle trip). Topo maps (15') Marion Peak, Mt. Goddard; Profiles 11, 9, 10. Best mid or late season; 48 miles.

Grade	Trail/layover days	Total recommended days
Leisurely	- - -	- - -
Moderate	7/3	10
Strenuous	6/3	9

HILITES   This trans-Sierra route is relatively little used from Cedar Grove Roadend to the junction with the Muir Trail, and the hiker can count on a measure of solitude. Fine angling and magnificent panoramas are expectations to be realized, and the sweeping variety of flora and fauna encountered on this trail knows no equal in Sierra trips.

DESCRIPTION (Strenuous trip)

1st Hiking Day (Cedar Grove Roadend to Granite Lake, 8.5 miles): See 1st hiking day, trip 56.

2nd Hiking Day (Granite Lake to State Lakes, 7 miles): See 2nd hiking day, trip 57.

3rd Hiking Day (State Lakes to Simpson Meadow, 8 miles): Our ducked trail starts northward on the north side of the meadow at the northwest end of the lake. Wildflower fanciers will find the area around the State Lakes visited by the trail a plethora of color. Rank fields of false solomon's seal cover the open flats, and lush-foliaged shooting star waves above dense mats of moss and low-lying fern in the damp grottos along the streams. In the drier stretches along the trail that continues northward to the next of the State Lakes group, one will find the supine pussy paws, prim Douglas phlox, taller lupine, and the tall, stately bluebell. The grassy fringes of this next lake offer good campsites on the west side where the trail fords the outlet stream. (A warning note: this stream marks the last reliable water until the Middle Fork Kings River.) From State Lakes the trail turns westerly, going moderately down and then up, past the lateral to enchanting Horseshoe Lakes (not shown on the topo map), and then past the sandy junction with the Dougherty Meadow trail. Evidence of glacial action in the form of morainal debris is found along the westerly-trending trail, along with a moderate forest cover of lodgepole, silver and juniper. The trail crosses the divide ridge, descends moderately, and then steeply. Across the canyon of the Middle Fork Kings River, the unimposing heights of Tunemah Peak and the White Divide come into view, and, from several vantage points, one can see up rocky Goddard **Creek** and Enchanted Gorge to the Black Divide. The rapidly descending route continues via steep, eroded switchbacks through three life zones. Lodgepole, the predominant tree of the higher elevations, shows growing inclusions of juniper, silver, sugar pine and incense cedar. The mixed forest cover drops behind as the trail zigzags its final drop to the canyon floor. There the trail passes a drift fence and, winding through lush vegetation, it meets the Tehipite Valley trail. At this junction, our route turns right into Simpson Meadow. Used first by the Yokuts Indians, and then by sheepmen and cattlemen, this meadow is presently nearly forgotten. Its remoteness and difficulty of access have made it one of the least-visited meadows in this part of the Sierra, and today it is usually visited only by the wilderness traveler who seeks solitude and is not alarmed by the sight of an occasional rattlesnake around the area of Simpson Meadow. Our route passes the abandoned ranger station (about 200 yards above the junction) on a gently ascending, very rough trail, and arrives at the fair packer and primitive campsites on nearby Horseshoe Creek (6010'). Alternative primitive sites can be found along the river upstream. Firewood is abundant, and those with two layover days and an inclination to a lengthy side trip may wish to visit Tehipite Valley twelve miles downstream, there to see the magnificently polished granite facade of Tehipite Dome, and the adjacent impressive falls. (Warnings: (1) Rattlesnakes are commonly encountered enroute and at Tehipite Valley. (2) The high waters of the Summer of 1967 resulted in many washouts of the trail, and at this writing the trail was impassable to stock). Fishing on the Middle Fork Kings River is good-to-excellent for rainbow and golden (to 14").

4th Hiking Day   (Simpson Meadow to Grouse Meadows, 10 miles): Ascending gently, the poorly maintained trail continues northeasterly through alternating meadow and moderate forest of white fir, incense cedar, Jeffrey and quaking aspen. Sagebrush frequently overhangs the trail, making footing sometimes difficult, and in the wetter sections the eroded trail is obliterated. As the trail rounds the talus-ridden slopes of Windy Peak, it offers good views of Goddard Creek canyon, and the evidence of a decade-old fire that swept unchecked up Middle Fork Kings River and Goddard Creek canyons is painfully evident in their brush-choked, black-stumped slopes. Still ascending gently, the sandy trail swings somewhat more easterly as it fords multi-branched Windy Canyon Creek. To the northeast, the east canyon wall shows the break carved there by the feeder glacier emanating from the upper reaches of Cartridge Creek. Just beyond the ford of Windy Canyon Creek, the trail turns north, and the canyon walls narrow dramatically. The trail then fords Cartridge Creek by a substantial bridge, and passes the Cartridge Creek trail, branching right from the packer's campsite. Ascending more steeply now, the trail crosses rocky stretches broken by pockets of timber cover, and the visible waters of the Middle Fork are white with rapids and cascades. The trail keeps to the canyon walls, usually fifty to a hundred feet above the stream, and the drop to the river's waters is frequently a sheer face of polished granite. Heavy winter fall across the trail (uncleared at this writing) makes progress by foot a laborious affair over jumbled talus, and exceedingly difficult for stock. Flowers seen along this stretch are generally of the dry country variety, including Indian paintbrush, pentstemon, Collinsia, forget me not, lupine and fleabane. The trail climbs steeply to the flats just below Devils Washbowl. To the right, the east canyon walls provide a fascinating study in convoluted glacial polish, and the views to the west and northwest of the Great Cliffs and the heavily fractured rock of Devils Crags portend later, equally exciting views of the Black Divide. The trail touches the river briefly near some sandy campsites, and then switchbacks up to awesome Devils Washbowl. The latter is a wild, spectacular falls and cataract in a granite gorge setting, bearing an apt scientifically applied title of "plunge basin." Leaving the tumult of the water behind, the trail continues to ascend over rock to the innocuous looking but treacherous ford of the unnamed creek draining Windy Cliff to the southeast. This ford is impassable to stock at this writing. The flora around these tributary fords deserves the traveler's attention because of both its lushness and the presence of the very rare copper birch. Among the wildflowers one is sure to find are Indian paintbrush, pentstemon, pennyroyal, white Mariposa, white cinquefoil, tiger lily, lupine, red columbine and elderberry. Ascending and descending steeply, the vacillating trail is sometimes at river's edge, and other times two hundred feet above. The underfooting is very rocky and treacherous until it approaches the Palisade Creek crossing. This crossing is preceded by a drift fence, and a reacquaintance with a timber cover of Jeffrey, lodgepole, white fir and silver pine. Just after the steel bridge crossing of Palisade Creek, our route meets and turns left onto the John Muir Trail and passes several excellent campsites. Continuing north, the trail crosses an easy ridge. (The topo map is incorrect in showing that the trail just above the junction fords the Middle Fork Kings River, and refords just south of Grouse Meadows.) The trail then fords the unnamed tributary draining the west slopes of Giraud Peak, and arrives at the excellent campsites at the south end of Grouse Meadows. Firewood is plentiful, and the intimate views are excellent of the lush meadows, and the now-almost-turgid waters of the meandering river. Fishing for rainbow, some golden and brook (to 13″) is good.

5th Hiking Day (Grouse Meadows to Dusy Basin, 8 miles): Leaving the pleasant grasslands of Grouse Meadows behind, the trail continues its gentle but steady ascent. On the left, the river foregoes the placid temperament of its winding meadow course and resumes its mad, white-water plunge. Beyond the river to the west, The Citadel's granite face stands guard over the south side of an obvious hanging valley, and the early-morning traveler is often treated to a burst of reflected sunlight from glacially polished surfaces high on the canyon's west wall north of the hanging valley. The trail undulates up and down the east wall, sometimes 80 to 100 feet above the river, sometimes right alongside it. The thin lodgepole forest cover occurs mostly in stands, with intermittent stretches of grassy pockets, and the underfooting is mostly rocky. Ahead, the canyon narrows, and the trail crosses Dusy Branch via a substantial steel footbridge, and meets the Dusy Basin trail. A few yards north of this junction is the Le Conte Ranger Station, where emergency services are available. Our route turns right (east) and begins the steep, switchbacking ascent of the east canyon wall. This ascent is broken into two distinct steps that gain 2000′ in about 2 miles, but the steepness of the slope is tamed by the well-graded switchbacks. Touching the creek at strategic intervals (a cold drink on this climb is always welcome), the trail offers magnificent views of the monolithic granite structures on the far side of the canyon. Near the creek, the wildflower lover will find lush shooting star, fireweed, pentstemon, pennyroyal and some yellow columbine nestling next to damp, moss-covered, rocky grottos. Along the switchbacks, occasional lodgepole and juniper break the monotony of the slab granite, and one particular juniper stands out with a near-record girth. Like a beetle-browed sentinel this ancient specimen guards the north end of one of the switchbacks near the top of the first step. Views of the chutes and cascades of Dusy Branch reward the dusty trail-pounder as he finishes the first climb and enters the cooling bower of a mixed stand of lodgepole and aspen. The trail crosses the creek (bridge) and then returns to continue the switchbacking up through a sparse forest cover of aspen. This ascent levels out near the lowest of the Dusy Basin lake chain, and emerges to open, breathtaking views of Mt. Winchell, Mt. Agassiz and Columbine Peak. Rounding the north side of the lower Dusy Basin lake chain, the trail turns north and climbs a series of grass-topped ledges. A short, well-worn spur trail branches right, leading to alternative campsites situated both alongside Dusy Branch and

Lake Italy and Mt. Hilgard   E. P. Pister

Don Denison

Tyndall Creek lateral moraine. Mt. Kaweah and Kaweah Peaks Ridge in distance.

Upper Lost Lake.

Mt. Humphreys in distance.

E. P. Pister

Washington State Department of Game

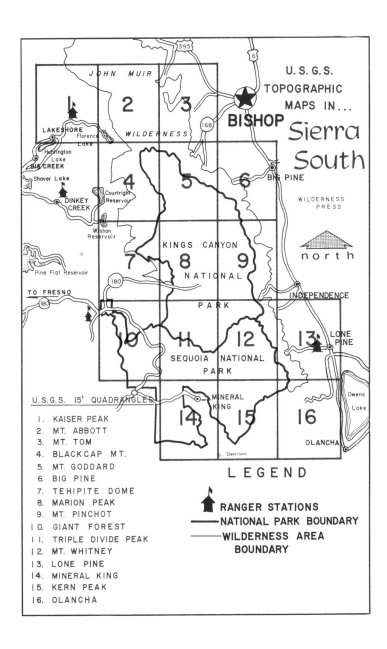

U.S.G.S.
TOPOGRAPHIC
MAPS IN...

BISHOP Sierra South

JOHN MUIR

2   3

WILDERNESS

LAKESHORE
Florence Lake
Huntington Lake
BIG CREEK
Shaver Lake

4   5   6   BIG PINE

WILDERNESS PRESS

Courtright Reservoir

DINKEY CREEK

Wishon Reservoir

KINGS CANYON

north

7   8   9

NATIONAL

Pine Flat Reservoir

TO FRESNO

PARK

INDEPENDENCE

10   11   12   13   LONE PINE

SEQUOIA NATIONAL
PARK

MINERAL KING

Owens Lake

14   15   16

OLANCHA

D. DENISON

LEGEND

U.S.G.S. 15' QUADRANGLES

1. KAISER PEAK
2. MT. ABBOTT
3. MT. TOM
4. BLACKCAP MT.
5. MT. GODDARD
6. BIG PINE
7. TEHIPITE DOME
8. MARION PEAK
9. MT. PINCHOT
10. GIANT FOREST
11. TRIPLE DIVIDE PEAK
12. MT. WHITNEY
13. LONE PINE
14. MINERAL KING
15. KERN PEAK
16. OLANCHA

RANGER STATIONS
NATIONAL PARK BOUNDARY
WILDERNESS AREA
BOUNDARY

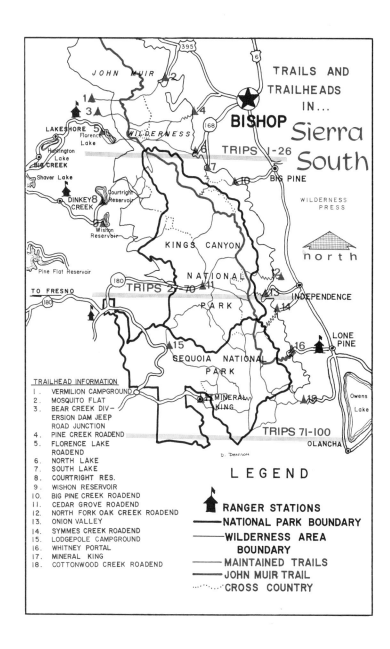

TRAILS AND
TRAILHEADS
IN...
BISHOP Sierra
South
TRIPS 1-26

WILDERNESS
PRESS

north

TRIPS 27-70

TRIPS 71-100

JOHN MUIR

WILDERNESS

LAKESHORE

Florence Lake

Huntington Lake

BIG CREEK

Shaver Lake

DINKEY CREEK

Courtright Reservoir

Wishon Reservoir

Pine Flat Reservoir

TO FRESNO

KINGS CANYON

NATIONAL

PARK

SEQUOIA NATIONAL PARK

MINERAL KING

D. DENISON

BIG PINE

INDEPENDENCE

LONE PINE

Owens Lake

OLANCHA

TRAILHEAD INFORMATION

1. VERMILION CAMPGROUND
2. MOSQUITO FLAT
3. BEAR CREEK DIV-
   ERSION DAM JEEP
   ROAD JUNCTION
4. PINE CREEK ROADEND
5. FLORENCE LAKE
   ROADEND
6. NORTH LAKE
7. SOUTH LAKE
8. COURTRIGHT RES.
9. WISHON RESERVOIR
10. BIG PINE CREEK ROADEND
11. CEDAR GROVE ROADEND
12. NORTH FORK OAK CREEK ROADEND
13. ONION VALLEY
14. SYMMES CREEK ROADEND
15. LODGEPOLE CAMPGROUND
16. WHITNEY PORTAL
17. MINERAL KING
18. COTTONWOOD CREEK ROADEND

LEGEND

RANGER STATIONS
NATIONAL PARK BOUNDARY
WILDERNESS AREA
   BOUNDARY
MAINTAINED TRAILS
JOHN MUIR TRAIL
CROSS COUNTRY

Forester Pass seen from the south   Don Denison

Royce Peak and Royce Lakes   E. P. Pister

Wanda Lake and Mt. Goddard   E. P. Pister

Tunemah Lake with ice   Karl Schwenke

Upper Chocolate Lake,

Bishop Creek

E. P. Pister

on the middle lakes of the Dusy Basin chain (11300'). Our route veers away from the creek, climbing above it, and where it rejoins the creek while on an eastward jog, our route turns right a short cross-country distance and descends through an alpine fell field to the good campsites near the west side of the northernmost lake in the basin. Fishing for golden and golden hybrids is good (to 8"). Firewood is scarce. This campsite offers the camper a fine base for further explorations of Dusy and Palisades basins and a granite outcropping just east of the lake provides the finest panoramic viewpoint in the entire basin. Those with a bent for angling will find the fishing on the outlet of the large lake to the east rewarding (golden and golden hybrids to 23").

6th Hiking Day (Dusy Basin to South Lake, 6.5 miles): See 1st hiking day, trip 45.

TRIP   From CEDAR GROVE ROADEND to VIDETTE MEADOW (round trip). Topo maps (15') Marion Peak, Mt. Pinchot; Profile 13. Best early-to-mid season; 28 miles.

Grade	Trail/layover days	Total recommended days
Leisurely	4/1	5
Moderate	3/0	3
Strenuous	2/0	2

HILITES   Climbing 4000', this trip follows an old Indian trade route paralleling Bubbs Creek. Beyond the realm of the Park's dayhiker, the trail climbs the path of an old glacier to beautiful Vidette Meadow, a "high country crossroads." Here in the shadow of the spectacular Kearsarge Pinnacles this route meets the famous John Muir Trail.

DESCRIPTION (Moderate trip)

1st Hiking Day (Cedar Grove Roadend to Campsites, Sphinx Creek Trail Junction, 4 miles): From the paved roadend loop (5035') the trail ascends gently through a mixed forest cover of ponderosa, incense cedar, black oak, sugar pine and a few rare (for this side of the Sierra crest) pinon pine. This tree, whose fruit provides the delicious pine nut, is of the single-needle group, and may be identified by either its single needle or its distinctive spherical cone. Most noticeable about the cone is its very thick, blunt, four-sided scale. The balmy climate usually characteristic of the gently sloping canyon floor made this area a favorite of the Monache tribe, who had their summer hunting camps here. Foraging parties of Indians made their "spur" camps along Bubbs Creek at many of the same spots chosen by today's back-country traveler. The murmur of the South Fork Kings River, sometimes near, sometimes far, accompanies the traveler as he winds up the gentle ascent and passes the Paradise Valley/Woods Creek trail (branching north) just before crossing a succession of bridges to the north side of Bubbs Creek. The last bridge crossing marks the beginning of a series of steady switchbacks that ascend to the Sphinx Creek trail junction. This ascent offers fine views back into the dramatic U-shaped South Fork Kings River canyon. On the south side of the Bubbs Creek canyon the dominating landmark is the pronounced granite point known as The Sphinx. To the east its namesake stream cuts a sharp-lipped defile on the peak's east shoulder. Here at the junction (6280') are several fair campsites with ample firewood. Evidence of Indian camps in this vicinity was found just upstream. Fishing for rainbow and brown trout (fry) is poor. Grazing is restricted to burros (one night only).

2nd Hiking Day (Campsites, Sphinx Creek Trail Junction to Vidette Meadow, 10 miles): Keeping to the north side of Bubbs Creek, the trail ascends steadily up the canyon. The sparse-to-moderate forest cover reflects the altitude gain, with inclusions of lodgepole and fir and some Jeffrey. Beautiful stands of these trees offer those who would come to know the trees a splendid opportunity to study and identify them. The lodgepole, the most common, is usually identified by its straight, slender trunk, although in higher elevations the tree is frequently stunted, twisted and weathered. The tree's normal shape gave it its name, for it caused the Indians of the Great Plains to journey far into the Rocky Mountains in search of poles for their skin lodges, or tepees. Even more distinctive are the two needles to a bunch and the grayish, thin-scaled bark. A close look at the bark will reveal that the scales have yellow edges, and those with discriminating noses will discern an odor from the bark which very much resembles that of a newly opened bottle of gin. Continuing up Bubbs Creek canyon, the trail fords several small, unnamed tributaries, and then Charlotte Creek. On the north wall of the canyon, one can see the cleft of the Charlotte Creek drainage, guarded to the west by Charlotte Dome (unmarked on the topo map). The south wall presents several avalanche chutes, which are responsible for the patch of bent and broken trees on the near side of the canyon — they all lean north, away from the onslaught of the snow mass. Beyond Charlotte Creek the forest cover becomes more dense, with increasing amounts of Jeffrey pine. After a short, steep stretch of rocky going, the trail travels through fine stands of quaking aspen and black cottonwood to beautiful Junction Meadow. Views through the trees of Mt. Bago to the north reveal two interesting septa of metavolcanic rock in black stripes. Beyond several good campsites at the west end of the meadow, our route passes the East Lake/Lake Reflection trail. This meadow is closed to grazing because of serious deterioration brought on by overgrazing in the past. At the east end of the meadow, the trail switchbacks up a dry manzanita slope, sometimes distant from the creek and sometimes right alongside. The steepest part of the climb ends at the conclusion of the switchbacks, and the trail then proceeds on a moderate ascent to the junction with the John Muir Trail. Looking back, one has fine views of the avalanche-scarred north face of West Vidette. Our route turns right, fords the tiny outlet creek from Bullfrog Lake and arrives at the excellent campsites (9600') at beautiful Vidette Meadow, scattered along Bubbs Creek. Fishing for brook, rainbow and some brown (to 8") is fair, and firewood is ample.

3rd Hiking Day (Vidette Meadow to Cedar Grove Roadend, 14 miles): Retrace steps of 1st and 2nd hiking days.

 60

TRIP   From CEDAR GROVE ROADEND to CHARLOTTE LAKE (round trip). Topo maps (15') Marion Peak, Mt. Pinchot; Profile 13. Best mid or late season; 33 miles.

Grade	Trail/layover days	Total recommended days
Leisurely	5/1	6
Moderate	4/1	5
Strenuous	2/1	3

HILITES   Striking right into the heart of the high country, this route ascends a lengthy stretch of the Bubbs Creek drainage to the charming meadows at the foot of the Kearsarge Pinnacles and the Videttes. The terminus of this trip, Charlotte Lake, is an exciting base camp location for trips to 4 major lake basins.

DESCRIPTION (Leisurely trip)
1st Hiking Day (Cedar Grove Roadend to Campsites, Sphinx Creek Trail Junction, 4 miles): See 1st hiking day, trip 59.

2nd Hiking Day (Campsites, Sphinx Creek Trail Junction to Vidette Meadow, 10 miles): See 2nd hiking day, trip 59.

3rd Hiking Day (Vidette Meadow to Charlotte Lake, 2.5 miles): Retrace steps to the junction of the John Muir Trail and the Bubbs Creek trail. Following the Muir Trail as it switchbacks up the steep north side of the canyon, the traveler is treated to breathtaking views of the Kearsarge Pinnacles to the east, and the Videttes and snow-necklaced Deerhorn Mountain to the south. It is easy, while viewing this spectacle, to understand the popularity of the Muir Trail, and it is with a sense of loss that one leaves the Bubbs Creek valley and crosses the lip of the Bullfrog Lake basin. Our route bypasses Bullfrog Lake, continuing northwest on a series of switchbacks to the Charlotte Lake trail. This trail leaves the Muir Trail and after providing one last look back to the Bubbs Creek drainage and far south into Center Basin, with the Kings-Kern Divide in the background, zigzags down to Charlotte Lake. High on the left of the switchbacks tower the several summits of red-rocked Mt. Bago. The forest cover encountered along this descent includes lodgepole, foxtail and whitebark pine. Good campsites may be found along the north side of the lake (10370'), where firewood is abundant. Emergency services are available from the resident summer ranger. Fishing for rainbow and brook trout (to 10") is good. The meadows around and above the lake are closed to grazing. A great side trip is the one into Gardiner and Sixty Lake basins. From Charlotte Lake the traveler with four extra hiking days' time and the inclination to visit spectacular, lonely country can circuit this country using a cross-country route joining the two basins, returning via Rae Lakes and Glenn Pass. This route climbs the north wall above Charlotte Creek, and, passing north of Charlotte Dome, climbs Gardiner Pass. On the north side of the pass the trail drops down along a chain of lakes, the largest (just west of point 11156) being a good leisurely day's walk from Charlotte Lake. From this lake the trail switchbacks down to ford Gardiner Creek. Then, ascending steadily, the trail goes eastward up the Gardiner Creek drainage to the beautiful lakes of the upper basin. Excellent campsites will be found around the outlet of Lake 11394. Fishing in most of these lakes for brook trout (to 18") is excellent. The cross-country travel from Gardiner Basin to Sixty Lake Basin is best accomplished by continuing past several unnamed, rockbound lakelets to the south end of Gardiner Basin, and crossing the steep southeast cirque wall. This crossing will bring the hiker to the uppermost lake of the Sixty Lakes chain. Excellent campsites are along the meadowed west side of the next large lake (the long lake southeast of Mt. Cotter). As in Gardiner Basin, the fishing for brook (to 16") is excellent on most of the lakes, and in the intervening stream. From these campsites, the newly found trail crosses the intervening stream, circles around the south end of Fin Dome, and switchbacks down to beautiful Rae Lakes, where it joins the John Muir Trail. Turning south, the trail then switchbacks up over rocky Glen Pass, and meets the Charlotte Lake lateral, described in the 3rd hiking day.

4th Hiking Day (Charlotte Lake to Vidette Meadow, 2.5 miles): Retrace steps of 3rd hiking day.

5th Hiking Day (Vidette Meadow to Cedar Grove Roadend, 14 miles): Retrace steps of 1st and 2nd hiking days.

61

TRIP	From CEDAR GROVE ROADEND to RAE LAKES via Vidette Meadow, Glen Pass (round trip). Topo maps (15') Marion Peak, Mt. Pinchot; Profile 13. Best late season; 40 miles.

Grade	Trail/layover days	Total recommended days
Leisurely	5/2	7
Moderate	4/2	6
Strenuous	4/1	5

HILITES   Rae Lakes have long been a favorite of the high-country hiker and photographer — and with good cause. Situated beyond Glen Pass, and between the Sierra crest and the King Spur, these lakes are a scenic paradise. Because of this, and because of the central location, anyone contemplating this trip should plan on spending some layover days for exploring the Sixty Lake Basin.

DESCRIPTION   *(Leisurely trip)*

1st Hiking Day (Cedar Grove Roadend to Campsites, Sphinx Creek Trail Junction, 4 miles): See 1st hiking day, trip 59.

2nd Hiking Day (Campsites, Sphinx Creek Trail Junction to Vidette Meadow, 10 miles): See 2nd hiking day, trip 59.

3rd Hiking Day (Vidette Meadow to Rae Lakes, 6 miles): From Vidette Meadow our route follows the John Muir Trail north as it climbs out of Bubbs Creek canyon. This climb parallels and sometimes crosses the outlet stream from Bullfrog Lake in a series of switchbacks. Excellent views of the Kearsarge Pinnacles to the east complement the view of the Videttes to the south. Beyond the Videttes tower the peaks of the Kings-Kern Divide, foregrounded by the barren granite of Center Basin. As the trail tops the lip of the Bullfrog Lake basin, the peaks of the main Sierra crest appear to the northeast, and although mostly white granite, some of the higher peaks reveal the more ancient sedimentary and metamorphic red rock. Our route passes trail laterals to Bullfrog Lake and Charlotte Lake, staying on the John Muir Trail. Anglers wishing to do a bit of fishing before continuing will find angling fair for brook (to 10") on beautiful Bullfrog Lake. Because of the heavy traffic and camping impact from the Muir trail and the Kearsarge Pass lateral, this lake is closed to camping and grazing. From the Bullfrog Lake trail our route swings west, turns northerly on a long, steady ascent that rounds a granite promontory, passes two small lakes, and switchbacks steadily up to Glen Pass (11978'). This climb offers good views of Charlotte Lake, the Charlotte Creek drainage, and Charlotte Dome. At the summit of Glen Pass one can look down on the several unnamed glacial lakes immediately to the north, and part of the Rae Lakes below. The immediate descent from the pass is made by zigzagging, rocky switchbacks that terminate at the granite bench holding the unnamed lakes cited above. After crossing the outlet stream from these lakes, the trail resumes its switchbacking descent, re-enters a forest cover of lodgepole and occasional whitebark and juniper, and then levels off as it skirts the west shore of the upper Rae Lake. Just before the trail crosses the narrow isthmus separating the upper lake from the rest of the chain, our trail passes the spur trail branching west to Sixty Lake Basin. Crossing the sparsely timbered isthmus, this route swings north, passes the short lateral to Dragon Lake, and arrives at the many excellent campsites on the east shore of middle and lower Rae Lakes (10560'). Firewood is somewhat scarce owing to the heavy impact, but the fishing for brook trout and some rainbow (to 16") is good. Views from the campsites across the beryl-green lake waters to the dramatically exfoliating Fin Dome and the King Spur beyond are among the best and longest remembered of the trip. (No grazing permitted around the lakes.)

4th Hiking Day (Rae Lakes to Vidette Meadow, 6 miles): Retrace steps of 3rd hiking day.

5th Hiking Day (Vidette Meadow to Cedar Grove Roadend, 14 miles): Retrace steps of 1st and 2nd hiking days.

 62

TRIP   From CEDAR GROVE ROADEND to RAE LAKES, return via South Fork Woods Creek, Paradise Valley (loop trip). Topo maps (15') Marion Peak, Mt. Pinchot; Profiles 13, 14. Best late season; 43.5 miles.

Grade	Trail/layover days	Total recommended days
Leisurely	6/2	8
Moderate	5/2	7
Strenuous	4/1	5

HILITES   Known as the "Rae Lakes Loop," this fine trip circles the King Spur. The landscape viewed enroute is dramatic enough to challenge the most accomplished photographer or artist as the route circles beneath the Videttes and the Kearsarge Pinnacles and traverses a lengthy stretch of the Sierra crest.

DESCRIPTION   (Leisurely trip)

1st Hiking Day   (Cedar Grove Roadend to Campsites, Sphinx Creek Trail Junction, 4 miles): See 1st hiking day, trip 59.

2nd Hiking Day   (Campsites, Sphinx Creek Trail Junction to Vidette Meadow, 10 miles): See 2nd hiking day, trip 59.

3rd Hiking Day   (Vidette Meadow to Rae Lakes, 6 miles): See 3rd hiking day, trip 61.

4th Hiking Day   (Rae Lakes to Campsites, Woods Creek Crossing, 6.5 miles): The trail covered in this hiking day is an easy downhill stretch that traces the length of the South Fork Woods Creek. Beginning from the campsites along the east side of Rae Lakes, the trail continues along the east side of the lake chain and the intervening stream on a moderate ascent. Fin Dome drops behind, and the outstanding landmark is Diamond Peak (to the east). The long black striations seen along the face of Diamond Peak and the continuing ridge to the north are metamorphosed lava, one of the few remaining bits of volcanic evidence to be found in this area. Just west of Diamond Peak the trail fords the South Fork Woods Creek and skirts the west side of the lowest lake of the Rae Lakes chain. At the outlet our route passes the turnoff to Baxter Pass, and then descends more sharply over rocky stretches that are interrupted by pockets of alluvial sand. The moderate forest cover is mostly clumps of lodgepole that show evidence of the lodgepole needle-miner, a tree-killing insect. The valley floor is relatively open as the trail descends and crosses the stream draining the Sixty Lake Basin and the stream draining Lake 10296. Rounding the northernmost prominence of the King Spur, the trail swings westerly, and its moderate descent levels off as it approaches the Woods Creek Crossing. A few yards above this crossing the traveler should keep an eye peeled for one of this region's most interesting historic landmarks, one of Shorty Lovelace's unusual line cabins which still stands on the east side of the creek. Those who take time out to examine this structure will soon discern its unique character. Appearing to be almost a miniature replica of the real article, it was erected to suit the needs of its builder, and it would scarcely accommodate the average person — standing or sleeping. It was from this cabin and several others in this general area that Shorty worked his trap line before it was included within the Park's boundaries. The trail fords just below the confluence of the South and North forks of Woods Creek via a footlog (8492'). Good campsites may be found along the stream, firewood is abundant, and forage for stock is good. Fishing on the creek is good for brook and rainbow (to 10").

5th Hiking Day   (Campsites, Woods Creek Crossing to Paradise Valley, 10 miles): Leaving the John Muir Trail our route turns west, staying on the north side of Woods Creek. Underfooting is alternately sandy and rocky as the trail descends gently between the narrowing canyon walls. The forest cover, still predominantly lodgepole, shows inclusions of red fir as the altitude lessens, and clumps of the water-loving quaking aspen dot the stream banks. This smooth-barked, whispering tree is the most conspicuous member of the deciduous group found in the high country. Always found near running water or at the edge of porous seepage areas (lava, talus, gravel), it acts as a native water locator, and its ghostly white trunk can be seen for great distances. Hikers who have camped in a grove of aspen will always remember the tree's gentle rustling sound as the leaves, responding to the slightest breeze, tremble against one another. The trail passes a burn scar (caused by a careless camper's campfire), and winds through Castle Domes Meadow, named for the obvious landmarks to the north. Undulating up and down the north canyon wall, the trail descends on a moderate grade, fords two unnamed right-bank tributaries, and then descends more steeply to the ford of South Fork Kings River. In contrast to the manzanita-covered slopes to the south, the steep walls up the South Fork canyon to the north are barren and forbidding. Known as Muro Blanco ("white wall"), they are part of the largest untrailed area in the Park. After the ford, the trail turns southwest and descends gently past a drift fence to the open expanses of Paradise Valley (6640'). Good camp-sites line the stream, firewood is ample, and fishing for rainbow and some brown is fair (to 8"). Grazing is restricted to burros — overnight only.

6th Hiking Day (Paradise Valley to Cedar Grove Roadend, 7 miles): On a gentle descent through a mixed forest cover of lodge-pole, red fir, white fir, Jeffrey, and some juniper and aspen, the trail continues southwest. At the lower end of Paradise Valley, the descent steepens, and the smooth, serpentining South Fork Kings River straightens out and dashes down the canyon floor. Views during this descent include the already familiar landmark, The Sphinx. Midway down this stretch the trail pauses in its de-scent near Mist Falls, a cascade that deserves its name only dur-ing times of high water. By midsummer this white-water tumble becomes sedate and subdued. Beyond Mist Falls the trail dips steeply over a rocky surface, and zigzags before leveling out on the wide valley floor. A short distance farther on, our route meets and joins the Bubbs Creek/Cedar Grove Roadend trail, and returns over the short 2-mile stretch described in the 1st hiking day.

63

TRIP   From CEDAR GROVE ROADEND to OAK CREEK ROADEND via Bubbs Creek, Glen Pass, Rae Lakes, Baxter Pass (shuttle trip). Topo maps (15') Marion Peak, Mt. Pinchot; Profiles 13, 14, 15. Best late sea-son; 35.5 miles.

	Trail/layover	Total recom-
Grade	days	mended days
Leisurely	5/2	7
Moderate	4/2	6
Strenuous	4/1	5

HILITES   This trans-Sierra crossing makes a delightful S-curve as it journeys from the Bubbs Creek drainage to Rae Lakes and emerges on the east side via little-used Baxter Pass. The scenic lakes and towering, alp-like peaks of this route make this a fine route for photography.

DESCRIPTION (Leisurely trip)

1st Hiking Day (Cedar Grove Roadend to Campsites, Sphinx Creek Trail Junction, 4 miles): See 1st hiking day, trip 59.

2nd Hiking Day (Campsites, Sphinx Creek Trail Junction to Vidette Meadow, 10 miles): See 2nd hiking day, trip 59.

3rd Hiking Day (Vidette Meadow to Rae Lakes, 6 miles): See 3rd hiking day, trip 61.

4th Hiking Day (Rae Lakes to Baxter Lakes, 5 miles): The first 2.5 miles of this day's hike follow the gentle-to-moderate descent of the South Fork Woods Creek. From Rae Lakes the trail passes through granite slab areas broken by stands of dwarfed lodgepole as it skirts the east side of the lower lakes of the Rae Lakes chain. Anglers will want to try their luck for the good brook trout fishing on some of these lakes and the stream flowing between them. The trail fords the stream between the lowest and next-to-lowest lakes, and circles the west side of the lowest lake before branching east on the Baxter Pass trail. The route refords the South Fork Woods Creek, and leaves the John Muir Trail, climbing the steep east wall of the valley. This ascent climbs steeply on a long northerly traverse that drops down temporarily into the Baxter Creek drainage before swinging east and continuing the steep ascent into the Baxter Lakes basin. The sparse lodgepole forest cover thins as the route fords Baxter Creek and passes several tiny lakelets. Campsites may be found along the stream, but the better ones are situated on the north side of the next to the highest (11040') of the chain. (The upper lake campsites have fine views, but no firewood.) Fishing for brook trout (to 10") is good.

5th Hiking Day (Baxter Lakes to Oak Creek Roadend, 10.5 miles): Rounding the north side of the highest and largest lake of the basin, the trail turns south as it ascends the steep granite scoop above the lake. Excellent views of Mt. Baxter to the north accompany the climb, and rockhounds can marvel at the dramatic striping on the nearby granite, known as mafic diking. These dikes, glaciated remnants of ancient magma intrusions, are evidence of the substantial volcanic action that played a part in the petrology of this area. The trail switchbacks up to Baxter Pass (12300'), where one has fine views of the crest, including Diamond Peak and Black Mountain; and as the trail zigzags down the south side of the pass, the views include the Oak Creek drainage and the

Owens River Valley beyond. The trail is extremely rocky as it descends rapidly past Summit Meadow, and here one can enjoy the russet and copper colors of the nearby rocks. Thence, the trail stays well above the tumbling waters of the North Fork Oak Creek. Among the flowers along the trail are lupine, mountain mint, Labrador tea, shooting star, pentstemon and red heather. After Summit Meadow the trail fords the creek, and, staying at or near timberline, follows the sharply cut defile of the stream. Midway down this descent the trail rises above the creek bed, and one can see the heavy concentrations of metavolcanic rock which was vented nearby and which characterizes the remaining descent onto the alluvial apron below. As the trail drops to the final ford of the creek, one encounters a good sampling of typical east-side flora including Indian paintbrush, rabbit brush, bitter brush, sagebrush, juniper, Jeffrey pine and mountain mahogany. The trail fords the North Fork Oak Creek and a tributary a short distance beyond, and then arrives at the dirt road (6000′) west of Oak Creek Camp.

TRIP   From CEDAR GROVE ROADEND to LAKE REFLECTION (round trip). Topo maps (15′) Marion Peak, Mt. Pinchot, Mt. Whitney; Profiles 13, 16. Best mid or late season; 33 miles.

Grade	Trail/layover days	Total recommended days
Leisurely	6/1	7
Moderate	4/1	5
Strenuous	3/1	4

HILITES   Those who appreciate the serenity of high, alpine lake basins will find this trip to the upper reaches of East Creek a rewarding choice. Excellent fishing amidst spellbinding surroundings makes this a fine angling trip, and if one doesn't fish, it is time well spent just "soaking up the country."

DESCRIPTION   (Moderate trip)
1st Hiking Day   (Cedar Grove Roadend to Junction Meadow, 11.5 miles): Proceed to Junction Meadow as described in the 1st and part of the 2nd hiking day, trip 59.

2nd Hiking Day   (Junction Meadow to Lake Reflection, 5 miles): At Junction Meadow our trail branches right, fords Bubbs Creek, and ascends East Creek canyon. This ascent is accomplished via rocky switchbacks that zigzag through a sparse-to-moderate forest cover of lodgepole, fir, Jeffrey and some aspen. The view back to the north is dominated by the red metamorphic rocks of Mt. Bago, and as one tops the first rise of the ascent, the peaks of the Kings-Kern Divide come into view. Anglers trying their luck along East Creek will find rainbow and brook trout to 8″, and the trout are somewhat larger in East Lake. After a brief stretch of moderate uphill going, the trail again steepens for one more climb before leveling off at East Lake. One's first view of these picturesque waters with their grassy fringe may be accompanied by a sighting of one of the many mule deer that frequent the canyon. The barren, unjointed granite walls that rise on either side—especially Mt. Brewer on the west—are an impressive backdrop for leisure moments spent on the shores of this mountain gem, and it is always with some reluctance that visitors move on. After crossing the inlet to East Lake, the trail climbs steadily through rock-broken stands of lodgepole and hemlock. The right canyon wall breaks, and one can clearly make out the cirque in which Lake Reflection, the end of this hiking day, lies. The turnoff to this lake is at an unmarked junction just above the confluence of the outlet stream from Lake Reflection and the stream draining the lakes at the foot of Harrison Pass. This short spur takes one to the excellent campsites at the northeast end of Lake Reflection (10005′), where the angler will find excellent fishing for golden, brook and hybrids (to 16″). Firewood is ample. When a breeze is not stirring the waters of this lake, the tableau of peaks reflected in their depths is a memorable scene of a scope seldom matched in the Sierra. At the head of the cirque basin, all side excursions are up, but the expenditure of sweat and effort required to explore the surrounding lakes is repaid by views and a sense of achievement that has been shared by many mountaineers since those of the Brewer Party first ascended these heights.

3rd Hiking Day   (Lake Reflection to Junction Meadow, 5 miles): Retrace steps of 2nd hiking day.

4th Hiking Day   (Junction Meadow to Cedar Grove Roadend, 11.5 miles): Retrace steps of 1st hiking day.

TRIP   From CEDAR GROVE ROADEND to UPPER KERN RIVER DRAINAGE via Bubbs Creek, Forester Pass, return by Harrison Pass, Lake Reflection (semiloop trip). Topo maps (15′) Marion Peak, Mt. Pinchot, Mt. Whitney; Profiles 13, 16. Best late season; 54.2 miles.

	Trail/layover	Total recom-
Grade	days	mended days
Leisurely	8/3	11
Moderate	6/3	9
Strenuous	5/3	8

HILITES   Crossing two little-used passes, this trip explores the glaciated upper reaches of the Kern Trench and circumnavigates a good piece of the Kings-Kern and Great Western divides. This is a long and rugged route that is recommended for the hearty back-country traveler possessed of a sense of adventure and a liking for high, barren surroundings.

DESCRIPTION   *(Moderate trip)*

1st Hiking Day   (Cedar Grove Roadend to Junction Meadow, 11.5 miles): Proceed to Junction Meadow as described in the 1st and part of the 2nd hiking day, trip 59.

2nd Hiking Day   (Junction Meadow to Campsites, Upper East Fork Bubbs Creek, 4.5 miles): Proceed to Vidette Meadow as described in 2nd hiking day, trip 59, where our route joins the John Muir Trail and turns southeast, ascending the East Fork Bubbs Creek. About ½ mile above Vidette Meadow our route passes an old trapper's cabin. Shorty Lovelace trapped this country until it was made into a national park, and a network of his cabins remains to remind today's travelers of an era of the not-too-distant past. After the initial steep ascent above Vidette Meadow, the trail levels out to a moderate but steady ascent along the east bank of the creek through a moderate forest cover of lodgepole and occasional hemlock. Several campsites line the East Fork Bubbs Creek, but those just below the creek ford (10200') offer fine campsite views of University Peak to the east, Center Peak to the southeast, and East Vidette and East Spur to the west. Fishing for brook (to 7") is good, and firewood is ample. Side excursions for golden-trout fishing or mere pleasure can be made via the old Muir trail route through Center Basin.

3rd Hiking Day   (Campsites, Upper East Fork Bubbs Creek to Campsite, Outlet Stream of Lake 11440, 12.2 miles, part cross country): From these campsites the trail fords the creek and two tiny tributaries before recrossing just below the Junction Pass trail junction. Our route (the "new" John Muir Trail) keeps to the right, ascending steeply over the barren granite west of Center Peak. This climb takes one above timberline as it winds back and forth over the tributary that drains Lake 12248, and over one's shoulder the peaks of the Sierra crest march away on the northern horizon. Rounding the steep west shore of Lake 12248, the trail hugs the west wall of the canyon, and then switchbacks steeply up to the narrow notch in the Kings-Kern Divide which is Forester Pass (13200'). Views from the pass to the north and east include Mt. Pinchot, Junction Peak, Mt. Keith, Center Peak, Mt. Bradley and University (once University of California) Peak. Mt. Stanford and Caltech Peak are to the west. To the south are Mt. Kaweah and the Kaweah Peaks Ridge, the Red Spur, Picket Guard Peak and Kern Point. Leaving this windy orientation point behind, the trail descends steeply by numerous, short switchbacks, some of which are barely more than shelves carved into the steep face of the Junction Peak ridge. A few hardy polemonium and some yellow hulsea share the high slope with scurrying conies, and the traveler who lifts his eyes is sometimes treated to a sighting of a golden eagle soaring high above the granite peaks. After the trail levels off somewhat, the rocky route winds among a number of unnamed, granitoid lakes making up the headwaters of Tyndall Creek. To the east the unusual formation called Diamond Mesa appears as a sheer-walled, flat-topped ridge dangling from the jumbled heights of Junction Peak. Here, the trail passes through "marmot land," and the traveling human intruder is looked upon indulgently as a seasonal part of the scenery — accepted, at a respectful distance. Near timberline, our route intersects the signed Lake South America/Milestone Creek trail and turns right onto it. This trail soon turns west, and then ascends gently at timberline for ½ mile to another signed junction, where the Lake South America trail turns north and our route veers southwest. At the outlet stream of Lake 11440, the hiker should turn left and descend cross country to the good campsite (11200') at the edge of the meadow one quarter mile south. Firewood is adequate, but the stream is barren of fish.

4th Hiking Day (Campsite, Outlet Stream of Lake 11440 to Lake Reflection, 9.5 miles, part cross country): Retrace steps of the previous hiking day to the Lake South America/Milestone trail junction, where this day's route turns north and ascends gently up the east side of a long, boulder-strewn meadow. At the head of this ascent, the trail becomes steeper, and switchbacks up 500' of barren, broken granite to a saddle which gives access to the large cirque basin at the head of the Kern River. Beside a charming little lake that feeds the Kern River our route meets the trail coming up from the river and turns right, toward Lake South America (so called from its shape), where the angler may wish to try the good fishing for golden to 12". From here the trail is ducked (inadequately) as it climbs toward Harrison Pass. Ahead, locating the pass by visual sighting is difficult, as the lowest point on the headwall of the canyon is nearer Mt. Ericsson than the actual pass is. Our ducked route veers eastward, toward Mt. Stanford, where the best descent on the north side may be had. This descent is often snow-choked until late summer, and should not be attempted with stock (despite the record of precedent). Views from Harrison Pass to the south include Mt. Kaweah, Kaweah Peaks Ridge, Milestone Mountain and Mt. Guyot. Looking north, Deerhorn Mountain with its avalanche chutes and talus fans stands athwart the view, but Mt. Goddard can be seen far in the distance to the left of it, and Middle Palisade in the distance to the right. From the pass, the route leads down the talus (sometimes over snow) to the small, granitoid lakes visible from the summit. This descent encounters a faint trail by the time it reaches timberline, and the trail continues its steep descent between Deerhorn Mountain and Ericsson Crags. The rocky trail levels off as it skirts the north side of another small lake, and then it drops steeply to meet East Creek. Here, at an unmarked junction, our route branches south toward the obvious cirque holding Lake

Reflection. This short spur trail brings one to the good campsites at the northeast end of Lake Reflection (10005'). Wood is ample, and fishermen will find the angling good for golden, brook and hybrids (to 16").

5th Hiking Day (Lake Reflection to Junction Meadow, 5 miles): See 2nd hiking day, trip 64.

6th Hiking Day (Junction Meadow to Cedar Grove Roadend, 11.5 miles): See 1st hiking day and part of 2nd hiking day, trip 59.

TRIP

From ONION VALLEY to FLOWER LAKE (round trip). Topo map (15') Mt. Pinchot; Profile 15. Best early or mid season; 7 miles.

Grade	Trail/layover days	Total recom- mended days
Leisurely	2/0	2
Moderate	- - -	- - -
Strenuous	- - -	- - -

HILITES

Employing one of the "easiest" east side entries, this trip climbs to the friendly lakes making up the headwaters of Independence Creek. The ample opportunities for good angling, and the exciting alpine scenery occupy one's weekend time in grand style.

DESCRIPTION (Leisurely trip)

1st Hiking Day (Onion Valley to Flower Lake, 3.5 miles): The trail leaves the road a few yards north of the campground and switchbacks up over a dry, manzanita-covered slope. Switchbacks always seem to come in bunches, and this ascent is no exception. The hiker can look forward to three distinct steps in the climb between Onion Valley and Flower Lake. The first set of switchbacks is relatively open and exposed, offering fine views back on Onion Valley and south to the heavily diked summit of Independence Peak. After a brief, moderately ascending stretch, the trail resumes its steady zigzagging climb, and encounters the first concentrations of timber cover. It is predominantly lodgepole, but one finds large stands of foxtail pine mixed into the trees that line the trail. This forest cover gives way to rocky going over a terminal moraine just before arriving at Gilbert Lake. Alternative campsites dot the shores of this fine swimming lake, and fishing for rainbow and brook is good — particularly in early season. This tiny lake absorbs most of the day-hiking impact from those camping at Onion Valley — an impact not shared by Matlock and Slim

Lakes ¼ mile to the south. The short spur trail to Flower Lake leaves the Kearsarge Pass trail just beyond the next set of switchbacks, leading to several good campsites along the north and east sides of this shallow lake (10540'). Firewood is ample in early season (winter fall) but is usually picked over by mid season. Fishing for rainbow and some brook trout is fair on this tiny lake, but serious anglers should wander across to the more distant lakes in the timbered cirque basin to the south.

2nd Hiking Day (Flower Lake to Onion Valley, 3.5 miles): Retrace steps of 1st hiking day.

TRIP — From ONION VALLEY to CEDAR GROVE via Kearsarge Pass, Charlotte Lake, Glen Pass, Rae Lakes, South Fork Woods Creek, Paradise Valley (shuttle trip). Topo maps (15') Mt. Pinchot, Marion Peak; Profiles 15, 13, 14. Best mid or late season; 38 miles.

Grade	Trail/layover days	Total recommended days
Leisurely	6/2	8
Moderate	5/2	7
Strenuous	4/2	6

HILITES — Kearsarge Pass, because of its relative low elevation and proximity to an east-side roadend, is a popular way to reach the John Muir Trail. Because of this popularity, many of the lakes and meadows en route have been overrun, and Park officials have felt it necessary to close these "impacted" areas to grazing and camping. Despite these restrictions, the country retains its popularity, and anyone planning to tramp the Muir trail in the vicinity of this pass should expect company.

DESCRIPTION (Leisurely trip)

1st Hiking Day (Onion Valley to Flower Lake, 3.5 miles): See 1st hiking day, trip 66.

2nd Hiking Day (Flower Lake to Charlotte Lake, 5.5 miles): Retracing the short spur trail to the main Kearsarge Pass trail, our route turns left (west) and crosses an easy rise to a viewpoint overlooking Heart Lake. From this point the trail switchbacks up to another overlook — this time the lake is the nearly perfect blue oval of Big Pothole Lake. In the course of this climb, one can look back across the Owens River Valley to the White Mountains. From the trail high above the water, the lake, with its backgrounding granite finger, is particularly photogenic. From the switchbacks on, the trail rises above timber (excepting a few hardy whitebark specimens) and then makes two long-legged traverses across an exposed rocky slope to the low saddle of Kearsarge Pass (11823'). To the west, the view is impressive, as it includes the Kearsarge Lakes, Bullfrog Lake and the serrated spires of the Kearsarge Pinnacles. Our route drops down on the west side of the pass on a long traverse that later resolves into the inevitable switchbacks. Passing a spur trail branching left to the Kearsarge Lakes, the route continues westward through a moderate and then dense forest cover of lodgepole, hemlock, and some whitebark pine to Bullfrog Lake. Anglers wishing some variation in their sport may wish to try the waters of the Kearsarge chain for the rainbow and brook trout. Our route rounds the north end of Bullfrog Lake, and meets the John Muir Trail, where our route follows north onto the signed Charlotte Lake spur trail. This trail switchbacks down steeply for a short mile, arriving at the good campsites along the north side of the lake (10370'). Firewood is abundant, and fishing for rainbow and brook (to 10") is good. Emergency services are available from the resident summer ranger. An exciting route alternative via Gardiner and Sixty Lake basins can be taken from this point (see 3rd hiking day, trip 60).

3rd Hiking Day (Charlotte Lake to Rae Lakes, 5.5 miles): Retrace steps to the John Muir Trail, and then proceed as described in the 3rd hiking day, trip 61.

4th Hiking Day (Rae Lakes to Campsites, Woods Creek Crossing, 6.5 miles): See 4th hiking day, trip 62.

5th Hiking Day (Campsites, Woods Creek Crossing to Paradise Valley, 10 miles): See 5th hiking day, trip 62.

6th Hiking Day (Paradise Valley to Cedar Grove Roadend, 7 miles): See 6th hiking day, trip 62.

 68

TRIP From ONION VALLEY to CEDAR GROVE via Kearsarge Pass, Vidette Meadow, Bubbs Creek (shuttle trip). Topo maps (15') Mt. Pinchot, Marion Peak; Profiles 15, 13. Best mid or late season; 23.5 miles.

Grade	Trail/layover days	Total recommended days
Leisurely	3/1	4
Moderate	- - -	- - -
Strenuous	- - -	- - -

HILITES   There is no finer, shorter, more representative trans-Sierra route than this one. Because of these qualities, it is an ideal shuttle trip for the beginner who wants to survey Sierra flora, walk the John Muir Trail and cross the Sierra crest.

DESCRIPTION   (Leisurely trip)
1st Hiking Day   (Onion Valley to Flower Lake, 3.5 miles): See 1st hiking day, trip 66.

2nd Hiking Day   (Flower Lake to Vidette Meadow, 6 miles): Proceed to the junction with the Muir Trail as described in the 2nd hiking day, trip 67. At this junction our route turns left onto the Muir Trail, and, passing through alternating meadow and forest stands, arrives at the switchbacks that drop into Bubbs Creek canyon. At the floor of the canyon, the Muir trail meets and passes the Bubbs Creek trail (we return to it on the following hiking day), and reaches the excellent campsites scattered along Bubbs Creek at Vidette Meadow. Fishing for brook, rainbow and some brown (to 8″) is fair. Firewood is ample.

3rd Hiking Day   (Vidette Meadow to Cedar Grove Roadend, 14 miles): Retrace steps of 1st and 2nd hiking days, trip 59.

 69

TRIP   From ONION VALLEY to UPPER KERN RIVER DRAINAGE via Kearsarge Pass, Vidette Meadow, Forester Pass, return via Harrison Pass, Lake Reflection, Junction Meadow (semiloop trip). Topo maps (15′) Mt. Pinchot, Mt. Whitney; Profiles 15, 13, 16. Best late season; 50.2 miles.

Grade	Trail/layover days	Total recommended days
Leisurely	8/3	11
Moderate	7/3	10
Strenuous	6/3	9

HILITES   One soon learns that good back-country loop trips are hard to come by, and excellent loops are as rare as honey on a bear's nose. This trip is an excellent semiloop that circles a significant portion of the Kings-Kern Divide.

DESCRIPTION   (Moderate trip)
1st Hiking Day   (Onion Valley to Flower Lake, 3.5 miles): See 1st hiking day, trip 66.

2nd Hiking Day (Flower Lake to Vidette Meadow, 6 miles): See 2nd hiking day, trip 68.

3rd Hiking Day (Vidette Meadow to Campsite, Outlet Stream of Lake 11440, 14.2 miles, part cross country): See part of 2nd hiking day, trip 65, and 3rd hiking day, trip 65.

4th Hiking Day (Campsite, Outlet Stream of Lake 11440 to Lake Reflection, 9.5 miles, part cross country): See 4th hiking day, trip 65.

5th Hiking Day (Lake Reflection to Vidette Meadow, 7.5 miles): See 2nd hiking day, trip 64, and part of 2nd hiking day, trip 59.

6th Hiking Day (Vidette Meadow to Flower Lake, 6 miles): Retrace steps of 2nd hiking day.

7th Hiking Day (Flower Lake to Onion Valley, 3.5 miles): Retrace steps of 1st hiking day.

	Trail/layover	Total recom-
Grade	days	mended days
Leisurely	5/2	7
Moderate	4/2	6
Strenuous	4/1	5

TRIP From ONION VALLEY to OAK CREEK ROADEND via Kearsarge Pass, Glen Pass, Rae Lakes, Baxter Pass (shuttle trip). Topo map (15′) Mt. Pinchot; Profiles 15, 13, 14. Best late season; 30 miles.

HILITES Utilizing a brief but beautiful segment of the Muir trail, this shuttle trip enters the high country by the most popular pass in the Sierra and leaves by one of this range's least-known passes. The enchantment of Rae Lakes, the halfway point of this horseshoe-shaped route, is well known to every experienced Sierra mountaineer, and their fame is deserved.

DESCRIPTION (Leisurely trip)
1st Hiking Day (Onion Valley to Flower Lake, 3.5 miles): See 1st hiking day, trip 66.

2nd Hiking Day (Flower Lake to Charlotte Lake, 5.5 miles): See 2nd hiking day, trip 67.

3rd Hiking Day   (Charlotte Lake to Rae Lakes, 5.5 miles): Retrace steps to the Muir Trail, and then proceed as described in the 3rd hiking day, trip 61.

4th Hiking Day   (Rae Lakes to Baxter Lakes, 5 miles): See 4th hiking day, trip 63.

5th Hiking Day   (Baxter Lakes to Oak Creek Roadend, 10.5 miles): See 5th hiking day, trip 63.

BUBBS CREEK TO LOWER KERN

This stretch of country composes the least visited, least known, and least trampled region in the Sierra. It owes its integrity not to its lack of scenic or recreational potential, but rather to the presence of a fortuitously placed series of natural barriers — Great Western Divide, Kings-Kern Divide, and the Sierra crest. Joined together in an upside-down U, they protect the first 24 miles of the Kern River watershed with a wall of mountains crossed only by 1) people who have business here (rangers, packers, etc.), 2) people who have a love for the high country, and 3) people who fly over in airplanes. There are those among us who would restrict the third category because of the objectionable sonic booms.*

The one area described in this section that sits outside this protective cup of divides and ranges is the Roaring River Country. Remoteness from roads and a convoluted terrain guarantee its sanctuary. And sanctuary it is, for in the remote headwaters of Roaring River a hiker can walk for one, two, or even three days without seeing a soul.

With the notable exceptions of Mineral King and Horseshoe Meadow, this section is protected from commercial exploitation by national park status and a wilderness area title. At this writing, private business concerns are at work to establish large ski resorts at these vulnerable spots, over the objections of Park officials, conservation organizations, mountaineers and others sympathetic to the maintenance of primitive Sierra country. The establishment of major roads, and the breach of the "buffer" zone, cannot help but affect the peace, serenity and pristine wilderness quality of this hitherto remote section. With these road intrusions and the resulting concentrations of people, there cannot help but be a consequent, devastating impact upon this region's fragile ecology.

The delicate balance between plant and animal life is nowhere more manifest than in the alpine fell fields over Cottonwood Pass just west of Horseshoe Meadow, or around the subalpine meadows just south of Little Clair Lake over the crest from Mineral King. Here, in an incredibly brief 6-7 week span, some 40 varieties of hardy-yet-vulnerable grasses, sedges and flowering plants grow, bud, blossom, seed, and are harvested, running their appointed course under the daily threat of killing frost, and before the juggernaut deadline of the first winter snows. Caught in the complex "web of life," year-round resident animals like the cony, marmot, pocket gopher and Belding ground squirrel stake their

*Should the reader and the writers ever meet and share a backcountry campfire, remind us to recount the hairy tale of the mountain climber who was hanging by his fingertips beneath an overhanging snow cornice when one of these supersonic jets went by.

very existence on the plants' explosively short summer tenure. Inexorably linked in the ecological chain, the migrating and hibernating carnivores, such as the coyote, mountain lion, black bear, red fox, marten, weasel and wolverine, would perish without their dependable rodent and squirrel food supply. So fragile and tenuous is this balance that the trampling by man and his livestock of a high, grassy meadow — particularly during the early, wet days of spring — can have and has had catastrophic effects upon the food chain.

This is not to argue that man does not have a place in this setting. His trails, within strict practical and esthetic limitations, are as legitimate as those of the deer. He has the right to share the fish of the streams and the berries of the hillside with the bear. Like the marmot, he has his place in the sun — preferably a big flat rock where he too can laze away a warm afternoon. Man's propensity for mountaintops and places of quiet solitude is as valid as the bighorn sheep's. And, like the Hermit thrush at nesting time, or the Brewer blackbird at sundown, he has the right to sing of his exultation at being alive and here.

But, because he knows the devastation wrought by large, concentrated numbers of his species upon this country, he owes it to his co-habiters, and to himself, to expand rather than constrict the size of primitive country, and to disperse his impact upon the country. Implicit within both of these obligations should be a profound respect for the ecological chain, of which man is a part, for this respect will give birth to a deeper knowledge and appreciation of the re-creating benefits of a region such as this. Apart from sharing their appreciation of and passion for this grand part of the Sierra, it was the hope of the authors that they might, with this modest guide, call the attention of the prospective traveler to the less traveled byways, and thereby contribute, in small measure, to the distribution of human impact. Because many of the routes described here are the lesser traveled, they are therefore sometimes faint, but that is as it should be. The passes are sometimes steeper than those used on the more traveled routes, but the rewards of scenery and solitude are commensurate.

As the quality of the wilderness experience is important, so is the quantity. For it is only through public support that requisite public legislation and administrative decisions will reflect man's desire and need for wild areas. The more people that are introduced to basic wilderness values, perhaps through guides like this, the greater will be the demand for more and better wilderness areas and national parks. Pieces of untrammelled country like that between the Kings-Kern Divide and the lower Kern River will remain bastions of peace and solitude, not because of the shallow artifices designed to discourage and restrict wilderness travel (poor signing and other Park policies, high packer's rates, etc.), but because of the addition of more wilderness alternatives. The sooner Park officials and conservation organizations recognize this fact, the sooner the current trend to wilderness attrition will be reversed.

There are five trailheads cited in the text that give access to this region — 2 on the west side, and 3 on the east. On the west side, both Lodgepole Campground and Mineral King can be reached via State Route 198 from Visalia, or State Route 180 from Fresno. To reach Mineral King, turn east for 25 miles on the road (partly paved, mostly dirt) that leaves Hiway 198 at Hammond. On the east side, the Symmes Creek Roadend is reached by branching south from the Onion Valley road 3 miles west of Independence (dirt road). To reach Whitney Portal, take the paved road that leaves Hiway 395 at Lone Pine. The partly paved road leading to the Cottonwood Creek Roadend leaves the same hiway about 3 miles south of Lone Pine.

 # 71

TRIP From SYMMES CREEK ROADEND to WRIGHT LAKES via Anvil Camp and Shepherd Pass (round trip). Topo map (15') Mt. Whitney; Profile 16. Best mid or late season; 24 miles.

Grade	Trail/layover days	Total recommended days
Leisurely	- - -	- - -
Moderate	3/1	4
Strenuous	3/0	3

HILITES This trip provides the great satisfaction of reaching the high, remote back country via a tough climb up the canyon of Shepherd Creek, one of the immense gashes that typify the eastern Sierra escarpment. The great elevation gain makes it a trip only for those in excellent physical condition.

DESCRIPTION (Moderate trip)

1st Hiking Day (Symmes Creek Roadend to Anvil Camp, 7 miles): Leaving the Symmes Creek corral, the sandy trail winds through sagebrush on a gentle desert ascent for the first mile. As it enters the Symmes Creek canyon, pinon pine appears, and, at streamside, alders. Our trail fords the creek several times, passing stands of showy early and midseason columbine, and then begins a long series of rocky switchbacks that climb 2300' to the saddle straddling the Shepherd and Symmes Creek watersheds. Above 8000' red fir and then silver pine form a moderate forest cover, and the entire hot slope supports sagebrush, mountain mahogany and creamberry. From the saddle at the head of this slope, the great peak to the south is Mt. Williamson, second highest in California — though, surprisingly, it is not on the Sierra crest. The deep, steep gash that contains Shepherd Creek falls away at one's feet, and it is an impressive introduction to the immense canyons of the eastern escarpment. After a short ascent, the sandy trail descends to cross an unnamed creek which normally is the only water between Symmes Creek and Anvil Camp. From here the trail approaches Shepherd Creek, but turns away before reaching it and switchbacks up to Mahogany Flat, which is a gently sloping hillside where fire killed all the mountain mahogany. At the upper end of this flat, the trail enters a cover of sparse lodgepole, Jeffrey, silver and foxtail pine, and then switchbacks up a rocky slope to gain the elevation of the cascade visible to the southwest on Shepherd Creek. As the route passes a large talus slope, the entire surroundings change dramatically within a few hundred feet. The trail has been largely decomposed granite, and the vegetation generally sparse and desertlike. But as the trail reaches Anvil Camp (10000') the experienced Sierra traveler suddenly recognizes that he is in the High Sierra: there is duff, a burbling stream, a good campsite, willows, grass, and young lodgepole pines. Firewood is adequate, and fishing is fair in Shepherd Creek for rainbow (to 9").

2nd Hiking Day (Anvil Camp to Wright Lakes, 5 miles, part cross country): From Anvil Camp the trail ascends moderately over rocky slopes on the south side of Shepherd Creek. After a mile the trail to Junction Pass turns off to the right. (Until Forester Pass was opened in 1931 the John Muir Trail, in passing from the Kings River to the Kern River drainage, detoured to the east side of the Sierra crest over Junction Pass, down to this trail junction, and recrossed westward over Shepherd Pass.) The route crosses the area labeled "The Pothole" on the topo map, and ascends through great boulders to the giant declivity, below the pass, for which that label should have been reserved. Here is a gargantuan jumble of great jagged rocks that have been weathered out of the headwall of the cirque. The last 500' ascent to Shepherd Pass (12050') is on switchbacks up a steep scree slope which often has patches of snow that remain into August. At the summit the route enters Sequoia National Park and begins a descent down a broad boulder-strewn field to alpine meadows and stands of foxtail pine. Immediately to the south is the northern flank of Mt. Tyndall (14018'), which the famous mountaineer Clarence King climbed in 1864 believing it to be the highest Sierra peak. He did not realize his error until he reached the summit. At the 11600' level the hiker should leave the trail and traverse southwest cross-country to the saddle between Peak 13540' and Peak 12345'. The panoramic view from this saddle includes Junction Peak, Mts. Keith, Brewer, Kaweah, Guyot, Young, and Hale and the top of Mt. Whitney, as well as the Kern River trench. Even in this high, rocky saddle there are flowers, including the blue, multiheaded polemonium, or "sky pilot." Our route traverses down the east wall of the cirque that lies south of the saddle, to the fair campsites in a grove of foxtails where the outlet stream of Lake 11952 meets the other two draining the upper basin. Firewood is scarce, but fishing is good for golden (to 8"). The hiker who is willing to forego a wood supply may camp on Lake 11952, a classic cirque lake under the south slope of Mt. Tyndall which boasts good fishing for rainbow (to 14"). One should note that the trail shown on the topo map from the John Muir Trail up the Wright Lakes basin has never been maintained and cannot be followed as a trail.

3rd Hiking Day (Wright Lakes to Symmes Creek Roadend, 12 miles, part cross country): Retrace steps of 1st and 2nd hiking days.

| | TRIP | From SYMMES CREEK ROADEND to MILESTONE BASIN via Anvil Camp and Shepherd Pass (round trip). Topo map (15') Mt. Whitney; Profile 16. Best mid or late season; 37 miles). |

Grade	Trail/layover days	Total recommended days
Leisurely	- - -	- - -
Moderate	4/2	6
Strenuous	4/0	4

HILITES Milestone Basin is a fine choice for the lover of high country who wants to be alone. Many fish-filled lakes lie under the prepossessing heights of the Great Western Divide, where the delicate quality of the light and the air work their magic on all who come.

DESCRIPTION (Moderate trip)

1st Hiking Day (Symmes Creek Roadend to Anvil Camp, 7 miles): See 1st hiking day, trip 71.

2nd Hiking Day (Anvil Camp to Milestone Basin, 11.5 miles): See description of 2nd hiking day, trip 71, from Anvil Camp to where that day's route leaves the Shepherd Pass trail. Our route continues down the trail beside Tyndall Creek, through a huge, boulder-strewn, sloping meadow, with the 13000′ peaks of the Great Western Divide filling the western horizon. After fording Tyndall Creek, the trail diverges from the stream and enters a sparse cover of lodgepole and foxtail pine, meeting the stream again at the John Muir Trail. Our route turns right (north) onto the John Muir Trail, fords Tyndall Creek, and ascends a moderate slope to timberline. Three-fourths of a mile from the last ford our route turns left onto the Lake South America trail. A half mile farther on across alpine fell fields, it turns left again, onto the Milestone Basin trail. Views in this upper Kern basin are at all times panoramic, and the traveler will mentally record pictures of the skyline that are not soon forgotten. At the outlet stream of Lake 11440 the angler may wish to veer north and sample that lake's waters for the good fishing for golden (to 12").The trail then skirts along the north side of a small lake (not ¼ mile north of it, as on the topo map), and makes a short, rocky climb to a ridge where the descent to the Kern River begins. From the ridge the traveler has closer views of Mt. Jordan, Thunder Mtn., Milestone Mtn., Midway Mtn., Kern Ridge and Red Spur. The trail descends moderately through rocky and meadowy sections with a moderate cover of foxtail, lodgepole and some whitebark, and arrives at a picturebook lake that is fast (geologically speaking) turning to meadow. One may regret that all these high lakes are doomed, but one may enjoy the blend of meadows and lakes existing in the time to which he was born. After climbing slightly, our route begins the last, steep descent to the Kern River, where it emerges at an unnamed lake at 10700' elevation (good fishing for golden and rainbow-golden hybrids to 10"). Our route turns left at the east side of this lake and descends gently beside the infant Kern River for about 200 yards to the signed trail turning west to Milestone Basin. Fording the river, the trail contours to meet Milestone Creek and then veers west up a rocky slope away from the creek. After another half mile it rejoins the creek at a bench where, beside a waterfall, there is a good campsite (11100'). Wood is ample, and fishing in Milestone Creek is good for rainbow (to 10"). Those who wish to camp as high as possible may climb to the high lake (11900') just to the right of "Midway Mtn." on the topo map. The trail shown on the topo map beside Milestone Creek above the confluence of the north fork does not exist, and the hiker should follow the ducked route that turns right up the north fork, passes through a defile, skirts a small lake barren of fish, and traverses up to the high lake, where fishing is good for golden (to 12"). There are fair campsites with scarce wood below this lake on the outlet stream.

3rd Hiking Day (Milestone Basin to Anvil Camp, 11.5 miles): Retrace steps of 2nd hiking day.

4th Hiking Day (Anvil Camp to Symmes Creek Roadend, 7 miles): Retrace steps of 1st hiking day.

TRIP   From SYMMES CREEK ROADEND to MINERAL KING via Anvil Camp, Shepherd Pass, Upper Kern River, Rattlesnake Creek and Franklin Pass (shuttle trip). Topo maps (15') Mt. Whitney, Kern Peak, Mineral King; Profiles 16, 27, 25. Best mid-to-late season; 55.7 miles.

	Trail/layover	Total recom-
Grade	days	mended days
Leisurely	- - -	- - -
Moderate	6/2	8
Strenuous	5/0	5

HILITES   This long shuttle trip provides a grand sample of everything the High Sierra has to offer: sweeping vistas, intimate groves, barren granite, streamside meadows, rainbow, golden, brook and brown trout, pages of geological history, access to the highest Sierra peaks, the marks of great glaciers, thick pine forests, alpine fell fields—and that feeling of grandeur which calls the backpacker to the Sierra again and again.

DESCRIPTION (Moderate trip)

1st Hiking Day (Symmes Creek Roadend to Anvil Camp, 7 miles): See 1st hiking day, trip 71.

2nd Hiking Day (Anvil Camp to Lake on Upper Kern River, 10.2 miles): Follow 2nd hiking day, trip 72, to the lake on the Kern River at 10700' elevation, where the Milestone Basin trail meets the Kern River trail. There are good campsites at the lake inlet, and fishing is good for golden and hybrids (to 10"). Wood is ample.

3rd Hiking Day (Lake on Upper Kern River to Junction Meadow, 7 miles): From the lakeside campsites the trail proceeds south along the east shore of the lake, where red pentstemon, or mountain pride, is especially abundant in the broken granite slopes. After several hundred yards the Kern River trail passes the Milestone Basin trail branching right, and soon begins the steep 600' descent of a granite-slabbed slope where, in the shade of lodgepole pines, one sees yarrow milfoil, paintbrush, pentstemon, fleabane, and red mountain heather. Despite the topo map indication, the trail remains on the east side of the river. As the descent begins to level off, the trail passes through a bank of shield fern among which grows the delicate, white-headed Queen Anne's lace. At the foot of the descent our route enters a dell where lodgepole pines with notably straight trunks form a thick stand. The yellow groundsel flowers dominate the ground cover under these pines, complemented by the hues of orange tiger lily, purple swamp onion and red columbine. Fording the outlet stream of Lake 11440, the trail begins a dusty section where the sagebrush is spottily shaded by a few lodgepole and foxtail pines. Shortly before the junction with the Tyndall Creek trail there is a good packer campsite beside the river, and here one begins to see red fir and aspen, indicating arrival in the Canadian life zone. The sandy, exposed trail continues its gentle descent to the Tyndall Creek ford (difficult in early season), where a stock drift fence bears a sign indicating that Junction Meadow (ahead) is closed to grazing. Beyond this ford, the canyon becomes steeper, and the trail becomes more dufflike and tree-shaded. The first Jeffrey pines of this trip appear, along with a few mountain juniper, and the trail passes a now roofless cabin that was used as a powder magazine by crews doing trail work in this area. One-half mile beyond, our route meets the High Sierra trail coming down from Wallace Creek, and from here down to Upper Funston Meadow the Kern River trail and the High Sierra trail are "superimposed." From this junction it is a steep descent of 1 mile to Junction Meadow. Views on this descent are good down the Kern canyon, an immense U-trough which was given that shape by the main Kern glacier. The glacier left the tributary valleys hanging, but erosion and weathering since then has decreased the slope of Wallace Creek (to the east) for the last several miles before it enters the Kern. The Kern-Kaweah River, to the west, rushes more precipitously down to the master stream. The forest cover on this descent is sparse lodgepole and Jeffrey, along with clumps of aspen, on a slope dominated by manzanita and currant. As the trail levels off, it enters a parklike grove of stalwart Jeffrey pines that provide a noble setting for the good campsites on the Kern River. Firewood is ample and fishing is good for rainbow and some brook (to 10").

4th Hiking Day (Junction Meadow to Campsites, Rattlesnake Creek/Kern River, 11.5 miles): This day's hike is entirely beside the young Kern River, but it is not lacking in contrasts and discoveries. Fording Wallace Creek (high water in early season) the trail descends gently down the U-trough of the Kern River. This trough is remarkably straight for about 25 miles, as it traces the Kern Canyon fault. The fault, a zone of structural weakness in the Sierra batholith, is more susceptible to erosion than the surrounding rock. This deep canyon has been carved by both glacial and stream action: three times the glacier advanced down the canyon, shearing off spurs created by stream erosion and leaving some tributary valleys hanging above the main valley. The glacier also scooped and plucked at the bedrock, creating basins (like the lake at the start of this hiking day) in the granite which became lakes when the glacier melted and retreated. It is interesting to speculate that our trail probably passes over some of these ancient lake beds, now buried beneath river sediments. The descending trail becomes a little steeper as it fords Whitney Creek, where a thirsty hiker can sample water that coursed down from the highest point in the contiguous United States. Tributaries cascading down the east face of Red Spur provide excellent views as the trail steepens again and fords the stream that drains Guyot Flat. Rounding the most salient part of Red Spur, the trail turns slighlty west as it skirts the steep bluffs on the east canyon wall. The gravelly, flat canyon floor widens as the trail approaches the fords of the branchlets of Rock Creek. Just beyond the first of these is the delightful mountain spa of Kern Hot Spring — a treat for the tired, dusty hiker. To the traveler, the crude cement bathtub here becomes a regal, heated (115°) pool. Only a few feet away, the great Kern River rushes past, and its cold waters can be dipped into to cool the hot-spring water as desired. Beyond Kern Hot Spring the valley floor widens and the river bifurcates as it flows past Chagoopa Falls. Chagoopa Creek descends 1700' from its hanging valley on Chagoopa Plateau, but the actual waterfall drops only 150'. (Note: the topo map indicates a "Chagoopa Falls Ranger Station" nearby. This station no longer exists.) A short distance to the south the route crosses a bridge to the west side of the Kern, and then continues its gentle descent past the Big Arroyo turnoff, thereby leaving the High Sierra Trail. Keeping away from the willow-infested banks of the Kern, the trail continues south past Upper Funston Meadow (grazing limited) through a moderate-to-heavy forest cover of white fir, Jeffrey, sugar pine and some black oak, birch and aspen. Heavy patches of bracken fern inhibit the going in the wetter stretches, and the trail crosses through the site of an old burn before passing a drift fence and crossing the steel cantilever bridge spanning Big Arroyo Creek. From the bridge it is but a mile of level going to the good packer campsite at the confluence of Rattlesnake Creek and the Kern River. Fishing on the Kern is excellent for rainbow and brown (to 18") and firewood is ample. Emergency services, should they be required, are available at the Kern Canyon Ranger Station 6 miles down-canyon. A cautionary note is warranted here: Rattlesnake Creek came by its name honestly, and one should exercise some care in hiking and climbing in the vicinity.

5th Hiking Day (Campsites, Rattlesnake Creek/Kern River to Campsites, Upper Rattlesnake Creek, 9.5 miles): See 2nd hiking day, trip 100.

6th Hiking Day (Campsites, Upper Rattlesnake Creek to Mineral King, 10.5 miles): See 1st hiking day, trip 96.

74

TRIP   From SYMMES CREEK ROADEND to CEDAR GROVE via Shepherd Pass, Upper Kern River, Junction Meadow, Colby Pass, Scaffold Meadows and Avalanche Pass (shuttle trip). Topo maps (15') Mt. Whitney, Triple Divide Peak, Marion Peak; Profiles 16, 27, 20, 18, 13. Best mid-to-late season; 59.2 miles.

Grade	Trail/layover days	Total recommended days
Leisurely	- - -	- - -
Moderate	8/4	12
Strenuous	7/1	8

HILITES   Staying entirely on trails sometimes limits one's experiences, but this route is diversified enough for any taste. Visiting four life zones, the trip offers a complete sampling of High Sierra ecologies, and affords grand views of deep canyons and serrated skylines.

DESCRIPTION (Moderate trip)
1st Hiking Day (Symmes Creek Roadend to Anvil Camp, 7 miles): See 1st hiking day, trip 71.

2nd Hiking Day (Anvil Camp to Lake on Upper Kern River, 10.2 miles): See 2nd hiking day, trip 73.

3rd Hiking Day (Lake on Upper Kern River to Junction Meadow, 7 miles): See 3rd hiking day, trip 73.

4th Hiking Day (Junction Meadow to Campsites, Kern-Kaweah River, 6 miles): See 4th hiking day, trip 79.

5th Hiking Day (Campsites, Kern-Kaweah River to Big West Meadow, 7 miles): Leaving the Kern-Kaweah drainage behind, the trail ascends steeply and quickly transcends the sparse cover of lodgepole pine. This steep climb offers magnificent views back into the headwaters of the Kern-Kaweah drainage and the back-grounding Kaweah Peaks Ridge. Just to the north of these distinctive summits rise the pyramidal heights of aptly named Triple Divide Peak — this landmark peak divides the drainages of the Kern, Kings and Kaweah rivers. The steep ascent levels briefly as it crosses the tributaries draining Milestone Bowl, and then, by a faint and unreliably ducked trail, resumes its steep, steady climb to Colby Pass (12000'). Here one has grand views down Cloud Canyon and of Glacier Ridge and the Cockscomb-like sentinels atop Whaleback Ridge. This pass is often snow-covered until late in the season, but the route down to Cloud Canyon is easy to discern as it drops down past occasional foxtail and whitebark and then around the northeast side of Colby Lake (campsites). Anglers may wish to sample the poor-to-fair fishing for rainbow at Colby Lake before continuing. The poorly ducked trail follows the outlet stream from the wooded area at its source, zigging and zagging back and forth across the stream in the descent. Dwarfed and twisted whitebark pines dot the slopes on either side as the route dips steeply down over the unjointed granite shoulder of Whaleback Ridge to the Cloud Canyon floor where it meets the trail descending from Glacier Ridge. Our trail turns right and crosses to the east side of Cloud Canyon Creek just north of Table Creek, and proceeds downstream through a lodgepole forest cover for about ½ mile to the good campsites located on the west side of the stream just south of Big West Meadow (8700'). Firewood is ample, and fishing for rainbow and golden is poor.

6th Hiking Day (Big West Meadow to Scaffold Meadows, 7 miles): Wildflowers abound along the descending trail, including lupine, corn lily, aster, shooting star and sneezeweed. The moderate-to-heavy stands of lodgepole occasionally give way to clumps of aspen as the trail passes the lower "Grand Palace Hotel Drift Fence" and a nearby packer campsite. The descent is moderate on a duff surface as it passes Cement Table Meadow (not marked on the topo map) and a nearby campsite. The gradual loss of altitude is reflected in the changing forest cover, which now shows red fir, juniper, and white fir mixed with the lodgepole. Views of the glacially smoothed granite, particularly on the west wall of the canyon, continue as the duff-and-sand trail takes the traveler down past the signed turnoff to Brewer Lakes and Brewer Creek. A few yards past the upper drift fence at Scaffold Meadows, our trail arrives at the campground that is signed "Austin Camp"

(7500'). Firewood is ample, and fishing in the river is fair for rainbow and some golden (to 10").

7th Hiking Day (Scaffold Meadows to Campsite, Sphinx Creek Ford, 9 miles): Crossing the bridge by the Ranger Station, the route takes the Avalanche Pass trail northward on a steady ascent over a sandy trail, through a heavy forest cover of Jeffrey pine, red and white fir, and juniper. At the Scaffold Meadows drift fence the ascent becomes moderate to steep as the trail climbs the lateral moraine whose morainal nature is identified by its rounded boulders and granite sand. From the crown of this moraine views are good up Deadman Canyon to the head of the cirque near Elizabeth Pass. Here another trail turns right to Brewer Lakes and Brewer Creek, as our route begins a short steady descent to the easy ford of Moraine Creek. The moist sections near the creek support a variety of wildflowers, including shooting star, sneeze-weed, cinquefoil, aster, groundsel and milfoil. Beyond the ford the duff-and-sand trail ascends steadily to moderately to the tributary that drains the Avalanche Pass area. The forest cover of lodgepole, red fir and a few juniper is moderate to heavy, and some aspen thrive along the creek. Contrary to the topo map, our trail remains on the east side of the creek, and has a number of switchbacks as it climbs from 8800' to 9200'. The trail becomes less steep, and finally level, as it nears Avalanche Pass (10000'). Views from the pass are inhibited by the moderate-to-heavy forest cover of foxtail and some lodgepole. Along the moderate descent north of the pass, foxtail pines disappear and red fir and silver pine join the lodgepole to compose a heavy forest cover over the trail on granite sand. After fording the westernmost tributary of Sphinx Creek, our trail descends moderately to ford a second tributary, and then drops again on a moderate descent to Sphinx Creek and a packer campsite, where firewood is ample.

8th Hiking Day (Campsite, Sphinx Creek Ford to Cedar Grove Roadend, 6 miles): Leaving Sphinx Creek via a short, steady descent, the trail then begins a long level traverse high above the creek on the east canyon wall. Part of the Sphinx Crest is visible to the south through the trees, a moderate cover of Jeffrey pine and red fir. The traverse ends as the trail begins a series of long, well-built switchbacks that descend to the banks of Sphinx Creek in its deep, V-shaped gorge. On this descent, red fir replaces Jeffrey as the dominant species and a few black oak trees begin to be seen. Both the creek and the trail follow along granite slabs for much of the way from the beginning of the switchbacks to the foot of the descent, and some of the trail has been blasted across these slabs. As the trail leads out onto the north side of a granite nose, there are very good views up the Bubbs Creek drainage, down the canyon to Kanawyers, and northwest to the peaks of the Monarch Divide, which separates the South and Middle Forks of the Kings River. The last portion of the descent to Bubbs Creek is moderate, via many more switchbacks than are shown on the topo map. Then the forest cover thickens and our route meets the Bubbs Creek trail, where it turns left and retraces the steps of 1st hiking day, trip 59.

TRIP   From WHITNEY PORTAL to MIRROR LAKE (round trip). Topo map (15') Mt. Whitney; Profile 17. Best mid or late season; 8 miles.

Grade	Trail/layover days	Total recommended days
Leisurely	2/1	3
Moderate	2/0	2
Strenuous	- - -	- - -

HILITES   This overnight trip offers an experience of the high country in the shadow of Mt. Whitney. Mirror Lake is a beautiful glacial lake that can be used as a base camp for climbing the great peak.

DESCRIPTION (Leisurely trip)

1st Hiking Day (Whitney Portal to Mirror Lake, 4 miles): At the roadend (8367') a register stands in the shelter of a 35-foot-high granite monolith, a foretaste of the great granitic buttresses and pinnacles that lie ahead. The trail begins on a steep ascent up switchbacks through a moderate forest cover of Jeffrey pine and red fir. After ½ mile the foot trail is joined by the stock trail coming from the pack station, and the route enters the John Muir Wilderness Area. Soon the forest cover thins, and the slope is covered with a chaparral that includes mountain mahogany, Sierra chinquapin and sagebrush. This steep slope can get very hot in mid-morning, and the trip is best begun as early as possible. Breather stops on this trail section provide a Veed view down the canyon framing the Alabama Hills. The trail levels off through several willow-covered flats having a moderate forest cover of lodgepole and foxtail, and passes fields of corn lilies, delphinium, tall lupine and swamp whiteheads as it approaches the ford of Lone Pine Creek. Beyond this log ford is the junction with a lateral that leads east to Lone Pine Lake. From here, our route switchbacks up another slope through a moderate lodgepole cover to Outpost Camp (called "Bighorn Park" on the topo map), a willow-covered meadow that was once a lake. A very large abandoned stove near the upper end of this park is evidence of the days when the "highest use" of this area was not for wilderness recreation. The trail veers away from the waterfall that tumbles down into Outpost Camp from the southwest, fords Lone Pine Creek and begins a short series of switchbacks beside the cascading creek, past blossoming (in season) creamberry, Indian paintbrush, Sierra chinquapin, mountain pride, currant, pennyroyal, fireweed and groundsel. Just after the trail crosses a footbridge it arrives at Mirror Lake (10640'), cradled in its cirque beneath the south face of Thor Peak. This cold lake has fair fishing for rainbow and brook (to 8"). Wood is scarce, and the fair campsites are heavily used. In summer, a ranger is stationed here (emergency services available). Those who wish to ascend Mt. Whitney will camp here or, if willing to camp above timberline, at Trail Camp (see trip 76).

2nd Hiking Day (Mirror Lake to Whitney Portal, 4 miles): Retrace steps of 1st hiking day.

	Trail/layover days	Total recommended days
Grade		
Leisurely	- - -	- - -
Moderate	4/1	5
Strenuous	3/0	3

TRIP From WHITNEY PORTAL to CRABTREE RANGER STATION (round trip). Topo map (15') Mt. Whitney; Profile 17. Best mid-to-late season; 30 miles.

HILITES Despite the elevation at the pass where this route crosses the Sierra crest, it offers the fastest way into the high country of Sequoia National Park. Just beyond the pass is the spur trail to the top of Mt. Whitney, an easy amble from there.

DESCRIPTION *(Moderate trip)*

1st Hiking Day (Whitney Portal to Mirror Lake, 4 miles): See 1st hiking day, trip 75.

2nd Hiking Day (Mirror Lake to Crabtree Ranger Station, 11 miles): (This hiking day is a long one, owing to a lack of campsites short of Crabtree Ranger Station, and it involves an ascent of 3100'. The prudent hiker will start early.) Leaving Mirror Lake, the trail ascends the south wall of the Mirror Lake cirque via switchbacks. At the top of the ascent the trail passes timberline, as a last foxtail pine and a broken, weathered, convoluted whitebark snag are seen, along with a few last willows. Soon Mt. Whitney comes into view, over Pinnacle Ridge. From here, the rocky trail ascends moderately alongside the gigantic boulders on the north side of the South Fork Lone Pine Creek. In the cracks in the boulders the hiker will find ivesia, cinquefoil, creamberry, currant and much gooseberry, and looking across the canyon he will see the cascading outlet of Consultation Lake. Beside a rock bridge that crosses the stream are specimens of the moisture-loving shooting star. After ascending over some poured concrete steps —

which unfortunately detract from the wilderness feel of this country — the trail arrives at the last campsite before the crest — Trail Camp (12000'). Here beneath Wotan's Throne is also the last reliable water in late season. There are numerous level campsites, but no wood. As the trail begins the one hundred or so switchbacks to Trail Crest (the name of the pass) Mt. Whitney passes from view behind a sharp spire and Mt. Russell, farther north, comes into view. This rocky, barren talus slope is not entirely barren, for one may see a dozen species of flowering plants, climaxed by the multiflowered, blue "sky pilot." The building of this trail section involved much blasting with dynamite, and the natural fracture planes of the granite are evident in the blasted slabs. Finally the 1700' ascent from Trail Camp ends at Trail Crest (13777'), and the hiker suddenly has vistas of a great part of Sequoia National Park to the west, including the entire Great Western Divide. To the east, far below, are Consultation Lake and several smaller, unnamed lakes, lying close under the Whitney crest, which may not be free of ice the whole summer. From Trail Crest the route descends for a short half mile to the junction with the 2-mile lateral to Mt. Whitney (14495'). The highest mountain in the United States until Alaska was admitted as a state, this peak was first climbed on August 18, 1873, by three fishermen, who made the ascent up the southwest slope. The present trail between this junction and the summit lies close to the crest on the western slope. As our switchbacking descent on the west side of the Sierra crest begins, one can make out the Hitchcock Lakes below in a cirque basin that has been changed but little since its glacier melted. The parallel avalanche chutes on the northeast wall of Mt. Hitchcock all terminate at the upper limit of glacial erosion. Along the switchbacks, the most prominent flower is hulsea, alpine gold. The switchbacks end and the trail follows a moderate descent on a traverse of the "back" side of Mt. Whitney, leveling off at the first possible campsite, overlooking Guitar Lake (good fishing for golden to 10"). The nearest wood is one half mile down the canyon. From this campsite our route crosses the outlet of Arctic Lake, descends on a moderately steep, rocky trail into a sparse cover of lodgepole, and arrives at Timberline Lake (no camping or grazing, but fair fishing for golden to 7"). After skirting the shore of this lake (viewpoints for focusing the camera on Mt. Whitney and its reflection), the trail passes through a small meadow (good campsite) and descends down the narrow valley of Whitney Creek to the good campsites near Crabtree Ranger Station. Emergency services are available at the ranger station. Wood is adequate, and fishing in Whitney Creek is fair for golden (to 7"). (During times of heavy trail traffic, the hiker who wants more solitude may choose to camp at Upper Crabtree Meadow, ½ mile southwest of the Ranger Station, or Lower Crabtree Meadow, 1 mile southwest. These sites are reached by taking the Rock Creek trail at the junction west of the ranger station.)

3rd Hiking Day (Crabtree Ranger Station to Mirror Lake, 11 miles): Retrace steps of 2nd hiking day.

4th Hiking Day (Mirror Lake to Whitney Portal, 4 miles): Retrace steps of 1st hiking **day**.

TRIP   From WHITNEY PORTAL to WALLACE LAKE via Mirror Lake, Trail Crest, Crabtree Ranger Station and Wallace Creek (round trip). Topo map (15') Mt. Whitney; Profiles 17, 27. Best late season; 49 miles.

Grade	Trail/layover days	Total recommended days
Leisurely	7/3	10
Moderate	6/1	7
Strenuous	5/0	5

HILITES   Wallace Lake, lying in the heart of the Mt. Whitney region, is thought by many to be the finest fishing lake in the region. Well off the "beaten track" it is also a base from which to climb Mts. Barnard and Russell.

DESCRIPTION   (Moderate trip)

1st Hiking Day   (Whitney Portal to Mirror Lake, 4 miles): See 1st hiking day, trip 75.

2nd Hiking Day   (Mirror Lake to Crabtree Ranger Station, 11 miles): See 2nd hiking day, trip 76.

3rd Hiking Day   (Crabtree Ranger Station to Wallace Lake, 9.5 miles): From Crabtree Ranger Station our route branches right (north) onto a sandy trail and climbs the north slope of Whitney Creek canyon into a foxtail pine forest. On an overcast day, this foxtail forest, with its dead snags, fallen trees, and lack of ground cover, has an eerie, gloomy, otherworldly quality. The trail then switchbacks up to the junction with the Lower Crabtree Meadow/Army Pass trail. These switchbacks offer the hard-breathing hiker views of Mts. Hitchcock, Pickering and Chamberlain, and the flanks of Mt. Whitney, whose summit is over the horizon. From the ridge the route descends gently on a sandy trail through a moderate cover of lodgepole and foxtail to a ford (10636') of an unnamed creek. Beginning here the trail skirts what is called "Sandy Meadow" on the topo map, but it is neither flat nor grassy. Instead, it is a bowl whose lower slopes are bare and sandy. The small meadowy sections of trail that exist in the bowl lie beside several little streams not shown on the topo map, and in season they are graced with the yellow blossoms of groundsel and monkey flower. After these crossings the trail ascends a moderate slope with a lodgepole canopy and a heavy lupine ground cover to the saddle marked 10964' on the topo map. From this saddle the route descends gently on a sandy trail around the west shoulder of Mt.

Young. Leveling off, the trail winds among the massive boulders that make up a lateral moraine, and then leads down a rocky hillside from which the traveler has views of Mt. Ericsson, Tawny Point, Junction Peak, the flank of Mt. Tyndall, Mt. Williamson, Trojan Peak and, farthest right, Mt. Barnard. After the ford of a tributary of Wallace Creek the descent becomes gentle again, through a moderate cover of lodgepole, foxtail and whitebark pine. Beyond the next tributary ford the descent steepens, and the trail switchbacks ½ mile down to Wallace Creek. At the creek the High Sierra trail and the John Muir Trail, which have been "superimposed," diverge, the High Sierra trail turning left (west) toward Giant Forest and the Muir trail continuing north toward Yosemite. Our route turns right (east) up Wallace Creek canyon. Under a forest cover of sparse-to-moderate lodgepole the trail ascends gently amid sprinklings of western wallflower, pentstemon, groundsel, yarrow milfoil and Labrador tea. Contrary to the topo map trail, at the meadow where the outlet of Wales Lake joins Wallace Creek the trail fords the creek and then fords the tributary, staying on the south side of Wallace Creek. Here the ascent becomes moderate for a short distance, and then reverts to a gentler grade. This route up Wallace Creek canyon is sometimes indistinct and sometimes confused by multiple trail sections and inadequate ducking. Careful negotiation of the indistinct sections will bring one to the fair campsites at timberline (11400') about ½ mile below Wallace Lake, where wood is scarce. Those who prefer to camp at the lake will find sufficient shelter but no wood. Wallace Lake lies at the foot of the arête that connects Mt. Barnard with Tunnebora Peak. Fishing in Wallace Lake is good for golden (to 14"), and the same is true of Wales Lake, reached by cross country southwest from the inlet of Wallace Lake.

4th Hiking Day (Wallace Lake to Crabtree Ranger Station, 9.5 miles): Retrace steps of 3rd hiking day.

5th Hiking Day (Crabtree Ranger Station to Mirror Lake, 11 miles): Retrace steps of 2nd hiking day.

6th Hiking Day (Mirror Lake to Whitney Portal, 4 miles): Retrace steps of 1st hiking day.

TRIP   From WHITNEY PORTAL to MILESTONE BASIN via Mirror Lake, Trail Crest, Crabtree Ranger Station, Wallace Creek, Junction Meadow, Upper Kern River and Tyndall Creek (semiloop trip). Topo map (15') Mt. Whitney; Profiles 17, 27, 16. Best mid-to-late season; 64 miles.

Grade	Trail/layover days	Total recom- mended days
Leisurely	10/3	13
Moderate	8/2	10
Strenuous	6/1	7

HILITES This trip samples both well-traveled trails and little used trails, country above timberline and deep, dense forests. Milestone Basin, set under the giant finger of Milestone Mountain, is remote enough to suit the solitude-seeking hiker, and the lakes piscatorial enough to suit the most avid angler.

DESCRIPTION (Moderate trip)

1st Hiking Day (Whitney Portal to Mirror Lake, 4 miles): See 1st hiking day, trip 75.

2nd Hiking Day (Mirror Lake to Crabtree Ranger Station, 11 miles): See 2nd hiking day, trip 76.

3rd Hiking Day (Crabtree Ranger Station to Campsites, Upper Kern River, 9.5 miles): Follow the description of 3rd hiking day, trip 77 to the junction of the John Muir Trail and the High Sierra trail at Wallace Creek. Taking the High Sierra trail from this junction our route proceeds down Wallace Creek canyon on sandy underfooting, with views ahead of Mt. Kaweah and the Kaweah Peaks Ridge. The trail veers away from Wallace Creek and then meets it again after a short moderate descent on an exposed slope. Our trail passes campsites lining both sides as it winds among sparse-to-moderate lodgepole and a great variety of wildflowers, including fireweed, paintbrush, arnica, sulfur flower, wild buckwheat, pennyroyal, mountain pride and creamberry. After fording Wright Creek the trail descends more steeply through sparse lodgepole mixed with some foxtail pine. As the canyon widens and the trail veers more westerly, the timber cover diminishes almost to nothing, and the slope (hot in afternoon) is covered with manzanita, creamberry, hollyleaf redberry, mountain mahogany and Sierra chinquapin. The main splash of color in this chaparral is the red pentstemon, mountain pride. This exposed slope offers views down the great trough of the Kern River, south to Mt. Guyot and west to Kaweah Peaks Ridge. The descent now reaches the Canadian life zone as Jeffrey pines are seen, along with mountain juniper. Our route turns northward and traverses down the Kern Canyon wall to meet the Kern River trail, where it turns right (north), leaving the High Sierra trail. One mile up the canyon our route passes a roofless cabin that was a powder magazine used by crews constructing trails in this region. Beginning here there are several good campsites along the river, where firewood is ample and fishing is good for rainbow (to 10"). These are the Kern River rainbow, *Salmo gairdneri gilberti,* found only in the upper Kern River.

4th Hiking Day (Campsites, Upper Kern River to Milestone Basin, 6.5 miles): Once past the cabin, the trail ascends less steeply, and soon it reaches the ford of Tyndall Creek, difficult in early season. (Stock drift fence at the creek.) Beyond the ford, the trail becomes sandier and drier, and the red fir and aspen gradually disappear, leaving a forest cover of lodgepole and some foxtail that is sparse on the hillsides and moderate on the river terraces. There are numerous campsites along this stretch of trail, including a packer campsite ½ mile beyond the Tyndall Creek trail. Beyond the Tyndall Creek trail, our route becomes more exposed, with considerable sagebrush. The trail fords the outlet stream of Lake 11440 and soon comes to a dell thick with lodgepole trunks. The wildflower display in this large dell is dominated by groundsel, and includes also tiger lilies, swamp onion and red columbine. The trail ascends above the dell and passes through a bank of shield fern, Queen Anne's lace and bush chinquapin. Contrary to the topo map, the trail stays on the east side of the river. Our route ascends steeply through a sparse lodgepole cover on a rocky trail over granite slabs that rise 600′ to the upper Kern plateau. As of this writing, there is much evidence of dynamiting of the granite in the trailbed in this stretch, and yet many fallen trees block the way. The trail levels off and soon reaches the signed junction with the Milestone Basin trail, where our route turns left (west). From this junction, continue as in the last part of 2nd hiking day, trip 72.

5th Hiking Day (Milestone Basin to Tyndall Creek Tributary, 6.5 miles): Retrace steps of 2nd hiking day, trip 72, to the ford at the John Muir Trail/Shepherd Pass trail junction, where our route turns right (south) on the John Muir Trail. The rocky trail ascends gently along the east flank of Tawny Point through a sparse-to-moderate cover of lodgepole and foxtail pine past many poor campsites, and then arrives at the good campsites on a tributary of Tyndall Creek (11100′), near a small lake where swimming is good in late season. Firewood is adequate.

6th Hiking Day (Tyndall Creek Tributary to Crabtree Ranger Station, 9.5 miles): See 3rd hiking day, trip 80.

7th Hiking Day (Crabtree Ranger Station to Mirror Lake, 11 miles): See 2nd hiking day, trip 76.

8th Hiking Day (Mirror Lake to Whitney Portal, 4 miles): See 1st hiking day, trip 75.

TRIP   From WHITNEY PORTAL to CAMPSITES, KERN-KA-WEAH RIVER via Mirror Lake, Trail Crest, Crabtree Meadow, Wallace Creek, Junction Meadow (round trip). Topo map (15′) Mt. Whitney; Profiles 17, 27, 20. Best mid-to-late season; 61 miles.

Grade	Trail/layover days	Total recommended days
Leisurely	9/2	11
Moderate	8/1	9
Strenuous	6/1	7

HILITES   This route combines the high, rocky country along the Whitney crest with the alluvial meadows on the Kern River and the intimate camping on the little-visited Kern-Kaweah River canyon.

DESCRIPTION   (Moderate trip)

1st Hiking Day   (Whitney Portal to Mirror Lake, 4 miles): See 1st hiking day, trip 75.

2nd Hiking Day   (Mirror Lake to Crabtree Ranger Station, 11 miles): See 2nd hiking day, trip 76.

3rd Hiking Day   (Crabtree Ranger Station to Junction Meadow, 9.5 miles): See 3rd hiking day, trip 78 to junction of High Sierra trail and Kern River trail, where our trail turns left (south). From here the rocky trail descends steeply to Junction Meadow through stands of aspen and past occasional Jeffrey and lodgepole pines, the ground cover being manzanita and currant. As the trail levels off, it enters a parklike grove of stalwart Jeffrey pines that provide the setting for the good campsites on the Kern River (no grazing). It is interesting to note that the flora of this meadow are rooted in the highest alluvial deposit in the Kern Canyon. Firewood is adequate, and fishing is good for rainbow and some brook (to 10″).

4th Hiking Day   (Junction Meadow to Campsites, Kern-Kaweah River, 6 miles): This day's route is unmaintained and impassable to stock, but a knapsacker with any experience will have no trouble staying on the route. Soon after the ford of the Kern River (difficult in early season) the trail begins the steep ascent up the Kern canyon wall to the hanging valley above. Veering away from the Kern-Kaweah River, it ascends to the north side of a granite knob, or spine, and passes through what has been called "Kern-Kaweah Pass." This difficult climb is repaid by the delightful valley above it, one of the finest in the Sierra. From the "pass" the trail descends slightly to Rockslide Lake, with its crystal-clear, emerald-green water. Just beyond the lake, the canyon widens into a kind of granite amphitheater, where two tributary streams, meeting, dash into the main canyon over a rocky ledge, to meet the main river below the fall by which the river arrives at the bowl. The ascent through a sparse-to-moderate lodgepole cover is moderate as the trail threads the deep canyon lying between Kern Point and Picket Guard Peak. One more steep ascent is required to reach the bowl that contains Gallats Lake, a pond in a large, wet meadow (fishing is good for golden to 8″). Fair campsites are here, but the traveler will prefer those about one mile ahead where the trail turns away from the river toward Colby Pass. Firewood is ample, and fishing is excellent for golden (to 7″).

5th Hiking Day   (Campsites, Kern-Kaweah River to Junction Meadow, 6 miles): Retrace steps of 4th hiking day.

6th Hiking Day (Junction Meadow to Crabtree Ranger Station, 9.5 miles): Retrace steps of 3rd hiking day.

7th Hiking Day (Crabtree Ranger Station to Mirror Lake, 11 miles): Retrace steps of 2nd hiking day.

8th Hiking Day (Mirror Lake to Whitney Portal, 4 miles): Retrace steps of 1st hiking day.

TRIP   From WHITNEY PORTAL to SYMMES CREEK ROAD-
            END via Mirror Lake, Crabtree Meadow, Tyndall Creek,
            Shepherd Pass (shuttle trip). Topo map (15') Mt. Whit-
            ney; Profiles 17, 16. Best mid-to-late season; 39 miles.

Grade	Trail/layover days	Total recommended days
Leisurely	6/3	9
Moderate	5/2	7
Strenuous	4/0	4

HILITES   This high trip loops around "the Whitney group," the
            culmination of the Sierra spine, with five peaks stand-
            ing over 14000'. A spur trail will take the hiker to the
            highest point in the contiguous 48 states, 14495 feet
            above sea level. The vast panoramas of the upper
            Kern basin along this route are unequalled in the
            Sierra.

DESCRIPTION (Moderate trip)

1st Hiking Day (Whitney Portal to Mirror Lake, 4 miles): See 1st hiking day, trip 75.

2nd Hiking Day (Mirror Lake to Crabtree Ranger Station, 11 miles): See 2nd hiking day, trip 76.

3rd Hiking Day (Crabtree Ranger Station to Tyndall Creek Tributary, 9.5 miles): See description of 3rd hiking day, trip 77 to the
junction of the John Muir Trail and the High Sierra Trail. From
Wallace Creek, this day's route continues north on the John Muir
Trail. The sandy and rocky trail ascends moderately through a
sparse-to-moderate lodgepole cover, to an overlook that lensmen
will want to utilize for photographs of the Great Western Divide.
Here the trail becomes quite level as it crosses a sandy flat bearing a forest cover of lodgepole and foxtail pines. The trail crosses
Wright Creek via a rocky ford and passes good campsites located

east of the trail. From here, views are good up the valley of Wright Creek toward Mt. Tyndall, and the aspiring geologist will discern several terminal moraines athwart the valley. The trail passes a signed trail leading east, marked "Wright Lakes, 3.5 mi.," but this lateral, even though it shows on the topo map, peters out within 100 yards and cannot be found beyond that. From this sign, several short ascents separated by level stretches bring the hiker out onto Bighorn Plateau, where the panoramic view begins with Red Spur to the southwest and sweeps north along the Great Western Divide and east along the Kings-Kern Divide to Junction Peak. In addition, one can see, to the southeast, Mts. Whitney, Young and Russell. A small lake west of the trail presents great photographic possibilities in the morning, and any time of day is good for photographing the lateral moraine of the Tyndall Creek glacier, which follows a contour along the west side of the plateau. Color is provided by a large field of lupine sweeping up the slope to the east. From here a gentle descent on a rocky trail through a sparse foxtail cover leads to the good campsites (11100′) where the trail crosses the outlet of a small lake (no fish) which offers good swimming in late season. Firewood is ample.

4th Hiking Day (Tyndall Creek Tributary to Anvil Camp, 7.5 miles): As the day begins, the John Muir Trail descends gently on a rocky trail through a forest cover of mixed lodgepole and foxtail to the junction with the Shepherd Pass trail. Our route turns right (east) off the Muir Trail and begins a long, steady ascent up the meadowy, boulder-strewn upper basin of Tyndall Creek. Views improve constantly as the traveler gains elevation, and the peaks of the Great Western Divide take on new aspects as they are seen from new angles. To the north, the southern escarpment of Diamond Mesa hides an upper surface that is one of the most level areas in this region. The traveler who has read the incredible first chapter of Clarence King's *Mountaineering in the Sierra Nevada* may speculate on where King and Richard Cotter crossed the Kings-Kern Divide and traversed this basin on their way to ascending Mt. Tyndall — which, in naming, they believed to be the highest Sierra peak until they were on top of it and saw other, higher ones nearby. The appearance of Lake 12002 heralds the approach to Shepherd Pass (12050′), which from this side of the crest is merely the end of a long, gentle ascent. The east side of the pass is a total contrast, with its steep scree and talus slopes which are often not passable to stock until August. From the pass, the trail switchbacks down a 500′ scree slope into a gigantic, barren bowl scooped out by the plucking action of the Shepherd Creek glacier. Winding among boulders and topping a slight rise, the trail begins a moderate descent to timberline and a poor campsite near the junction with the Junction Pass trail. The rocky trail continues to descend moderately through a cover of sparse lodgepole to a ford of Shepherd Creek and the good campsites at Anvil Camp (10000′), where fishing for rainbow (to 9″) is fair, and firewood is adequate.

5th Hiking Day (Anvil Camp to Symmes Creek Roadend, 7 miles): See 1st hiking day, trip 71.

81

TRIP   From LODGEPOLE CAMPGROUND to RANGER LAKES via Silliman Pass (round trip). Topo map (15') Triple Divide Peak; Profile 18. Best mid-to-late season; 17 miles.

Grade	Trail/layover days	Total recom- mended days
Leisurely	2/1	3
Moderate	- - -	- - -
Strenuous	- - -	- - -

HILITES   Crossing the Silliman Crest on the boundary of Sequoia and Kings Canyon parks, this trip terminates at picturesque Ranger Lakes. Enroute, the trail passes through sedate fir forests, traces rambling brooks, and circles crystal clear lakes.

DESCRIPTION (Leisurely trip)

1st Hiking Day (Lodgepole Campground to Ranger Lakes, 8.5 miles): The trail crosses the Marble Fork Kaweah River via a bridge (6800'), and after a few yards of northerly travel turns west on a moderate ascent through a dense forest cover of fir and cedar. This ascent, over alternating rocky and sandy stretches, then turns north and levels to the first ford of Silliman Creek. These woods teem with wildlife, and the traveler is very apt to see a few mule deer, many squirrels, and a host of birds that will include Steller jay, pygmy nuthatch, Hammond flycatcher (until late summer), Williamson sapsucker, Brewer blackbird, fox sparrow and Lincoln sparrow. After two more fords of Silliman Creek, the trail continues the moderate up over duff and sand underfooting through patchy, dense stands of red and white fir and some meadow sections to Cahoon Gap (unmarked on the topo map). The trail then descends moderately to the ford of the unnamed tributary just south of the East Fork Clover Creek. One fourth mile beyond this ford the new trail fords the East Fork Clover Creek, and then turns east, passing the JO Pass trail. (This new trail that travels on the north side of the creek does not show on the topo map.) The sometimes gentle, sometimes moderate ascent up the East Fork Clover Creek witnesses the inclusion of lodgepole and silver pine in the forest cover, and as the trail approaches Twin Lakes, open ground stretches between the trees are a tide of colors. One will find rank, knee-high corn lily, blue and white lupine, white mariposa lily, orange wallflower, purple larkspur, lavender shooting star, white cinquefoil, violet aster and golden groundsel. The last mile to the heavily timbered flats around Twin

Lakes is a steep ascent, and the traveler may well contemplate a quick swim in the largest lake, whose shallow waters quickly warm to a midsummer's sun. This same lake has several campsites that are frequently utilized by contingents of Boy Scouts from nearby Wolverton Boy Scout Camp. Fishing at these lakes is poor. Continuing toward Silliman Pass, the view of the two large boulder stands of exfoliating granite (Twin Peaks) dominates the horizon during the steep progress to the pass' saddle. This ascent marks the end of the fir, and the almost exclusive domination of the lodgepole pine. At the pass (10165') one has a good view of flat-topped Mt. Silliman to the south, the heavily wooded Sugarloaf Creek drainage to the northeast, Glacier Ridge to the east, and the barren flats of the Tableland to the southeast. Unlike the topo map, the trail descent from the pass drops steeply and then turns north to the nose of a granite ridge before switchbacking down. From the switchbacks one has fine views of the dome called Sugarloaf. At the foot of the switchbacks a level, duff trail leads off to the larger of the Ranger Lakes (9180'), and to the excellent campsites on the southwest side of the lake. Firewood is abundant, and anglers working their way around the red fir, lodgepole and silver pine border of the shallow lake plying their art on the fair to good fishing for brook trout (to 8"), will also enjoy the carpet of shooting stars and the rose-purple blossom of the heather. A layover day spent in this pleasant environment will allow the traveler to visit the nearby scenic settings of Beville (rainbow and brook), Lost (brook) and Seville (brook) lakes.

2nd Hiking Day (Ranger Lakes to Lodgepole Campground, 8.5 miles): Retrace steps of 1st hiking day.

TRIP   From LODGEPOLE CAMPGROUND to SCAFFOLD MEADOWS via Silliman Pass, Ranger Lakes, Sugarloaf Valley (round trip). Topo map (15') Triple Divide Peak; Profile 18. Best mid or late season; 41 miles.

Grade	Trail/layover days	Total recommended days
Leisurely	6/2	8
Moderate	5/2	7
Strenuous	4/2	6

HILITES   Scaffold Meadows, the terminus of this long trip, makes a superb location for a base camp. From here, one can explore the upper reaches of several remote drainages, and in the course of these explorations enjoy some of the finest fishing of the Roaring River country.

DESCRIPTION (Leisurely trip)

1st Hiking Day (Lodgepole Campground to Ranger Lakes, 8.5 miles): See 1st hiking day, trip 81.

2nd Hiking Day (Ranger Lakes to Comanche Meadow, 5.5 miles): Rounding a rocky prominence on the east side of the larger of the Ranger Lakes, the faintly ducked trail undulates northward and circles Ball Dome past the turnoffs to Lost Lake and Seville Lake. Passing through a moderate-to-heavy forest cover of lodgepole and red fir (some Jeffrey and silver) the trail emerges at a meadowed crossing of the outlet stream from Seville Lake. The junctions for Seville Lake and the Marvin Pass trails are poorly marked, but the trails are clear. Keeping right, on the north side of Sugarloaf Creek, our route descends sometimes steadily and sometimes moderately over duff and sand underfooting. This descent crosses an unnamed tributary, and a short distance beyond passes another trail lateral to Marvin Pass. About ¼ mile farther on, the trail passes the South Fork Sugarloaf Creek trail (unmarked on the topo map), and then fords the rocky creek emptying Comanche Meadow (7680'). Good campsites will be found on Sugarloaf Creek before and after this ford. Firewood is abundant, and fishing for brook trout (to 8") is fair.

3rd Hiking Day (Comanche Meadow to Scaffold Meadows, 6.5 miles): The cattle that one is apt to see in the vicinity represent the last remaining grazing right of a cattleman in this part of the Park. One quarter mile after the ford the trail drops moderately on sandy underfooting over a heavily forested slope. The general downward course of this route is reflected in the presence of Jeffrey pine mixed with the lodgepole. The red fir stands are also showing inclusions of the lower-altitude white firs. As the trail levels out on the floor of Sugarloaf Valley, the dome from which the name is derived can be seen through the trees. More resistant than the surrounding rock, this granite island withstood the onslaught of the ice, and today stands as a round, smooth 1000'-high reminder of the ice river that formed the valley. Following the course of this old glacier through sporadic meadows, the trail veers away northerly from Sugarloaf Creek, and at the ford of its northernmost tributary passes another trail lateral to Marvin Pass. (This trail is not shown on the topo map.) On the east side of this wide, shallow ford, the trail passes more campsites before crossing a series of sharp wrinkles in the terrain to Ferguson Creek and still more campsites. Fording this creek via rocks, the trail then rounds a long, dry, timbered ridge nose before dropping down a steady slope to the drift fence just below Scaffold Meadows. Living up to its name, Roaring River can be heard a few yards to the left, and with this pleasant accompaniment the trail ascends the last, gentle ½ mile to the good, signed (Bluejay Camp) campsites (7360'). Wood is ample, and fishing for rainbow and some golden trout (to 10") is fair to good. Emergency services are available from the resident ranger, whose cabin is nearby.

Grazing is restricted to overnight — maximum of 12 head of stock. These campsites make a fine base camp for further explorations of the surrounding headwaters of Deadman Canyon Creek (see trip 84), Roaring River (see trip 74) and Brewer Creek.

4th Hiking Day (Scaffold Meadows to Comanche Meadow, 6.5 miles): Retrace steps of 3rd hiking day.

5th Hiking Day (Comanche Meadow to Ranger Lakes, 5.5 miles): Retrace steps of 2nd hiking day.

6th Hiking Day (Ranger Lakes to Lodgepole Campground, 8.5 miles): Retrace steps of 1st hiking day.

TRIP	From LODGEPOLE CAMPGROUND to RANGER MEADOW via Silliman Pass, Ranger Lakes, Sugarloaf Valley, Scaffold Meadows, Deadman Canyon, return via Elizabeth Pass, High Sierra Trail, Panther Gap (loop trip). Topo map (15') Triple Divide Peak; Profiles 18, 19, 21. Best late season; 50.5 miles.

Grade	Trail/layover days	Total recommended days
Leisurely	7/2	9
Moderate	6/2	8
Strenuous	5/2	7

HILITES   The climax of this trip is the high, wildflower-filled meadows at the head of Deadman Canyon. Seldom visited because of its remoteness, this glaciated canyon nestles against the craggy summits of Glacier Ridge in solitary splendor.

DESCRIPTION (Moderate trip)

1st Hiking Day (Lodgepole Campground to Ranger Lakes, 8.5 miles): See 1st hiking day, trip 81.

2nd Hiking Day (Ranger Lakes to Comanche Meadow, 5.5 miles): See 2nd hiking day, trip 82.

3rd Hiking Day (Comanche Meadow to Scaffold Meadows, 6.5 miles): See 3rd hiking day, trip 82.

4th Hiking Day (Scaffold Meadows to Upper Ranger Meadow, 7 miles): Our route passes the Avalanche Pass/Cedar Grove trail and the Cloud Canyon/Colby Pass trail, and, leaving Scaffold

Meadows, continues south while veering away from the river on a steady-to-moderate ascent. Views back over one's left shoulder include a fine example of a lateral moraine in the form of Moraine Ridge, the northeast wall of the canyon. About 1½ miles beyond the junctions mentioned above, our route ascends past the upper drift fence and several more campsites. Flowers seen during this short stretch include buckwheat, sagebrush, Indian paintbrush, white Mariposa, pennyroyal, pentstemon and shooting star. Continuing past the drift fence, the trail fords Deadman Canyon Creek, passes a packer campsite, and then the Moniere gravesite. Located at the north end of a large, wet meadow, about 50 yards southeast of the campsite cited above, the grave marks the derivation of the name Deadman Canyon. The citation on the grave reads: "Here reposes Alfred Moniere, sheepherder, mountain man, 18-- to 1887." This ascent continues along the east bank of the creek, offering good views up the canyon of the spectacularly smoothed, unjointed, barren walls. Crossing another long, wet meadow, the trail then refords the creek (the ford is marked by lush clumps of lupine and tiger lily) and climbs alongside a dramatic, green-water, granite slab chute. At the end of this ascent, the trail levels out as it passes through a dense stand of lodgepole and fir, and, passing a campsite, emerges at the north end of the open grasslands of Ranger Meadow. The precipitous canyon walls dominate the views while crossing the meadow, and the cirque holding Big Bird Lake is clear on the west wall. By midsummer, the meadow is a colorful carpet of wildflowers including shooting star, pentstemon, Labrador tea and red heather. From Ranger Meadow the trail resumes its steady ascent over duff and sand through stands of lodgepole and clumps of aspen. As the trail crowns the Upper Ranger Meadow flat, one has awesome glimpses of the headwall of the Deadman Canyon cirque, and this view continues to rule the skyline from the good campsites just beyond the drift fence at the north end of Upper Ranger Meadow. Firewood is ample, and fishing for rainbow, brook and hybrids is good (to 10″). One should not miss visiting scenic, deep, sheer-walled Big Bird Lake just a short climb to the southwest.

5th Hiking Day (Upper Ranger Meadow to Public Campground, Bearpaw Meadow, 11 miles): Just south of the campsites cited above the trail passes the spur trail leading to Big Bird Lake, and ascends gently across grassy Upper Ranger Meadow. Low-lying willows line the stream, and clumps of wildflowers dot the green expanse. The trail turns somewhat southeast as the ascent steepens to a moderate grade, and as it begins the steep ascent of the headwall, it parallels a dramatic series of cascades and falls. Near the top of the falls the trail fords the stream below a long, dashing granite chute, and climbs steeply by a faint, infrequently ducked route up the southwest wall of the cirque. This barren, rocky climb over light-colored granite slabs contrasts with the darker granite (around an old copper-mine site) seen to the east, and this contrast is even more marked from the tiny saddle of Elizabeth Pass (11360′). Views to the southwest include parts of the Middle Fork Kaweah River watershed, and the jumbled peaks of the southernmost prominences of the Tableland divide. From the pass, the ducked trail descends steeply via a long, smooth granite trough to a ford of an unnamed tributary that cascades and plunges down into River Valley. After a moderately descending traverse, the trail descends the steep northern wall of River Valley via a series of rocky switchbacks. At the foot of these zig-zags, our route passes the spur trail to Lonepine Meadow and Tamarack Lake, and then swings southwesterly across the sparsely timbered nose of the ridge above Bearpaw Meadow. (The trail continuing south, down River Valley, indicated on the topo map, is no longer maintained, and is hazardous during high water.) The descent from this ridge is steep, rocky and dry as it passes through stands of lodgepole and red fir and joins the High Sierra Trail ¼ mile north of Bearpaw Meadow. Our route turns right onto the High Sierra Trail for about 100 yards, and then branches left (south) on a 200-yard descent to the good campsites at the signed campground overlooking the Middle Fork Kaweah River canyon. Firewood is ample. Emergency services are available from the ranger station at Bearpaw Meadow, ½ mile east.

6th Hiking Day (Public Campground, Bearpaw Meadow to Lodgepole Campground, 12 miles): See 1st hiking day, trip 85.

 84

TRIP   From LODGEPOLE CAMPGROUND to CEDAR GROVE via Silliman Pass, Ranger Lakes, Sugarloaf Valley, Scaffold Meadows, Avalanche Pass, Bubbs Creek (shuttle trip). Topo maps (15') Triple Divide Peak, Marion Peak; Profiles 18, 13. Best late season; 35.5 miles.

Grade	Trail/layover days	Total recommended days
Leisurely	5/2	7
Moderate	4/2	6
Strenuous	4/1	5

HILITES   Touring the little-tramped Roaring River country, this route enters by Silliman Pass and emerges via Avalanche Pass. The many lakes and side trails found along the way offer the solitude-seeker respite from the "racetracks" of the more popular trails.

DESCRIPTION *(Leisurely trip)*
1st Hiking Day (Lodgepole Campground to Ranger Lakes, 8.5 miles): See 1st hiking day, trip 81.

2nd Hiking Day (Ranger Lakes to Comanche Meadow, 5.5 miles): See 2nd hiking day, trip 82.

3rd Hiking Day   (Comanche Meadow to Scaffold Meadows, 6.5 miles): See 3rd hiking day, trip 82.

4th Hiking Day   (Scaffold Meadows to Campsite, Sphinx Creek Ford, 9 miles): See 7th hiking day, trip 74.

5th Hiking Day   (Campsite, Sphinx Creek Ford to Cedar Grove Roadend, 6 miles): See 8th hiking day, trip 74.

 85

TRIP	From LODGEPOLE CAMPGROUND to WHITNEY PORTAL via Hamilton Lake, Kaweah Gap, Upper Funston Meadow, Junction Meadow, Wallace Creek, Crabtree Meadow and Trail Crest (shuttle trip). Topo maps (15′) Triple Divide Peak, Kern Peak, Mt. Whitney; Profiles 21, 27, 17. Best mid-to-late season; 72 miles.	

Grade	Trail/layover days	Total recommended days
Leisurely	11/4	15
Moderate	9/3	12
Strenuous	7/2	9

HILITES   Most of this dramatic trans-Sierra route follows the High Sierra Trail — a trail that is, in its early stages, literally carved out of the rock. Crossing the Great Western Divide, it descends to the Kern Trench, and emerges on the east side at Whitney Portal. The scenic terrain it visits, and the fine trout waters it crosses or camps near, make it a justly famous and popular route.

DESCRIPTION   (Moderate trip)

1st Hiking Day   (Lodgepole Campground to Public Campground, Bearpaw Meadow, 12 miles): The first 2.5 miles of this trip follow an old road that ascends in a long Z through meadows and dense, dry fir and Jeffrey pine stands covering the slope between Lodgepole Campground (6800′) and the Wolverton Ski Hut parking circle. One may elect to park his car at this parking circle (7250′), and thereby reduce the length of this hiking day. To join the trail from the parking circle, take the marked trail at the northeast side of the circle, and join the main trail (as per the topo map) a few yards beyond. Through dense stands of fir and Jeffrey, the duff and dust trail ascends steadily as it turns southeast, and passes the trail junction to Pear and Heather lakes. The trail crosses Panther

Meadow, and climbs through sparse timber to Panther Gap. Our route then continues eastward on a moderate ascent that brings the traveler to the point of the first breath-taking views south and southeast across the Middle Fork Kaweah River. It is these continuing views that make this trip such a scenic wonder. After descending steeply by switchbacks, the trail crosses Merten Creek (campsites nearby), and then resumes its steep descent through moderate stands of red fir, white fir and some Jeffrey. Wildflowers along the trail include lupine, forget-me-not, pennyroyal, pentstemon, and elderberry. As the trail levels out, it meets and turns east onto the High Sierra Trail and passes the Redwood Meadow trail, dropping down into the canyon. Our trail does not follow a "natural" route, but instead stays high on the north wall of the Middle Fork Kaweah River canyon. It is not a level traverse. Frequently, the trail undulates over 400' rises, only to drop down into a secondary tributary canyon, and then emerge to climb again. From the above junction, the trail descends to ford an unnamed tributary and then climb steeply. Views are all to the south and southeast, where the spectacular granite dome formations of Sugarbowl Dome and Castle Rocks rise above the timbered floor. With each ford of the unnamed tributaries flowing from the slopes of Alta Peak, the trail passes precariously perched campsites, and then as it rounds a hot, dry, sparsely timbered slope to the Buck Creek ford (bridge), it passes the Moose Lake trail. The high waters of 1967 washed out a piece of the trail immediately after the ford of Buck Creek, but the route is passable as it ascends through a dense fir forest cover to the signed turnoff to the campground 200 yards south. Here, good campsites (7700') enjoy fine views of the canyon to the south and southwest. Wood is ample. Emergency services are available from the ranger station at Bearpaw Meadow, ½ mile east.

2nd Hiking Day (Public Campground, Bearpaw Meadow to Hamilton Lakes, 5 miles): Returning to the High Sierra Trail, our route turns right (east), and 100 yards farther passes the Elizabeth Pass trail. A short distance beyond this junction, the trail passes by Bearpaw Meadow, said to have been named by early stockmen who found a bear's paw nailed to a tree. Today, most of the meadow is devoted to the outbuildings of Bearpaw Lodge (advance reservations for beds and board are advisable). Just across the trail from the lodge is the ranger's rustic cabin. The magnificent views from the meadow and the subsequent trail include Mt. Stewart and Eagle Scout Peak on the Great Western Divide, Black Kaweah beyond, the Yosemite-like depths of Hamilton Creek and Middle Fork Kaweah River, and the Cliff Creek drainage below. Continuing past Bearpaw Ranger Station, the trail descends moderately through mixed, sparse forest stands of red and white fir and yellow pine. As the trail rounds the slope and descends to River Valley, it traverses a section blasted from an immense, exfoliating granite slab. Educational views of clearcut avalanche chutes on the south wall of the canyon accompany the descent to the bridge fording the Middle Fork Kaweah River. (The trail indicated on the topo map ascending River Valley is no longer maintained.) This stream cascades and plunges down a narrow granite chasm below the bridge, and the force of the torrent is clear evidence of the cutting power of the water. From the bridge, the trail ascends an exposed slope, and, after it rounds the nose of the ridge separating the Tamarack Lake and Hamilton Lakes drainages, it passes a trail lateral to Elizabeth Pass. (This trail is not shown on the topo map, and the trail indicated on the topo switchbacking down into the Middle Fork Kaweah River valley is no longer maintained, and is not signed.) Continuing the steady ascent, the traveler is overwhelmed with the gigantic scale of the rock sculpting by ice, rock and snow to the east and southeast. The trail surface, while mostly rocky, passes occasional clumps of brightly colored wildflowers, including scarlet gilia, Douglas phlox, fleabane, Indian paintbrush, pentstemon, mountain blue-bell, red columbine and larkspur. Overhead, the mixed forest cover, mostly in sparse stands, includes black oak, juniper, Jeffrey and sugar pine. Overshadowing the final climb to the ford of Hamilton Creek, the sheer granite wall to the north called Angels Wing, the sharply pointed granite sentinels atop the south wall, and the wall's avalanche-chuted sides are a constant source of wonderment and awe. The trail climbs alongside the stream and then boulder-hops across just below the lowest lake of the Hamilton Lakes chain. From this ford the trail climbs steeply over shattered rock to the good improved campsites at the northwest end of Lake 8235. Views from the campsites, including the silver waterfall ribbon at the east end, are superlative, but firewood is scarce owing to the heavy and concentrated camper impact. Fishing for brook and rainbow (to 10") is fair to good.

3rd Hiking Day (Hamilton Lakes to Campsites, Big Arroyo Trail Junction, 7 miles): The steep climb to Kaweah Gap is an engineering marvel of trail construction, which has literally blasted the way along vertical cliff sections. Beginning at the northwest end of the lake, the trail ascends steadily through an open forest cover of juniper and red fir with constant views of the lake and its dramatic walls. Despite the rocky terrain, many wildflowers line this ascent, and among the manzanita and chinquapin one will find lush lupine, yellow columbine, pentstemon, Indian paintbrush, white cinque-foil, false Solomon seal and Douglas phlox. After some doubling back the trail turns south on a steep ascent to a point just above the north shore of the uppermost of the Hamilton Lakes. The jagged summits of the peaks of the Great Western Divide dominate the skyline to the east during the final, tarn-dotted ascent to the U-shaped Kaweah Gap, but as one approaches the gap one can see the equally spectacular summits of the Kaweah Peaks Ridge beyond. This colorful ridge governs the views from Kaweah Gap (10700'), and it is not until the east-side descent that one can see the Nine Lake Basin watershed to the north and the Little Five Lakes basin to the south. Those with a bent for exploring barren high country, or interested in the good brook-trout fishing, may elect to detour across granite slab and ledge routes north to the Nine Lake Basin. Our trail continues its steady-to-moderate southerly descent along the west side of the headwarters of Big Arroyo Creek, crossing over to the east side midway down. This descent crosses unjointed granite broken by substantial pockets of grass and numerous runoff streams (even in late season) and the open stretches afford fine views of the U-shaped, glacially wrought Big

Arroyo below, and the white, red and black rocks of Black and Red Kaweah peaks to the east. The trail then re-enters timber cover (lodgepole) and arrives at the good campsites along the stream (9800'). These campsites are about ¼ mile above the Little Five Lakes/Black Rock Pass trail junction. Fishing for brook trout to 7" is fair to good, and firewood is abundant. For those anglers with extra time, the short (2-mile) side trip to Little Five Lakes offers fine angling for golden.

4th Hiking Day (Campsites, Big Arroyo Trail Junction to Moraine Lake, 8.5 miles): Continuing past the Little Five Lakes trail junction, the trail there begins a long, steady traverse of the north side of Big Arroyo which culminates at the Chagoopa Plateau. This route parallels the course of a trunk glacier that once filled Big Arroyo, overflowed the benches 3 miles on either side, and contributed to the main glacier of Kern Canyon. As our route climbs the wall of this trough, one has the feeling of climbing through geologic ages as he treads over glacial outwash that dates back to Pleistocene times. The timber cover of this ascent is sparse, but there is no shortage of wildflowers tucked among the sage, manzanita and chinquapin. Most colorful are the yellow columbine, Indian paintbrush and lupine. The sparse forest cover increases in density near the Chagoopa Plateau, and one will find lodgepole and foxtail, and an occasional juniper. The ascent levels off near a small, mirror-faced tarn, and, swinging away north from the lip of Big Arroyo, it begins a gradual descent through alternating timber and meadow stretches. Tree-interrupted views of the jagged Great Western Divide skyline accompany the descent to the meadowed junction, on the south side of the tributary of Chagoopa Creek (the topo map is incorrect in showing the ford and reford of this stream). At this junction our route leaves the High Sierra Trail, branching right (south) through meadowed clumps of shooting star. This descent becomes steeper (moderate) over a coarse granite sand, through dense stands of lodgepole and foxtail pine. It is time well spent during this descent to step a few yards to the west of the trail for the superlative views down into Big Arroyo and across the Arroyo to the drainages of Soda and Lost Canyon creeks. This steady down-winding trail brings one to the wooded shores of Moraine Lake. Excellent campsites on the south side of the lake (9290') provide lake-fronted views back to the Kaweah Peaks. Firewood is abundant, and fishing for brook trout (to 12") is good.

5th Hiking Day (Moraine Lake to Kern Hot Spring, 8 miles): Crossing the rather old moraine just east of Moraine Lake, the trail turns north through a long, beautiful meadow, and passes an old stockman's cabin before rejoining the High Sierra Trail at Sky Parlor Meadow. Views back across this lupine-filled grassland, particularly of the Kaweahs and Red Spur, are excellent. Turning right (east) onto the High Sierra Trail, one begins the first moderate and then steep descent into the Kern Trench. The initial descent sees the lodgepole being replaced by the lower-altitude red fir, white fir, and Jeffrey pine; and still lower down, the trail descends steeply through manzanita and snowbrush that are overshadowed by an occasional juniper and oak. Views of the unmistakably U-shaped Kern Trench, typical of glacially formed valleys, are instructive — particularly to the south. The final climb down to the valley floor is accomplished via a series of steep, rocky switchbacks generally paralleling the plunging drop of Funston Creek. At the Kern Canyon floor, our route turns north (upstream) and retraces the steps of part of the 4th hiking day, trip 73 to Kern Hot Spring. Firewood is adequate, and fishing is good for Kern River rainbow (to 18″) and possibly some brown trout.

6th Hiking Day (Kern Hot Spring to Junction Meadow, 7 miles): Retrace steps of most of 4th hiking day, trip 73.

7th Hiking Day (Junction Meadow to Crabtree Ranger Station, 9.5 miles): The trail leaves the parklike Jeffrey pines of Junction Meadow and ascends steeply on rocky underfooting over a slope covered by manzanita and currant. Views down the Kern Trench improve constantly, as the occasional Jeffrey, lodgepole and aspen offer frames for the lensman who would compose a "shot" of the great cleft. After one mile the route arrives at the junction of the Kern River trail and the High Sierra trail, where it turns right (southeast) back toward Wallace Creek Canyon. From here, retrace steps of most of 3rd hiking day, trip 78.

8th Hiking Day (Crabtree Ranger Station to Mirror Lake, 11 miles): See 2nd hiking day, trip 76.

9th Hiking Day (Mirror Lake to Whitney Portal, 4 miles): See 1st hiking day, trip 75.

 86

TRIP   From COTTONWOOD CREEK ROADEND TO HORSE-SHOE MEADOW (loop trip). Topo map (15′) Olancha; Profile 22. Best early season; 8 miles.

Grade	Trail/layover days	Total recom- mended days
Leisurely	2/0	2
Moderate	- - -	- - -
Strenuous	- - -	- - -

HILITES   Long given over to the utilitarian purposes of stockmen, Horseshoe Meadow is now a pleasant wilderness retreat. Dense forests, clear streams and wildflower-dotted meadowland line the route of this weekend trip, making it a fine choice for the beginner and the experienced backpacker.

DESCRIPTION (Leisurely trip)

1st Hiking Day   (Cottonwood Creek Roadend to Upper Horseshoe Meadow, 4 miles): The newly extended road leaving Hiway 395 south of Lone Pine now rounds the south shoulder of Wonoga Peak, and terminates just west of the old Cottonwood Sawmill site (the sawmill was burned by vandals in 1965). The trailhead (9520') is located just west of the roadend pack station, and the trail leaves the road on a gentle ascent through a dense stand of lodgepole and foxtail pine. At a signed junction ⅛ mile beyond the trailhead, our route passes the Mulkey Meadow/Horseshoe Meadow trail, and continues west on a steady ascent. Along the trail, the traveler will find patches of sweet-smelling lupine, delicate pentstemon, low-lying, pink pussypaws, ochre-red Indian paintbrush, yellow monkey flower, and isolated representatives of the showy columbine. Underfoot, the sand-and-duff trail of the densely forested trailhead area gives way to rock and sand as the trail climbs. Then, leveling out on the east fringes of open meadowland, the footing reverts to duff and sand. Cottonwood Creek, now close on the left, is frequently willow-choked, but the more open stretches reveal it to be a placid, clear-running stream — ideal for fly-rod action. Beaver reintroduced in this region in the 1940s have flooded many of these meadows with their penchant for damming running water. As a consequence, government officials of the Forest Service and the DF&G differ as to their continued value on this drainage. Rarely seen during daylight hours, these rodents still inhabit these waters, and a little scouting around should reveal some of their latest handiwork. The trail swings northward, and then branches left away from the Golden Trout Camp trail at the signed junction. Immediately thereafter the trail fords Cottonwood Creek, and, after passing an unmarked trail (branching right) which ascends the South Fork, continues southerly to ford the South Fork Cottonwood Creek. This trail section is newly constructed; the lateral (no longer maintained) shown on the topo map leading to mid-Horseshoe Meadow branches left from our route before the ford. Our route then crosses the ridge to the south, staying close under the south face of the granite prominence marked 10661, and descends to join the Cottonwood Pass trail at the stockman's line cabin at the head of Horseshoe Meadow (this newly constructed trail is not shown on the topo map). Good campsites can be found along the creek above the 75-year old line cabin, where firewood is abundant. Fishing for brook trout is good (to 10").

2nd Hiking Day   (Upper Horseshoe Meadow to Cottonwood Creek Roadend, 4 miles): Winding east on a long, gently descending grade, our route sticks to the densely timbered northern fringe of Horseshoe Meadow. Views of these meadows, flanked by symmetrical Trail Peak, are excellent. Those getting on the trail early in the morning are sure to come upon a few late-grazing deer, and along with many other birds they may well make a sighting of the long-eared owl, a resident of these grasslands. Usually, this predatory bird is seen while swooping down upon its prey (meadow mice, deer mice and other rodents) but in very early season it is sometimes seen in family groups among the willows near the stream. Early-season anglers will find the going along the stream very wet going in the flooded meadow sections, but the fishing for brook trout continues to be good. Near the east end of the long meadow, the sometimes faint trail passes the Mulkey Pass/Mulkey Meadow trail (branching south), and veers northerly across a gentle, densely wooded saddle. Just beyond this saddle the trail passes another turnoff to Mulkey Pass/Mulkey Meadow, and then switchbacks down steadily to the Cottonwood Creek ford. Ascending on the north side of the ford, the trail meets the Golden Trout Camp/Cottonwood Creek Roadend trail, where our route turns right for the short remaining ⅛ mile to the roadend.

TRIP   From COTTONWOOD CREEK ROADEND to SOUTH FORK LAKES, return via cross country down South Fork Cottonwood Creek (loop trip). Topo map (15′) Olancha; Profile 22. Best mid or late season; 13.5 miles.

Grade	Trail/layover days	Total recommended days
Leisurely	2/1	3
Moderate	- - -	- - -
Strenuous	- - -	- - -

HILITES   A fine weekend loop trip, this route affords grand scenery, and a good exposure to east-side ecology that will benefit both beginner and old hand.

DESCRIPTION (Leisurely trip)

1st Hiking Day (Cottonwood Creek Roadend to South Fork Lakes, 7 miles): Proceed to the junction where the route described in the 1st hiking day, trip 86, leaves the Golden Trout Camp trail, where our route continues north. This steadily ascending route follows close along the east side of Cottonwood Creek, traverses a long meadow, and then passes Golden Trout Camp, a private resort. Here, our route passes the Little Cottonwood Creek trail branching east, and then swings west, passing through meadow clearings and moderate-to-dense stands of lodgepole and foxtail pine. The ascent levels during these meadow stretches, and then the trail begins a steady ascent that passes a trail which parallels our route up the creek drainage. Our route fords Cottonwood Creek midway between Golden Trout Camp and Cottonwood Lakes, and continues up a steep slope covered with willow and foxtail pine to the South Fork Lakes trail junction. Keeping to the right, our route ascends the steep morainal switchbacks, climbing eastward to the meadowed foot of the lowest of the Cottonwood Lakes chain (Lake 11005). Passing another trail that rounds the north side of the lake, our route follows the well-defined south-shore route across rolling tundra. (Note: All the Cottonwood Lakes are closed to fishing.) These lakes were used at one time for research and breeding of golden trout. Beyond this lake the trail touches the south shore of a lake just to the east, and then turns southward on an undulating ascent through and across a "rock garden." This rock-garden route is a slight deviation from the route indicated on the topo map, and from the point where the trail turns west-northwest a short spur trail descends a few yards to the good campsites at the west end of the westernmost of the South Fork Lakes (11000'). These campsites are located in a grove of sparse foxtail pine with fine views of Cirque Peak to the west. Firewood is ample, and fishing for golden is poor (fry). Anglers will fare better at nearby Cirque Lake and the easternmost of the South Fork Lakes.

2nd Hiking Day (South Fork Lakes to Cottonwood Creek Roadend, 6.5 miles, part cross country): With the raucous squall of the Clark nutcracker echoing around the rocks, the traveler works his way across the rocky, tarn-dotted terrain to the east of the lake. Intermittent seepage leads the way to the easternmost of the South Fork Lakes, where anglers can try for the lake's golden trout (to 7"). Keeping on the north and then the east side of the outlet stream, this route descends east and then south over heavily fractured granite to a timbered (foxtail) saddle where the stream cascades and falls from one rocky grotto to another. Clumps of shooting star topped by showy yellow columbine and orange tiger lily line the stream, and, as the route descends down the rocky draw, it meets a faint fisherman's trail just north of the large meadow section at the foot of the first descent. Old blazes mark the way when the trail disappears in the duff sections, but when in doubt one should keep to the north side of the stream. This route, following the creek's course, swings east, and enters another meadow with an old notched-log cabin at its head. From the east end of this meadow, the trail drops down to Cottonwood Creek on a clearly used northeasterly traverse. This traverse joins the Cottonwood Pass trail, and together they ford Cottonwood Creek to effect a junction with the trail described in the 1st hiking day. Our route turns south and retraces the steps of the 1st hiking day.

TRIP   From COTTONWOOD CREEK ROADEND to UPPER ROCK CREEK LAKE via Army Pass (round trip). Topo maps (15') Olancha, Kern Peak; Profile 23. Best mid or late season; 27 miles.

Grade	Trail/layover days	Total recommended days
Leisurely	4/4	8
Moderate	3/4	7
Strenuous	2/4	6

HILITES   Beautiful Rock Creek and its spectacular headwaters are the goal of this high-country trip. The tiny, unnamed lake at the end of this trip makes a fine base camp for further exploration of Mitre Basin and the Soldier Lake Chain.

DESCRIPTION   (Leisurely trip)
1st Hiking Day   (Cottonwood Creek Roadend to South Fork Lakes, 7 miles): See 1st hiking day, trip 87.

2nd Hiking Day   (South Fork Lakes to Upper Rock Creek Lake, 6.5 miles): From the westernmost of the South Fork Lakes, the trail ascends through thinning timber to Long Lake. At the east end of the lake our route passes a lateral branching east to the upper Cottonwood Lakes, and then begins a long, steadily rising traverse that takes the traveler above the campsites at the west end of Long Lake. Views of the lake from this traverse are favorites of photographers, but it is wise to save some film for the panoramic shots farther up. This traverse brings one above timberline, and the remainder of the climb is accomplished over granite slopes covered only with grass, willows and wildflowers. The first step of the climb tops a series of glacially smoothed ledges, and touches the south edge of granitoid High Lake. A pause for a drink of the icy water at High Lake's outlet will brace one for the forthcoming rocky switchbacks. The higher one climbs up this cirque wall, the better the views to the east of the lakes immediately below and of the Cottonwood Creek drainage. One frequently sights a scurrying marmot on the cirque floor, and their piping accompanies the hiker all the way to New Army Pass. At the summit (12300′) one should walk southwest on the knifelike crest for the majestic views across the Kern Trench to the Kaweah Peaks and the Great Western Divide. Back to the east, one can see across the Owens Valley to the White Mountains, and, on a clear day, make out the Saline Valley and Ubehebe Crater beyond. To the north towers the Mt. Whitney complex, and nearer one can make out the cirque basins of upper Mitre Basin. Descending from Army Pass into Sequoia National Park, the trail crosses a long, barren slope of coarse granite sand sprinkled with exfoliated granite boulders. Seepages with attendant grassy strips appear like creeping tendrils below, and up closer they are seen to be dotted with clumps of lupine. A few yards down this steady descent, our trail passes the trail that branches right to Old Army Pass. This pass, about ¼ mile to the northeast, was the original pass constructed by an army troop stationed in Owens Valley in the 1890s. Beyond this junction the route swings west and descends steadily over rocky trail, and then across run-off eroded meadow sections. The trail then re-enters a sparse-to-moderate forest cover of foxtail pine, and shortly thereafter passes a signed trail to Siberian Pass. There are excellent campsites on the south side of the stream just east of this junction (excellent grazing). Our route keeps to the right, continuing to descend through denser forest cover that includes lodgepole pine, and when the forest cover gives way to the open spaces of a lovely meadow, our trail meets and turns left onto the Rock Creek trail. This trail descends steeply alongside a willow-infested tributary of Rock Creek until the rocky slope gives way to the meadows just above Upper Rock Creek Lake. (This name is not employed on the topo map, but is generally used by mountaineers who frequent this country.) Around these meadows one may sight the relatively rare white-tailed jackrabbit. There are good campsites at the head of this meadow, but better ones are located at the lake outlet. These campsites are reached by fording Rock Creek and rounding the northern edge of the lake. Firewood is ample, grazing is fair and fishing for golden (to 10″) in the lake and adjoining stream is good to excellent. Several marmot families live in the granite to the north. This meadowed lake site makes a grand base camp for side trips to the rugged Mitre Basin and the adjoining "Soldier Lakes" (just south of The Major General). Fishing for golden in most of the lakes below the Mitre and The Major General is good, but the season is usually very short because of late ice melt. Other fine side trips include a looping cross-country exploration of the Boreal Plateau via Siberian Outpost; or the hardy and experienced knapsacker with a yen for adventure may wish to take the Guyot Flat trail to Crabtree Meadow and then take the scrambling cross-country route up the Crabtree Lakes chain which rounds Mt. Chamberlin, Mt. Newcomb, Mt. Pickering and Joe Devel Peak and returns via Mitre Basin.

3rd Hiking Day (Upper Rock Creek Lake to South Fork Lakes, 6.5 miles): Retrace steps of 2nd hiking day.

4th Hiking Day (South Fork Lakes to Cottonwood Creek Roadend, 7 miles): Retrace steps of 1st hiking day.

 89

TRIP	From COTTONWOOD CREEK ROADEND to UPPER ROCK CREEK LAKE via Army Pass, return via Siberian Pass, Big Whitney Meadow, Cottonwood Pass, Horseshoe Meadow (loop trip). Topo maps (15′) Olancha, Kern Peak; Profiles 23, 24. Best mid or late season; 29 miles.

Grade	Trail/layover days	Total recommended days
Leisurely	5/4	9
Moderate	4/4	8
Strenuous	3/4	7

HILITES   One of the finest loop trips in the Sierra, this route
tours peaks of spectacle and grandeur, visits unforgettable lakes, traces streams that plummet, seep
and meander, and blends them all together with a
carpet of green forest and open meadows that will
impress all who come with a sense of accomplishment and peace.

DESCRIPTION (Leisurely trip)
1st Hiking Day (Cottonwood Creek Roadend to South Fork Lakes,
7 miles): See 1st hiking day, trip 87.

2nd Hiking Day   (South Fork Lakes to Upper Rock Creek Lake,
6.5 miles): See 2nd hiking day, trip 88.

3rd Hiking Day (Upper Rock Creek Lake to Big Whitney Meadow,
6.5 miles): This hiking day begins by retracing the steps (1.5 miles)
to the meadowed Siberian Pass trail junction passed during the 2nd
hiking day. The trail from this junction ascends southward moderately over a densely forested slope of foxtail and lodgepole pine. An
old burn that swept over this hillside has left many darkened
stumps that, with subsequent wind and rain weathering, have
achieved beautiful sculptured forms. Overhead, the eastward-
pointing tree tops (prevailing wind) combine with the fire evidence
on the ground to give an otherworldly feeling to the whole hillside
— an impression that becomes even stronger as the trail crosses
the eastern end of barren Siberian Outpost. Named for its bleak
appearance in 1895 by Harvey Corbett, the entire area has the
look of a sterile meadow. (Most of the surface is a coarse granite
sand deposited as a result of mechanical and chemical erosion
of nearby granite slabs.) Grassy strips follow seepage lines as
they drain west from the trail, but otherwise the landscape seems
lifeless. After crossing the second "finger" of Siberian Outpost,
the trail ascends gently past a snowmarker site to the easy rise
called Siberian Pass (10900') and leaves Sequoia National Park.
At the pass our route passes the junction with the Lower Rock
Creek trail. The descent from this pass is steep at first, but becomes moderate to steady as it nears Big Whitney Meadow. The
moderate forest cover of foxtail pine near the pass increases in
density, and later includes lodgepole. Our trail crosses the headwaters of Golden Trout Creek midway down the descent, and
then, climbing gently, crosses a ridge before descending a moderate slope to the western edge of Big Whitney Meadow (several
campsites here). The underfooting of most of this descent has
been dust and some rock, but as it nears the meadow it is mostly
sand. Mats of yellow monkey flower color the forest floor, and as
the trail emerges in the opener sections, one finds lupine, pentstemon, white cinquefoil and sagebrush. Keeping to the forest
fringes on the west side of the very large grassland, our trail passes
the Cottonwood Pass trail, and a few yards beyond arrives at the
fair packer and primitive campsites at the Rocky Basin Lakes
trail junction. These campsites are just north of the Big Whitney
Tourist Pasture (fenced). Firewood is abundant. Anglers eager to
practice their art may wish to sample the good-to-excellent fishing
for golden and brook trout at Rocky Basin Lakes (see trip 90).

4th Hiking Day (Big Whitney Meadow to Upper Horseshoe Meadow, 5.5 miles): Crossing this enormous meadow entails a good deal of walking through sand as the trail strikes out due east. One sees some signs of erosion while crossing the meadow, a product of too early and too much stock grazing. Under the Forest Service's Multiple Use policy, this fine meadow and its smaller counterpart to the south are overrun with stock — a situation that does not contribute to the meadow's primitive aspect. The trail passes the raised, forested island in the middle of the meadow, and then crosses tiny, grassy-fringed tributaries of Golden Trout Creek, which hold an abundance of tiny golden trout. East of the meadow, the trail ascends through a moderate forest cover of lodgepole and foxtail on a steady grade. This ascent levels as the trail emerges at the Upper Meadow. The fringes of this meadow show the inevitable signs of lodgepole invasion as new growth of this tree makes up the shrinking periphery. In this meadow, the trail crosses Stokes Stringer, and then passes several fine campsites at the east edge of the meadow before beginning the steep ascent to the pass. This climb is accomplished without benefit of many switchbacks until it refords Stokes Stringer near the top. The stream, for the most part, remains hidden by a screen of willows, but wildflowers thrive near the stream and along the trail, and one will see lupine, wallflower, buttercup, white cinquefoil, Indian paintbrush, varicolored pentstemon, yellow columbine, monkey flower, lousewort, shooting star and Douglas phlox. The steepest part of the climb levels out into a charming alpine meadow (several good campsites) before turning northeast and making the final, long, sagebrush-dotted, meadow ascent to Cottonwood Pass (11200'). Views are best from the head of the alpine meadow cited above, and they include Kern Peak, Great Western Divide, Rocky Basin, and Boreal Plateau. Cottonwood Pass is a rocky saddle that looks east into the Cottonwood Creek drainage and across the Owens Valley to the White Mountains. The initial descent from the pass is over rocky, dusty switchbacks on a precipitous slope. This descent levels as it reaches the unnamed, willow-bound tributary that drains into Horseshoe Meadow. Lush, shoulder-high tiger lily graces this stream's banks, along with pentstemon, lousewort, yellow columbine and Indian paintbrush. Many sections of the subsequent moderate descent are heavily eroded and avalanche-ridden, making the descent to the tiny meadow above upper Horseshoe Meadow a scrambling affair. From this meadow, the descent becomes gentler, and just west of the old cabin our route crosses the jump-across stream to the good campsites just upstream. Firewood is abundant, and fishing for brook (to 10") is good.

5th Hiking Day (Upper Horseshoe Meadow to Cottonwood Creek Roadend, 4 miles): See 1st hiking day, trip 86.

90

TRIP	From COTTONWOOD CREEK ROADEND to ROCKY BASIN LAKES via Horseshoe Meadow, Cottonwood Pass, Big Whitney Meadow (round trip). Topo maps (15′) Olancha, Kern Peak; Profile 24. Best mid or late season; 27 miles.	

Grade	Trail/layover days	Total recom- mended days
Leisurely	6/2	8
Moderate	4/2	6
Strenuous	3/2	5

HILITES   The fine angling enjoyed at the culmination of this trip should make it a good selection for the intermediate hiker who wants good recreation as well as a challenging route.

DESCRIPTION *(Leisurely trip)*

1st Hiking Day   (Cottonwood Creek Roadend to Upper Horseshoe Meadow, 4 miles): See 1st hiking day, trip 86.

2nd Hiking Day   (Upper Horseshoe Meadow to Big Whitney Meadow, 5.5 miles): See 4th hiking day, trip 89.

3rd Hiking Day   (Big Whitney Meadow to Rocky Basin Lakes, 4 miles): The unsigned trail leaves the packer campsite on a moderate southwest ascent through dense and sometimes moderate stands of lodgepole, foxtail and hemlock. This ascent makes a long, dusty southwesterly traverse of the moraine just west of Big Whitney Meadow, and then descends to the banks of Barigan Stringer, where it meets and turns right onto the Barigan Stringer trail. The ascent following this junction is gentle, and then moderate over increasingly rocky underfooting. The foxtail and lodgepole pine forest cover lining either side of this ravine ascent is a favorite habitat for a great variety of birdlife, including the long-eared owl, Steller jay, robin, chickadee, junco, calliope hummingbird, Clark nutcracker and rosy finch. The latter is often one's only contact with birdlife at the higher elevations, and is a frequently seen companion on exploratory trips around the rocky, barren expanses of Funston Lake. The trail emerges at the sandy shores of the largest lake of the group (Lake 10745), where our route veers west across rock and sand to the westernmost lake of the group. The north and west walls of this high cirque basin are heavily fractured granite, and are a haven for marmots. Crossing to the northeast corner of the westernmost lake, our route finishes at the good campsites situated in the sparse stand of foxtail pine. Fishing for golden (to 16″) is good to excellent in all the lakes of this basin. The fish at Johnson Lake are generally smaller, but equally abundant. Large fish have also been taken from Funston Lake. Firewood is ample.

4th Hiking Day   (Rocky Basin Lakes to Big Whitney Meadow, 4 miles): Retrace steps of 3rd hiking day.

5th Hiking Day   (Big Whitney Meadow to Upper Horseshoe Meadow, 5.5 miles): Retrace steps of 2nd hiking day.

6th Hiking Day   (Upper Horseshoe Meadow to Cottonwood Creek Roadend, 4 miles): Retrace steps of 1st hiking day.

 91

TRIP   From COTTONWOOD CREEK ROADEND TO WHITNEY PORTAL via Army Pass, Rock Creek, Crabtree Meadow, John Muir Trail (shuttle trip). Topo maps (15′) Olancha, Kern Peak, Mt. Whitney, Lone Pine; Profiles 23, 17. Best mid or late season; 40.5 miles.

Grade	Trail/layover days	Total recommended days
Leisurely	6/2	8
Moderate	5/1	6
Strenuous	4/0	4

HILITES   This fine shuttle trip surveys the Sierra crest from Army Pass to Whitney Portal. Over 100 lakes are within a half day's walk from the campsites at the ends of these hiking days, making this selection a choice one for anglers.

DESCRIPTION   (Leisurely trip)

1st Hiking Day   (Cottonwood Creek Roadend to South Fork Lakes, 7 miles): See 1st hiking day, trip 87.

2nd Hiking Day   (South Fork Lakes to Upper Rock Creek Lake, 6.5 miles): See 2nd hiking day, trip 88.

3rd Hiking Day   (Upper Rock Creek Lake to Campsites, Lower Rock Creek Ford, 3 miles): This short hiking day is an easy tramp down Rock Creek. This tumbling rill slows to a murmuring brook in the meadow flats, and its fresh-from-the-source waters are crystal clear and icy cold. Leaving the shallow outlet of Upper Rock Creek Lake, the trail descends steadily alongside the now-cascading stream. The dense green panoply overhead of foxtail pine and occasional lodgepole allows only sparse, shade-loving clumps of gooseberry to grow along the trail, but the virile willow maintains its verdant stream-bank growth, shade or sun. Willow growth is synonymous with birdlife, and Rock Creek has its share of robins, white-crowned sparrows, chickadees, juncos, woodpeckers and olive-sided flycatchers. It is often the "oh-see view" call of this flycatcher that reminds the passerby of the beauty of his surroundings — surroundings that, on this canyon descent, include a chain of lovely meadows. Unfortunately, this native tour guide leaves these environs in August, and the late-season traveler is left to rely on his own initiative. In the middle of the second large meadow, the trail fords Rock Creek (difficult in high water) and veers away from the stream. Interestingly enough, most anglers ignore the waters of this tiny creek and thereby miss some fine fishing for golden. The fish are not too large, but there are several in every hole. The trail makes a reunion with the creek in the large, rolling meadow just above the ford by the campsites, where it passes the Siberian Pass trail. (The tiny fenced plots in the meadow are Park meadow research areas, and should not be tampered with.) At the west end of the meadow, the trail descends to the good campsites at the ford of lower Rock Creek (9500'). Here, fishing is good for golden (to 8") and firewood is abundant.

4th Hiking Day (Campsites, Lower Rock Creek Ford to Crabtree Ranger Station, 9 miles): Fording the stream, the trail climbs steeply up the north wall of the canyon, then levels somewhat to the ford of Guyot Creek. The jumbled, symmetrical crest of Mt. Guyot takes up the skyline to the west, and highly fractured Joe Devel Peak looms to the east as the trail begins another moderate ascent through a dense forest cover of lodgepole pine. This bouldery climb culminates at a saddle from which there are good views north across the Kern Canyon to the Kern-Kaweah drainage, Red Spur, Kern Ridge and the Great Western Divide. From the saddle, the trail descends moderately to the large sandy basin of Guyot Flat. Scientists estimate the sand of this basin is over 100' deep, and the resultant drainage affords little opportunity for plant seeding or growth. Like the Chagoopa Plateau across the canyon, this flat and the subsequent "shelf" traversed later in this hiking day were part of an immense valley floor (preglaciation). However, much of the granular sand deposits are a result of later weathering and erosion of the granite peaks to the east. Beyond Guyot Flat the trail undulates through a moderate forest cover of lodgepole and foxtail before dropping steeply into the Whitney Creek drainage. The descent into this drainage affords views eastward to Mt. Whitney — the long, flat-topped, avalanche-chuted mountain that towers over the nearer, granite-spired shoulder of Mt. Hitchcock. This descent concludes over a barren, rocky stretch to Lower Crabtree Meadow, where, just beyond a good campsite, our route fords Whitney Creek and turns right (east) along its north bank. A half mile of gentle ascent ends at Upper Crabtree Meadow, where the route passes the Crabtree Lakes trail. (This unmaintained trail leads to the good fishing on Crabtree Lakes for golden, to 14".) Continuing northeast beside Whitney Creek the trail ascends gently to meet the High Sierra/John Muir Trail immediately west of a ford of Whitney Creek. Beyond this ford is the Crabtree Ranger Station (emergency services available) and good campsites, where wood is adequate and fishing in Whitney Creek is fair for golden (to 7").

5th Hiking Day (Crabtree Ranger Station to Mirror Lake, 11 miles): See 2nd hiking day, trip 76.

6th Hiking Day (Mirror Lake to Whitney Portal, 4 miles): See 1st hiking day, trip 75.

TRIP   From COTTONWOOD CREEK ROADEND to WHITNEY PORTAL via Cottonwood Pass, Big Whitney Meadow, Siberian Pass, Rock Creek, Crabtree Meadow, John Muir Trail (shuttle trip). Topo maps (15') Olancha, Kern Peak, Mt. Whitney, Lone Pine; Profiles 24, 23, 17. Best mid or late season; 43.5 miles.

Grade	Trail/layover days	Total recommended days
Leisurely	6/2	8
Moderate	5/1	6
Strenuous	4/0	4

HILITES   Crossing three passes, this route tarries in four drainages offering a multitude of chances for angling that ranges from good to excellent. The scenery that graces most of this trail is exceeded nowhere in the Sierra, having an abundance of peaks exceeding 13000', and dozens of high, granitoid cirque basins.

DESCRIPTION (Leisurely trip)

1st Hiking Day (Cottonwood Creek Roadend to Upper Horseshoe Meadow, 4 miles): See 1st hiking day, trip 86.

2nd Hiking Day (Upper Horseshoe Meadow to Big Whitney Meadow, 5.5 miles): See 4th hiking day, trip 89.

3rd Hiking Day (Big Whitney Meadow to Campsites, Lower Rock Creek Ford, 10 miles): Keeping to the foxtail and lodgepole timber fringe along the west side of the meadow, the trail leads north over gentle, sandy swells to the easy step-across ford of a tributary of Golden Trout Creek. Then climbing moderately, the trail leaves the meadowland and enters dense concentrations of foxtail pine. This ascent levels briefly as it passes a wildflower-filled meadow (fields of monkey flower) and fords a second tributary.

Paralleling, but staying well above, this tributary, the trail jogs westward, and then begins a steep, rocky and sometimes dusty ascent of a ravine to Siberian Pass (10900′). The pass marks the boundary of Sequoia National Park. At the pass our route turns left, leaving the Army Pass/Mitre Basin trail, and descends across the open, gravelly expanses of Siberian Outpost. (Note: the topo map incorrectly shows the Siberian Outpost trail branching west *below* the pass.) Green-rimmed runoff streams wind through these barren reaches, but the feeling that usually attends these wide-open spaces is one of desolation. This impression is heightened by the presence of numerous golden foxtail snags that stand like lonely sentinels around the periphery. Along the stream the tell-tale network of wormlike dirt piles betrays the presence of pocket gophers. Consistently good views of Mitre Basin to the north attend the gentle descent along Siberian Pass Creek until the forest cover is reached two miles to the west. The pleasantly winding trail continues its gentle-to-moderate downgrade through meadowy sections. The nearby forest cover is first foxtail only, but later includes lodgepole. Leaving the last large meadow, the trail swings north away from Siberian Pass Creek on a descent that steepens and finally resolves into steep, rocky switchbacks. The forest cover, now predominantly lodgepole, thins as the trail levels and then emerges into lower Rock Creek meadow. Midway across the meadow our route meets the Rock Creek trail and turns left (west) onto it. This wild, grassy meadow is filled with wildflowers, and they make a colorful backdrop for the meandering stream that touches the eastern end. (The fenced plots of meadow are part of a Park meadow research project, and should not be tampered with.) From the meadow it is but a short distance to the good campsites at the ford of lower Rock Creek (9500′). Firewood is abundant and fishing for golden (to 8″) is good.

4th Hiking Day (Campsites, Lower Rock Creek to Crabtree Ranger Station, 9 miles): See 4th hiking day, trip 91.

5th Hiking Day (Crabtree Ranger Station to Mirror Lake, 11 miles): See 2nd hiking day, trip 76.

6th Hiking Day (Mirror Lake to Whitney Portal, 4 miles): See 1st hiking day, trip 75.

 93

TRIP   From COTTONWOOD CREEK ROADEND to MINERAL KING via Army Pass, Rock Creek, Siberian Pass, Big Whitney Meadow, Golden Trout Creek, Kern River, Rattlesnake Creek, Franklin Pass (shuttle trip). Topo maps (15′) Olancha, Kern Peak, Mineral King; Profiles 23, 24, 27, 25. Best mid or late season; 60 miles.

| | Trail/layover | Total recom- |
Grade	days	mended days
Leisurely	- - -	- - -
Moderate	7/4	11
Strenuous	6/4	10

HILITES   This excellent trans-Sierra route visits the finest fishing lakes and streams of the lower Kern River drainage. The severe altitude changes inherent in the route, however, recommend this trip for intermediate and experienced hikers only.

DESCRIPTION   (Moderate trip)
1st Hiking Day   (Cottonwood Creek Roadend to South Fork Lakes, 7 miles): See 1st hiking day, trip 87.

2nd Hiking Day   (South Fork Lakes to Upper Rock Creek Lake, 6.5 miles): See 2nd hiking day, trip 88.

3rd Hiking Day   (Upper Rock Creek Lake to Big Whitney Meadow, 6.5 miles): See 3rd hiking day, trip 89.

4th Hiking Day   (Big Whitney Meadow to Little Whitney Meadow, 10 miles): Passing the fenced "Tourist Pasture," the winding meadow trail continues south over rolling terrain. Cattle grazing permits are dispensed for this meadow and Little Whitney Meadow; hence the traveler may expect bovine company on these grassy sections. Many wildflowers line the route through the southern arm of the meadow and subsequent trail, including shooting star, monkey flower, lupine, wallflower, pentstemon, mountain aster, cream cup, scarlet gilia, white cinquefoil, Bigelow sneezeweed and pussy paws. The sandy surface of the meadow trail continues into the moderate-to-dense forest cover of lodgepole and foxtail pine below. Shortly after re-entering forest cover, the trail fords Barigan Stringer and passes several nearby campsites. The polished granite canyon walls narrow, and the stream quickens for about ½ mile, and then as the canyon opens somewhat our trail passes the Rocky Basin Lakes trail (several campsites here). Anglers who wish to sample the good fishing on Golden Trout Creek will find plentiful golden (to 8"). This creek was the original source for fish used in subsequent plantings throughout the higher lakes and streams of the Sierra. The first recorded account of the discovery of the golden of this stream reflects the excitement of the writer (Dr. Barton Evermann):

> "This is the most beautiful of all the trouts: the brilliancy and richness of its coloration is not equaled in any other known species; the delicate golden olive of the head, back, and upper part of the side, the clear golden yellow along and below the lateral line, and the marvelously rich cadmium of the under parts fully entitle this species to be known above all others as *the* golden trout."*

The Golden Trout of the Southern High Sierras, Bulletin, Bureau of Fisheries, 1905, V. 25, p. 28.

With patriotic fervor the doctor named this trout *Salmo roosevelti,* after then-President Theodore Roosevelt — fortunately, this name, labeling an animal with a man's name, has not gained widespread use. Beyond the Rocky Basin Lakes trail junction our trail continues a moderate sandy descent past several more campsites to the ford of Golden Trout Creek. (This ford is 2 miles south of the ford indicated on the topo.) Mounting a sandy shelf above the creek, the trail descends gently past the Tunnel Air Camp/Carroll Creek trail to the multi-building complex of Tunnel Guard Station (emergency services available here). The final descent to the Guard Station affords views of the open reaches of the valley, and of the red-topped volcanic hills to the southwest. Just beyond the Tunnel Guard Station our route passes the Ramshaw Meadow trail branching east, and then turns west to ford Golden Trout Creek. Fishing on Golden Trout Creek below Tunnel Guard Station is restricted to artificial lures. Across sandy, moderately forested, level terrain, the faint trail (boggy and heavily trampled by cattle) stays well north of the creek, and passes the unmaintained trail to Groundhog Meadow. Rejoining the creek, the trail continues westerly, winding along the northernmost edge of a large volcanic overlay (post-glacial) known as Malpais Lava. The largest single concentration of volcanic action in the upper reaches of the Kern, this basaltic flow shows itself near the trail in brilliant displays of colored rock. Predominant in the volcanic rock is a deep red, sometimes mixed with ochres and shades of tan. These colorful displays accompany the traveler all the way down this drainage, but the interested rock hound can see extensive fields of this rock by fording the creek and exploring the mile-wide strip of old lava flow to the south. Just east of Little Whitney Meadow, our trail drops steeply, and after passing the unmaintained trail to Salt Lick Meadow, fords Golden Trout Creek. On the west side of this meadowed ford are several good campsites with ample firewood (8420'). Fishing for golden in Golden Trout Creek (to 8") is good.

5th Hiking Day (Little Whitney Meadow to Campsites, Rattlesnake Creek/Kern River, 10 miles): The trail skirts the southern end of beautiful Little Whitney Meadow, and passes another "Tourist Pasture." Descending steadily over a dusty, granite sand surface, the trail then refords Golden Trout Creek. Then, as the trail continues its steady descent, the trail surface becomes pumice, and the forest cover of lodgepole gives way to Jeffrey and juniper. Large concentrations of wildflowers daub the opener stretches with yellows (monkey flower), whites (white Mariposa), mixed blues and purples (larkspur and pentstemon), and reds (red dogwood). Leveling out to a moderate descent, the trail then recrosses a tributary of Golden Trout Creek via a natural bridge of basaltic rock. Easily eroded, this pink rock shows extensive water cutting and sculpting. After Natural Bridge, the grade of the trail steepens to a steady descent over pumice and sand through a forest cover of Jeffrey, white fir and some lodgepole. At the switchbacks dropping to the Kern Canyon floor, one can see the clearly delineated volcanic overlay with its subsurface of granite where the underlying rock has been laid bare by subsequent stream cutting that has knifed through the basaltic layer and exposed a rainbow of blacks, reds, tans and whites. Some columnar basaltic formations, usually associated with these lava flows, may also be seen to the north. Volcano Falls provides excellent views on the right as the trail twines steeply down over pumice and rock, and far to the north, above the west canyon wall, one has fleeting glimpses of Mt. Kaweah. With the lower altitude come sugar pine and, on the canyon floor, quaking aspen, birch, black oak and incense cedar. It is not until the canyon floor is reached that one has views of domelike Tower Rock to the south. Through a sparse forest cover and clumps of sage, manzanita, willows and chinquapin, the trail veers south to cross the Kern River (footbridge), and then pass the Kern Canyon Ranger Station (emergency services available here). At the Ranger Station, our route meets and turns right onto the Kern Canyon trail, and ascends the Kern Canyon by a series of moderate ups and downs. The forest cover is usually dense, with tiny wet sections that are made difficult of passage by dense concentrations of bracken fern. Their luxuriant growth is commonly associated with canyon bottoms, and they are frequently found in conjunction with riverside stands of alder, laurel, aspen and birch. The approach to Lower Funston Meadow is heralded by passing the lower drift fence, and then the trail begins a steady climb over the alluvial fan that results from Laurel Creek's contribution of silt and rock on the canyon floor. Fording Laurel Creek is accomplished via two crossings, each marked by a campsite; during high water, the second ford is sometimes hazardous. Fishing in the Kern River, particularly near the confluences of the many tributary streams, is excellent. Angling is sometimes made difficult by the thickets of willows lining the river, but the rewards in rainbow trout (to 20″) more than make up for the casting problems. Fishermen, or those who simply enjoy the view from streamside, should keep a sharp eye out for beaver that work this section of the river. It is not surprising that one usually makes many wild animal sightings while traveling up this glacially carved trench. Animals, like men, are "channeled" down its steep-walled course, and within the canyon's relatively confined course, the hiker is apt to see bear, coyote, deer and the aforementioned beaver. From Laurel Creek the trail continues north through a moderate forest cover that includes an occasional sugar pine. Mostly duff, the trail surface makes pleasant walking, and the distance to the Rattlesnake Creek trail junction is rapidly covered. At this junction, and just across the sometimes difficult ford of Rattlesnake Creek, are excellent packer campsites (6600′), where campers will find ample firewood. Fishing is as cited above. (Note: Yes, there are rattlesnakes in this area.)

6th Hiking Day (Campsites, Rattlesnake Creek/Kern River to Campsites, Upper Rattlesnake Creek, 9.5 miles): See 2nd hiking day, trip 100.

7th Hiking Day (Campsites, Upper Rattlesnake Creek to Mineral King, 10.5 miles): See 1st hiking day, trip 96.

94

TRIP	From MINERAL KING to SPRING LAKE via Glacier Pass (round trip). Topo map (15') Mineral King; Profile 26. Best mid season; 10 miles.	

Grade	Trail/layover days	Total recommended days
Leisurely	- - -	- - -
Moderate	- - -	- - -
Strenuous	2/0	2

HILITES This "weekender" makes a fine exercise for the intermediate backpacker who has a couple of good conditioning trips behind him. This route sidesteps the main Great Western Divide crest, and crosses the Empire Mountain ridge by a little-used pass (some difficult route finding) to beautiful Spring Lake. Rugged peaks, mirrorlike tarns, possibilities for exploring old "prospects" and cascading streams are the rewards for a difficult climb. This trip is recommended for hikers only.

DESCRIPTION (Strenuous trip)

1st Hiking Day (Mineral King to Spring Lake, 5 miles, part cross country): Beginning from the dirt parking lot on the north side of the road, at the point where the road bends south toward the Mineral King store (7800'), our trail jogs north and then turns east on ascending switchbacks. This dusty, oft-eroded trail winds up a dry slope of manzanita and chinquapin, offering some views, from the south ends of the switchbacks, up the Mineral King valley to Farewell Gap. Keeping to the right, our trail passes the Timber Gap trail (branching north), and continues east up the Monarch Creek drainage. Few trees screen this trail from the sun, but the rank manzanita thickets along the trail are, as one old-timer put it, "shoulder high to a growed elephant." (Should you see an elephant, please report the sighting to the ranger on duty at the Mineral King Guard Station.) Sometimes but not always visible from the trail, Monarch Creek splashes down to the valley in a series of granite-bottomed falls from the "false cirque" just above. Our trail, nearing the brink of this false cirque, angles away from the creek and skirts the northern base of the granite bowl's walls. This bowl does, at first glance, appear to be a true cirque — the womb of a glacial *mer de glace* — but as the traveler continues, he will see that it is merely where the river of ice midway down the slope discovered a schistic weakness in the underlying rock, and ground down on its heel, carving, scraping and sculpting the resultant amphitheatre. Early local residents (the human sort) brought their eastern terminology to this country and, in honor of the many marmots that inhabit the rocky fringe of the grassy-bottomed bowl, named it Lower Groundhog Meadow. Beyond Lower Groundhog Meadow the rocky trail becomes very rough and sometimes faint as it climbs steeply on the northern wall of the amphitheatre. Views across the bowl are enhanced by the sparkling ribbon falls of Monarch Creek. Frequent runoff rills and loose rock make footing treacherous as the trail climbs past the turnoff to Crystal Lake and ascends the steep slope to the short Monarch Lakes spur trail junction. Anglers may wish to detour for the fair-to-good fishing for brook to be enjoyed in these lakes. Passing this junction the trail turns northerly, and by a series of short, rocky switchbacks climbs 800' to the signed Glacier Pass turnoff. Here our route (unmarked on the topo map) branches left (north) over coarse granite sand and then broken granite to Glacier Pass (11570'). This pass is not named on the topo map, but is the saddle just east-southeast of Empire Mountain on the Sequoia National Park boundary. Views of the Cliff Creek drainage and barren Mt. Eisen are impressive, and they attend the hiker as he scrambles down the north side of the pass. Those with an explora-tory bent may wish to detour across the barren granite slopes to the west, northeast of the summit of Empire Mountain, to the cairn-marked gold prospects and mines that dot the upper slopes. This side of the pass is frequently covered with late-melting snow, and care should be taken to keep to the tundra-topped granite ledges east of and above the tarn beginnings of the west tributary of Spring Lake. Here a faint trail (sometimes ducked, sometimes worn into the grass) descends steeply to ford the tributary just above its final plunge into Spring Lake. The trail then traverses the sparsely timbered west slope of the Spring Lake cirque to the good camp-sites (somewhat exposed) at the northwest end and at the outlet of the lake (10050'). Firewood is scarce, and fishing for brook (to 8") is good. Views from the campsites of the sheer, smoothed granite headwall at the south end of the lake fill the viewer with a sense of awe and respect for the glacier's power.

2nd Hiking Day (Spring Lake to Mineral King, 5 miles, part cross country): Retrace steps of 1st hiking day.

95

TRIP   From MINERAL KING to LOST CANYON via Saw-tooth Pass, Columbine Lake (round trip). Topo map (15') Mineral King; Profile 26. Best mid season; 13 miles.

Grade	Trail/layover days	Total recommended days
Leisurely	- - -	- - -
Moderate	- - -	- - -
Strenuous	2/1	3

HILITES   Strictly a knapsacker's route, this trail traces the Monarch Creek drainage to cross the **Great Western Divide** at Sawtooth Pass. High alpine scenery climaxed by the cold, often ice-filled waters of Columbine Lake make this a fine route for all who love the Sierra Nevada. The excellent fishing in the upper Lost Canyon drainage will reward the angler who is willing to "walk for his supper."

DESCRIPTION   (Strenuous trip)

1st Hiking Day   (Mineral King to Campsites, Upper Lost Canyon, 6.5 miles): Proceed to the Glacier Pass trail junction as described in 1st hiking day, trip 94, where our route angles sharply east toward the jagged ridge that is Sawtooth Pass. The final mile to this serrated summit is a scrambling climb over loose, fractured rock and coarse granite sand that have weathered from the rock above. From the summit of this high-ridged pass (11700′) there are vistas of the surrounding country exceeded only by those from the tops of nearby Sawtooth Peak and Needham Mountain. One can see the length of the Monarch Creek drainage to the west, and on down into the wooded drainage of the East Fork Kaweah River. Empire Mountain and the ridge to its southeast dominate the view to the north, Sawtooth Peak and Mineral Peak divide the skyline to the south, and to the east one looks across the barren reaches of Columbine Lake, Lost Canyon and Big Arroyo to the timbered reaches of the Chagoopa Plateau. Far on the eastern horizon, one can see the Mt. Whitney complex of peaks, and a part of the backbone of the Sierra. The descent on the east side of Sawtooth Pass, like the western ascent, is a steep, rocky, zigzagging affair that will leave the knapsacker little time for looking at the spectacular scenery. This descent continues steep as it makes a long traverse that crosses two inlet streams on the north side of granitoid Columbine Lake. Here glacially scoured granite slabs tilt into the lake's usually mirrorlike surface. The reflections of the nearby mineralized, rust-colored rocks blend with the chalkier whites of the lakeside granites to leave an indelible impression of mellowness in the passerby's mind—this despite the basin's look of harsh, treeless sterility. Rounding the north side of the lake, our route drops steeply down to the headwaters of Lost Canyon on a rocky surface that does not give way to grass and trees (lodgepole and some foxtail pines) until one is almost due north of the westernmost spire of Needham Mountain. Here good campsites will be found in an open, grassy setting (10200′) midst a sparse forest cover of stunted lodgepole pine. Firewood is ample, and fishing for brook trout further downstream is excellent.

2nd Hiking Day   (Campsites, Upper Lost Canyon to Mineral King, 6.5 miles): Retrace steps of 1st hiking day.

— 183 —

96

TRIP   From MINERAL KING to CAMPSITES, UPPER RAT-
TLESNAKE CREEK via Franklin Pass (round trip).
Topo map (15') Mineral King; Profile 25. Best mid or
late season; 19 miles.

Grade	Trail/layover days	Total recom- mended days
Leisurely	- - -	- - -
Moderate	- - -	- - -
Strenuous	2/1	3

HILITES   To call this trip a colorful one is an understatement.
The peaks cupping the Franklin Lakes cirque are an
artist's canvas of grays, shades of red, and various
tones of green. Across Franklin Pass the fine fishing
and beautifully intimate scenery of Rattlesnake Creek
beckon to anglers and appreciative naturalists.

DESCRIPTION (Strenuous trip)

1st Hiking Day (Mineral King to Campsites, Upper Rattlesnake
Creek, 10.5 miles): From the Mineral King village the dirt road
continues south along the floor of the valley to a point a few yards
past the pack station, where there is limited room for parking one's
car. A rough jeep road continues from this point for about 1 mile,
to an unimproved campground near the junction of Crystal Creek
and the East Fork Kaweah River. Looking upcanyon from this point,
V-shaped upper Farewell Canyon is clear, and one can readily
make out Farewell Gap at its apex. Just west of the trail the hurrying waters of the Kaweah River are hidden by a screen of willows,
and the early-morning hiker is very apt to see a late garbage-can-
breakfasting bear wandering a parallel course south through the
sagebrush of the valley floor. Scattered clumps of juniper and red
fir contrast with the ghostly white of aspen trunks just below the
point where the trail fords Crystal Creek and, passing the Farewell
Gap trail, begins a gentle-to-moderate ascent. Along the shaley
trail the fetid smell of corn lily assails the nostrils, and between
the snowbrush and manzanita of these lower slopes, spots of wildflower color provided by Indian paintbrush, fleabane, cow parsnip
and blue gentian dot the way. The trail then fords Franklin Creek,
and begins a steep ascent along a section of the Kaweah River
that flows down a deep wash. This wash breaks the typical U
shape of this glacially formed valley into the shape of a prone
brackets mark which is still evident as the trail levels out into
an open, treeless, alpine fell field. (This long southerly swing of
the trail is newly constructed, and deviates from that indicated on
the topo map.) Across the canyon, one can see the Farewell Gap
trail as it parallels our own route. About ½ mile north of Farewell

Gap our route doubles back north, passing an unmarked trail to Farewell Gap, and begins a stuttering, long traverse around the northwest end of Tulare Peak. This turn provides excellent views back down the Kaweah River watershed to Mineral King and beyond to Timber Gap. The long traverse enters a sparse forest cover of mature foxtail pine and crosses rocky stretches as it turns northeast into the Franklin Creek drainage. Descending briefly to ford Franklin Creek, the trail then rises steeply (rejoining the trail marked on the topo) to the rock- and concrete-dammed outlet of the lower of the Franklin Lakes. The colors in this dramatically walled cirque basin are a bizarre conglomeration. To the northeast Rainbow Mountain is a study of gray-white marble whorls set in a sea of pink, red and black metamorphic rock. To the south the slate ridge joining Tulare Peak and Florence Peak is a hue of vermilion red that sends color photographers scrambling for viewpoints from which to foreground the contrasting blue of Franklin Lake against this colorful headwall to the south. Anglers will find the fishing for brook (to 10") good on the lower lake, and even better at the upper lake. There are a few fair campsites along the northeast shore of lower Franklin Lake. From this lake the trail rises steadily, and then steeply on switchbacks. (These switchbacks are located somewhat north of the old ones indicated on the topo map.) Views of the Franklin Lakes cirque improve with altitude, and it isn't long before both the upper and lower lakes are in view. This ascent leaves the forest cover behind, as it crosses and recrosses a field of coarse granite granules. Despite the sievelike drainage of this slope, shooting star and wallflower are frequently seen — even at the pass. At Franklin Pass (11700') the traveler has the unique opportunity of dropping an "official" 200' with one step — and not breaking his neck in the process. The National Forest side of the sign at the pass indicates an elevation of 11500', while that of the Park indicates 11700'. Views from this windy pass are panoramic. Landmarks to the northwest include Castle Rocks and Paradise Peak; to the north the jumbled crests of Rainbow and Needham mountains; to the east the immediate, unglaciated plateau above the headwaters of Rattlesnake Creek, and Foerester Lake (on the wooded bench just north of Rattlesnake Creek). East of the Kern Trench and plateaus, one can make out Mt. Whitney on the Sierra crest. The initial descent from the pass is over the ancient (pre-Sierran uplift) bench seen from the pass. Mostly covered with a layer of disintegrated quartz sand, it is oddly dotted with miniature granite domes. After crossing this bench, the trail drops steeply over rocky, rough switchbacks that twine back and forth over the headwaters runoff of Rattlesnake Creek. This steep descent levels out on the north side of the creek, and enters a friendly forest of young lodgepole pine broken by pleasant meadow patches. Several excellent campsites (10300') line the creek here, and firewood is abundant. Fishing for brook trout (to 8") is good to excellent, and the stream is ideal for fly fishermen. These streamside campsites are fine base camps for angling side trips to the several nearby lakes situated on the benches on either side of the Rattlesnake Creek drainage.

2nd Hiking Day (Campsites, Upper Rattlesnake Creek to Mineral King, 10.5 miles): Retrace steps of 1st hiking day.

97

TRIP   From MINERAL KING to LITTLE CLAIRE LAKE via Franklin Pass, Rattlesnake Creek, Foerester Lake (round trip). Topo map (15') Mineral King; Profile 25. Best mid-to-late season; 26 miles.

Grade	Trail/layover days	Total recom- mended days
Leisurely	- - -	- - -
Moderate	- - -	- - -
Strenuous	3/2	5

HILITES   For fine fishing, superlative scenery and a whole range of side-trip possibilities, this trip is hard to beat. As the opportunities for recreation are varied, so are the watersheds that this trip visits. Crossing into Sequoia National Park via Franklin Pass, this route hooks around to visit the headwaters of two alpine headwaters of tributaries of the Kern River.

DESCRIPTION   (Strenuous trip)

1st Hiking Day   (Mineral King to Campsites, Upper Rattlesnake Creek, 10.5 miles): See 1st hiking day, trip 96.

2nd Hiking Day   (Campsites, Upper Rattlesnake Creek to Little Claire Lake, 2.5 miles): From the streamside campsites the trail descends moderately through an increasingly dense forest cover of lodgepole pine. At the first ford of Rattlesnake Creek, in the large meadowed area where the Rattlesnake Creek trail jogs south, our route branches left (east) away from the creek. A short distance beyond the junction, the trail fords the outlet stream from Foerester Lake, and ascends gently over a rocky slope. (This section of trail replaces the unmaintained trails to the east, and it is not indicated on the topo map.) The wetter sections of this short stretch of trail are lined with delicious swamp onion, a delightful addition to an evening's stew or soup. As the trail arrives at the charmingly meadowed west side of Foerester Lake, one sees occasional fox-tail pine among the lodgepole. Fine campsites on this shore look across the azure blue waters to a dense forest fringe, and an occasional dimpling on the surface indicates the presence of brook trout. Turning northwestward, the trail ascends stepladder fashion through a moderate lodgepole and foxtail pine forest cover and a meadowed bench, and then makes another ascent to the sandy crown of the ridge dividing the Rattlesnake and Soda Creek drainages. From this rounded summit the crests of Saw-tooth Peak and Needham Mountain are easily visible to the north, and they continue to be seen as the trail descends moderately to the south end of Little Claire Lake. The effervescent, burbling call of the Brewer blackbird and the raucous call of the Clark nutcracker frequently are heard as the traveler circles the east side of Little Claire Lake (10480′) to the excellent campsites at the north end of the lake, around the outlet. Firewood is ample, and fishing for brook is excellent (to 11″). Views to the east from the outlet-situated campsites should be ample reason for planning a stay here. Should the views not provide sufficient incentive, this camp is a fine starting point for discovery and fishing trips to the nearby lakes at the headwaters of Soda Creek.

3rd Hiking Day (Little Claire Lake to Mineral King, 13 miles): Retrace steps of 1st and 2nd hiking days.

TRIP From MINERAL KING to BIG FIVE LAKES via Franklin Pass, Rattlesnake Creek, Foerester Lake, Little Claire Lake, Soda Creek, Lost Canyon, return via cross country to Little Five Lakes, Black Rock Pass, Spring Lake, Glacier Pass (loop trip). Topo maps (15′) Mineral King, Kern Peak; Profiles 25, 26. Best mid or late season; 32.5 miles.

Grade	Trail/layover days	Total recommended days
Leisurely	- - -	- - -
Moderate	- - -	- - -
Strenuous	5/2	7

HILITES This is perhaps the best knapsacker's route for looping the fine fishing country east of Mineral King. Challenging cross-country routes and remote lakes are the attractions to the hiker. For the angler, the chance to wet a line in excellent golden trout waters should be sufficient inducement.

DESCRIPTION (Strenuous trip)

1st Hiking Day (Mineral King to Campsites, Upper Rattlesnake Creek, 10.5 miles): See 1st hiking day, trip 96.

2nd Hiking Day (Campsites, Upper Rattlesnake Creek to Little Claire Lake, 2.5 miles): See 2nd hiking day, trip 97.

3rd Hiking Day (Little Claire Lake to Lower Big Five Lake, 9 miles): The route along the west side of the outlet stream from

Little Claire Lake is a steep, scrambling climb down. Contrary to the topo map, there is no trail, but the tumbling outlet creek provides an easy guide. At the foot of this precipitous duff-and-rock slope, the route fords Soda Creek and meets the clearly defined Soda Creek trail on the north side. Turning right onto this trail, our route first descends gently over duff and sand through a moderate forest cover of lodgepole and foxtail pine, and then the grade steepens. Marmots on the rocky slopes south of the creek whistle excitedly as unexpected visitors to their domain pass by, but they do not usually stir from their watching posts unless the traveler shows more than passing interest. As the trail follows the steadily descending streambed, the creek's banks become willow-infested, and are separated from the trail by dells of birch, cottonwood and quaking aspen. Among the evergreens one now finds an occasional silver pine, and then red fir appears. Clumps of sagebrush space the stands of timber, and nestled next to their aromatic branches are much Douglas phlox and Indian paintbrush. The steadily descending trail crosses two jump-across tributaries before encountering the first Jeffrey and juniper of the trip. The appearance of these trees heralds the junction where the Big Arroyo trail branches right and our route, after a steep, rocky, exposed ascent to the waterfalls marking the foot of Lost Canyon, doubles back to the northwest. Just above these falls, our route fords Lost Canyon Creek and begins a steady ascent on a duff-and-sand trail. About 1 mile after the ford, the trail passes a series of streamside campsites located in the wooded sections between tiny meadows in a stepladdering series. At the first ford of Lost Canyon Creek, the obscurely marked trail to Big Five Lakes branches right (north), and, leaving Lost Canyon, climbs the steep north wall. This ascent, after its initial, faint, ducked beginnings, makes a clear series of short, steep switchbacks. These switchbacks afford fine views west to the barren headwaters of Lost Canyon Creek and the cirque holding Columbine Lake. Mostly lodgepole and foxtail pine, the timber cover thickens as the trail passes the tiny, unnamed lake (due east of the granite spur, in the Kern Peak topo map), and the hiker can enjoy the luxuriant growth of the wildflowers around its meadow fringes. Fields of shooting star, bunches of ground-hugging primrose, and a sprinkling of cheerful western mountain aster brighten the meadow and the adjoining trail. Circling the east side of this tiny lake, the trail fords the outlet stream, and then crosses a long, steady ridge that is heavily laid with fallen snags. The ground trail is sometimes faint, but it is well ducked. Above Big Five Lakes, the trail tops the ridge to fine views of Empire Mountain and Black Rock Pass to the west, and the lowest of the Big Five Lakes (9840') immediately below and to the west. The descent to the excellent campsites near the outlet and along the north side of this lake is a rocky, steep downgrade. Firewood around these campsites is ample, and fishing for golden trout is excellent (to 14").

4th Hiking Day (Lower Big Five Lake to Spring Lake, 5.5 miles, part cross country): Continuing west around the north side of the lake, the trail ascends along the north side of the lake's inlet through rank growths of ferns and moderate stands of foxtail.

This moderately ascending trail fords the stream ¼ mile below the outlet of the largest lake in the Big Five Lakes chain, and climbs over glacially smoothed granite to the lake's east shore. Our route fords the outlet and passes a packer campsite and several primitive campsites before crossing the swampy area around the north inlet of the lake. Just east of this inlet, the trail passes the Little Five Lakes trail branching right (north), and continues west up the Big Five Lakes basin. Fishermen will find the angling for golden good to excellent in all the lakes of the upper basin except the highest. The ascent to the third lake we pass is gentle over grass and swampy areas, and, near the outlet of this lake, the trail passes two primitive, exposed campsites. The grassy trail continues around the lake, but our cross-country route turns right (northwest) and ascends the steep granite ridge separating the Big Five Lakes and Little Five Lakes drainages. This ascent climbs by grass-topped ledges to the cairned saddle just south of the uppermost lake of the Little Five Lakes chain. From this ridge one can see across Big Arroyo to the Kaweah Peaks and Red Spur. To the west, aptly named Black Rock Pass stands out in startling relief from the surrounding white granite. The steep, rocky descent on the north side of the ridge is clearly ducked, and a minimum of scrambling is required to bring one to the edge of the uppermost lake. (Fishing for golden in the two lower lakes of this chain is good.) Crossing the outlet stream from this lake, our ducked route meets and turns left onto the Black Rock Pass trail. First ascending across alpine meadows, the trail veers north (not shown on the topo map) and then climbs a steep, very rocky series of switchbacks to the summit of Black Rock Pass (11600'). This pass provides one of the finer viewpoints on this trip. Looking east one can see the Kaweah Peaks Ridge, the wooded flats of Chagoopa Plateau, a considerable length of Big Arroyo, and both the Little and the Big Five Lakes basins. On the south side of the pass, there are heart-stopping panoramas of the deep Cliff Creek drainage and towering Empire Mountain, seeming to be almost at fingertip distance. Descending on the west side of the pass, the rocky trail makes one long traverse, and then drops by steady and steep zigzags to the grass-bottomed basin just north of Spring Lake. Here our route leaves the Black Rock Pass trail and contours around the head of this basin. Fording the tributary stream northeast of Spring Lake, our route ascends the waterfall outlet of Spring Lake itself, and arrives at the good campsites (somewhat exposed) on the east side of the outlet and in the sparse timber cover of the northwest shore (10050'). Views from these campsites of the massive cirque headwall and the ribboned waterfall inlets are satisfying. Firewood is scarce, and fishing for brook trout (to 8″) is good.

5th Hiking Day (Spring Lake to Mineral King, 5 miles, part cross country): See 1st hiking day, trip 94.

TRIP   From MINERAL KING to BIG FIVE LAKES via Saw-tooth Pass, Columbine Lake, Lost Canyon, return via cross country to Little Five Lakes, Black Rock Pass, Spring Lake, Glacier Pass (semi-loop trip). Topo maps (15′) Mineral King, Kern Peak; Profiles 26, 25. Best mid or late season; 21.5 miles.

Grade	Trail/layover days	Total recom-mended days
Leisurely	- - -	- - -
Moderate	- - -	- - -
Strenuous	4/2	6

HILITES   This fine, short, looping trip is an angler's delight. In this route's short mileage 5 creeks and 15 lakes are touched, providing a variety of fishing water — and trout — that the fisherman will certainly want to try.

DESCRIPTION   (Strenuous trip)

1st Hiking Day   (Mineral King to Campsites, Upper Lost Canyon, 6.5 miles): See 1st hiking day, trip 95.

2nd Hiking Day   (Campsites, Upper Lost Canyon to Lower Big Five Lake, 4.5 miles): From the alpine-meadowed bench below Columbine Lake, the trail enters forest cover (sparse lodgepole and foxtail), and then drops steeply over broken granite and mead-owy sections. This stepladdering descent keeps to the north side of Lost Canyon Creek for about 1 mile, and then fords the creek four times in the space of the next mile. The fourth ford returns to the north side of the creek, where our route branches north, away from Lost Canyon, on the poorly signed Big Five Lakes trail. From this junction, proceed as described in the 3rd hiking day, trip 98.

3rd Hiking Day   (Lower Big Five Lake to Spring Lake, 5.5 miles, part cross country): See 4th hiking day, trip 98.

4th Hiking Day   (Spring Lake to Mineral King, 5 miles, part cross country): See 1st hiking day, trip 94.

100

TRIP   From MINERAL KING to KERN RIVER via Franklin Pass, Rattlesnake Creek, Kern River, return via High Sierra trail, Little Five Lakes, Black Rock Pass, Spring Lake, Glacier Pass (loop trip). Topo maps (15') Mineral King, Kern Peak, Mt. Whitney, Triple Divide Peak; Profiles 25, 27, 21, 26. Best mid or late season; 60.5 miles.

Grade	Trail/layover days	Total recommended days
Leisurely	- - -	- - -
Moderate	8/3	11
Strenuous	7/2	9

HILITES   This loop trip is one that should be taken by all who would say, "I know the Great Western Divide country," or "I know the Kern Trench and its wooded plateaus." This route surveys a 5000' range of Sierran biota, and the scope of the glaciated terrain one travels over reads like the synopsis of a geology textbook.

DESCRIPTION (Strenuous trip)

1st Hiking Day (Mineral King to Campsites, Upper Rattlesnake Creek, 10.5 miles): See 1st hiking day, trip 96.

2nd Hiking Day (Campsites, Upper Rattlesnake Creek to Campsites, Rattlesnake Creek/Kern River, 9.5 miles): Traveling down through the upper reaches of Rattlesnake Creek is a delightful study in intimate meadows, dense stands of lodgepole pine and a classic, murmuring mountain creek. Within a mile from the timberline campsites, our trail passes the signed turnoff to Foerester and Little Claire lakes, and then jogs across the winding meadow stream, only to return to the north side a few yards downstream. Below this ford the creek picks up speed as its meandering course is constricted by narrowing canyon walls, and the trail climbs briefly on the north canyon wall. In the narrow canyon the trail stays high above the swiftly tumbling creek waters as it descends on a long, steady, rocky traverse of the canyon wall. Rounding the fractured granite nose of a ridge, the trail descends steeply to ford an unnamed tributary cascading down from the north wall, and then rejoins Rattlesnake Creek in the level stretches at Cow Camp Meadows. This green grassland, once a way-camp for stockmen, is now given over to the many mule deer in the vicinity and an occasional bear. Reflecting the lower altitude, the meadow's fringes show a forest cover of lodgepole, fir and some juniper, and as the trail continues to descend steadily, Jeffrey, laurel, aspen and birch begin to make their predictable appearance. Just above the final steep descent into the Kern Trench, our trail passes the trail to the Big Arroyo, branching north, and then switchbacks down abruptly to the good packer campsites just south of the junction with the Kern River trail. (Those wishing to take in the geologically instructive views from Rattlesnake Point should follow the fire trail leaving the Rattlesnake Creek trail at the Big Arroyo trail junction. From this point, one has unobstructed views of the canyon's distinctive, glacially formed U-shape, and the wooded plateaus that were part of a pre-uplift valley floor.) Firewood at these campsites is ample, and fishing for rainbow in the Kern is excellent (to 20").

3rd Hiking Day (Campsites, Rattlesnake Creek/Kern River to Moraine Lake, 8 miles): Retrace steps of last part of 4th hiking day, trip 73 to junction of Kern River trail and High Sierra trail. Then proceed west on High Sierra trail, retracing steps of first part of 5th hiking day, trip 85.

4th Hiking Day (Moraine Lake to Campsites, Big Arroyo Trail Junction, 8.5 miles): See 4th hiking day, trip 85.

5th Hiking Day (Campsites, Big Arroyo Trail Junction to Hamilton Lakes, 7 miles): See 3rd hiking day, trip 85.

6th Hiking Day (Hamilton Lakes to Public Campground, Bearpaw Meadow, 5 miles): See 2nd hiking day, trip 85.

7th Hiking Day (Public Campground, Bearpaw Meadow to Lodgepole Campground, 12 miles): See 1st hiking day, trip 85.

Bibliography

Books

American National Red Cross, *American Red Cross First Aid Textbook*

Mary Austin, *The Land of Little Rain*

David R. Brower, ed., *The Sierra Club Wilderness Handbook*

Boughton Cobb, *A Field Guide to the Ferns*

Gerry Cunningham and Margaret Hansson, *Light Weight Camping Equipment and How to Make It*

Vlad Evanoff, *The Fresh-Water Fisherman's Bible*

Francis P. Farquhar, *History of the Sierra Nevada*

————, *Place Names of the High Sierra*

Erwin G. Gudde, *1000 California Place Names*

Clarence King, *Mountaineering in the Sierra Nevada*

Oscar Lewis, *High Sierra Country*

Francois Matthes (edited by Fritiof Fryxell), *Francois Matthes and the Marks of Time*

————, *Glacial Reconnaissance of Sequoia National Park —* Professional Paper 504-A

————, *Reconnaissance of the Geomorphology and Glacial Geology of the San Joaquin Basin —* Professional Paper 329

———— (edited by Fritiof Fryxell), *Sequoia National Park, a Geological Album*

Charles McDermand, *Waters of the Golden Trout Country*

————, *Yosemite and Kings Canyon Trout*

James G. Moore, *Geology of the Mount Pinchot Quadrangle,* Geological Survey Bulletin 1130

John Muir, *My First Summer in the Sierra*

————, *Studies in the Sierra*

Philip Munz, *California Mountain Wildflowers*

Olaus J. Murie, *A Field Guide to Animal Tracks*

Roderick Peattie, ed., *The Sierra Nevada: the Range of Light*

Roger Tory Peterson, *A Field Guide to Western Birds*

Hal Roth, *Pathway in the Sky*

Genny Schumacher, ed., *Deepest Valley*

Seattle Mountaineers, *Mountaineering: the Freedom of the Hills*

Seattle Mountaineers Safety Committee, *Mountaineering First Aid*

Walter Starr, Jr., *Guide to the John Muir Trail and the High Sierra Region*

Tracy I. Storer and Robert L. Usinger, *Sierra Nevada Natural History*

W. Storrs, *The Sierra*

Lowell Sumner and Joseph Dixon, *Birds and Mammals of the Sierra Nevada*

Hervey H. Voge, ed., *A Climber's Guide to the High Sierra*

Pamphlets

Pat Adler, *Mineral King Guide*

Hasse Bunnelle and Winnie Thomas, *Food for Knapsackers*

A. B. Elsasser, *Indians of Sequoia and Kings Canyon National Park*

High Sierra Packers, Eastern Sierra Packers Association, Box 147, Bishop, California

Packers and Pack Trips, California State Chamber of Commerce, 350 Bush Street, San Francisco 94104

TRIP CROSS-REFERENCE TABLE

Trip No.	No. Hiking Days	Season			Pace			Trip Type			Semi-Loop
		Early	Mid	Late	Leis.	Mod.	Stren.	Round	Shuttle	Loop	
1	2	X		X	X			X			
2	2		X	X		X		X			
3	3	X		X		X			X		
4	4		X	X		X		X			
5	5		X	X		X					X
6	4		X	X		X		X			
7	6		X	X		X					X
8	4		X	X		X			X		
9	6		X	X		X					X
10	6			X		X					X
11	5			X		X			X		
12	7			X		X			X		
13	8			X		X					X
14	6		X	X		X			X		
15	6		X	X	X			X			
16	6		X	X	X				X		
17	2		X		X			X			
18	4		X		X			X			
19	4		X	X	X				X		
20	6		X	X	X				X		
21	7			X		X					X
22	7		X	X		X				X	
23	2		X	X	X			X			
24	3		X	X		X		X			
25	5		X	X	X				X		
26	4		X	X	X				X		
27	2	X →			X			X			
28	4	X →			X			X			
29	4		X →		X			X			
30	6		X →		X						X
31	6		X →		X			X			
32	7		X	X	X						X

Trip No.	No. Hiking Days	Season			Pace			Trip Type			
		Early	Mid	Late	Leis.	Mod.	Stren.	Round	Shuttle	Loop	Semi-Loop
33	7		X	X	X						X
34	6		X	X	X			X			
35	5		X	X		X			X		
36	6		X	X		X			X		
37	7		X	X		X			X		
38	9		X	X			X		X		
39	8		X	X	X			X			
40	10		X	X	X			X			
41	11		X	X	X				X		
42	9		X	X		X			X		
43	2		X	X	X			X			
44	2		X	X	X					X	
45	2		X	X	X			X			
46	4		X	X		X			X		
47	2		X		X			X			
48	3		X	X	X					X	
49	6		X	X		X					X
50	9		X	X		X			X		
51	10		X	X		X			X		
52	9		X	X	X				X		
53	9		X	X	X				X		
54	8		X	X	X				X		
55	11		X	X	X				X		
56	2	X		X		X		X			
57	4	X		X		X		X			
58	6		X	X		X			X		
59	3	X →				X		X			
60	5		X	X	X			X			
61	5			X	X			X			
62	6			X	X					X	
63	5			X	X				X		
64	4		X	X		X		X			
65	6			X		X					X
66	2	X	X			X		X			

Trip No.	No. Hiking Days	Season			Pace			Trip Type			
		Early	Mid	Late	Leis.	Mod.	Stren.	Round	Shuttle	Loop	Semi-Loop
67	6		X	X	X				X		
68	3		X	X	X				X		
69	7			X		X					X
70	5			X	X				X		
71	3		X	X		X		X			
72	4		X	X		X		X			
73	6		X →			X			X		
74	8		X →			X			X		
75	2		X	X	X			X			
76	4		X →			X		X			
77	6			X		X		X			
78	8		X →			X					X
79	8		X →			X		X			
80	5		X →			X			X		
81	2		X →		X			X			
82	6		X	X	X			X			
83	6			X		X					X
84	5			X	X				X		
85	9		X →			X			X		
86	2	X			X						X
87	2		X	X	X						X
88	4		X	X	X			X			
89	5		X	X	X						X
90	6		X	X	X			X			
91	6		X	X	X				X		
92	6		X	X	X				X		
93	7		X	X		X			X		
94	2		X				X	X			
95	2		X				X	X			
96	2		X	X			X	X			
97	3		X →				X	X			
98	5		X	X			X			X	
99	4		X	X			X			X	
100	6		X	X			X			X	

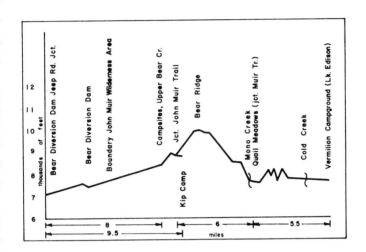

Profile 1

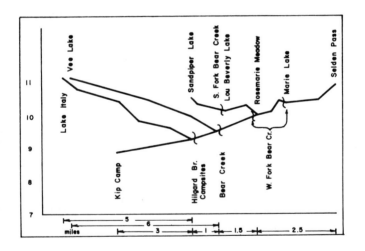

Profile 2

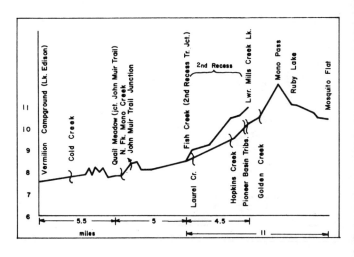

Profile 3

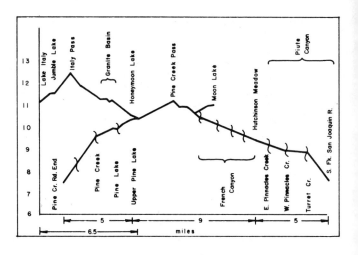

Profile 4

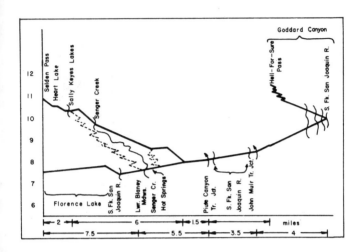

Profile 5

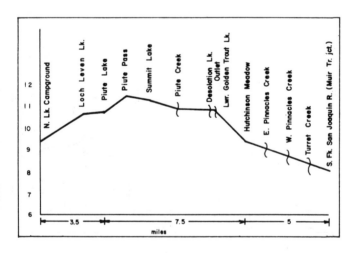

Profile 6

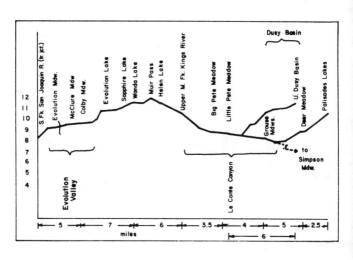

Profile 7

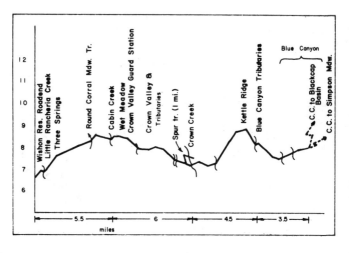

Profile 8

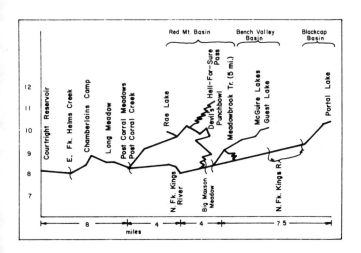

Profile 9

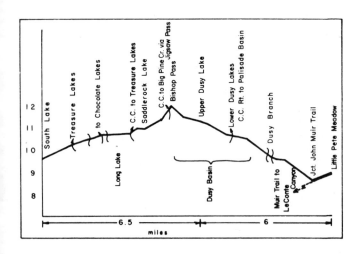

Profile 10

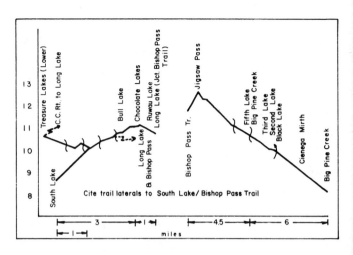

Profile 11

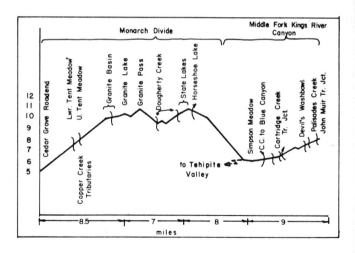

Profile 12

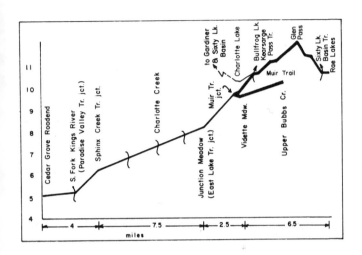

Profile 13

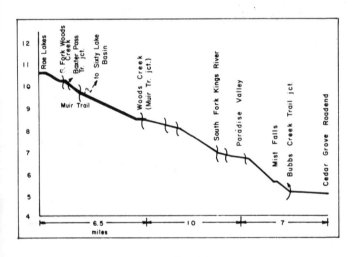

Profile 14

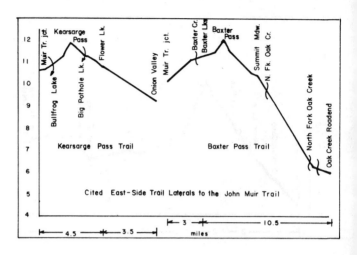

Profile 15

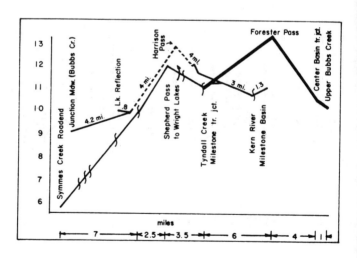

Profile 16

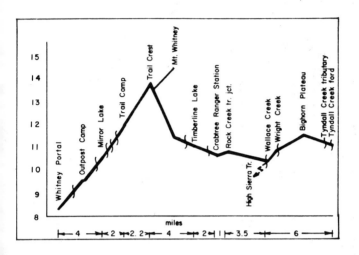

Profile 17

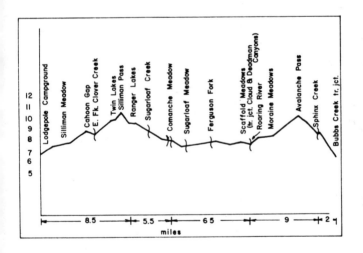

Profile 18

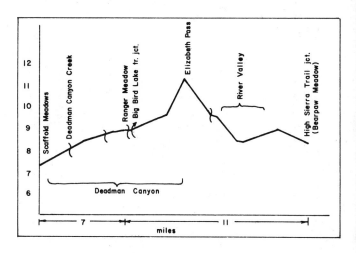

Profile 19

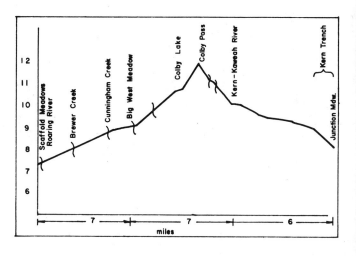

Profile 20

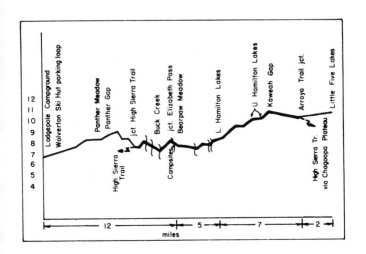

Profile 21

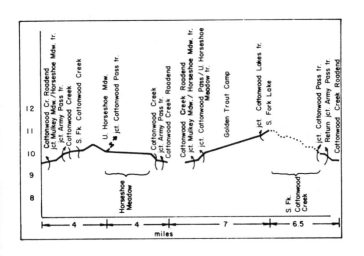

Profile 22

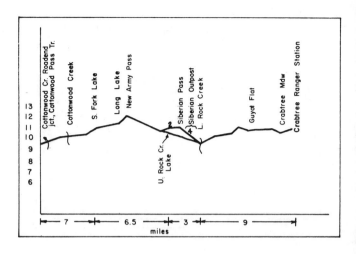

Profile 23

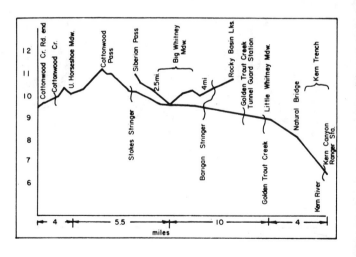

Profile 24

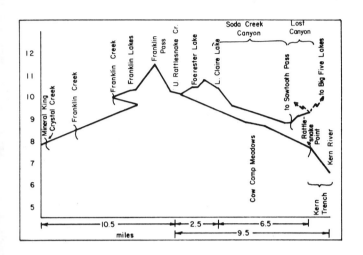

Profile 25

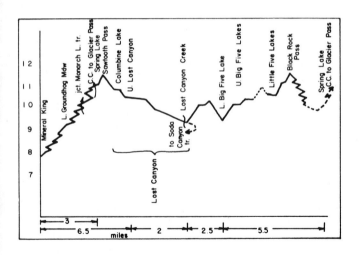

Profile 26

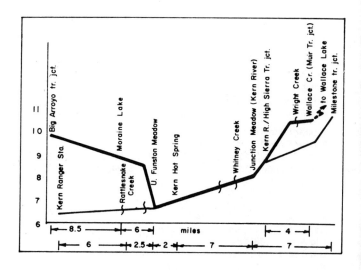

Profile 27

INDEX

Trail notes